I know nothing about the author of this work. Yet, somehow we´re connected.

I have travelled, by sheer coincidence, on the very same trains he took. I have also, at different times, been to the obscure tea shops his journal mentions. But what truly connects us are our fondness for old bookstores.

The defunct basement bookstore off Anna Nagar Roundtana in Chennai, the wastepaper dealer in Naraina, New Delhi, the hawker who sells pirated books off Civil Lines in Aligarh... he too had been to them all. I've been strangely linked to Thomas for close to a decade now, ever since I'd first encountered his journal in a moth-eaten pile of miscellaneous literature outside the Moore Market in Chennai.

Truth be told, I never wanted to publish the findings in his journal. The first time I found it, I did exactly as the journal instructed and returned it to the address mentioned. When I found it again in Prayagraj in 2009, I put it down to coincidence. I have sent this book back to its rightful owner at least 50 times, and somehow it has always found its way back to me. Even after I moved to the Netherlands.

I have now stopped questioning why. But fear sits coiled in the pit of my stomach.

—C.G. Salamander

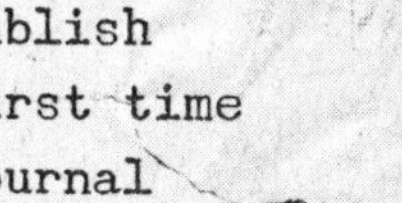

FIELD EXPLORATIONS OF MYTHICAL BEASTS ACROSS INDIA

Thomas Iravathur

THE ASUNAM
the asunam

15/5/2018

Kurinji Hills, TN

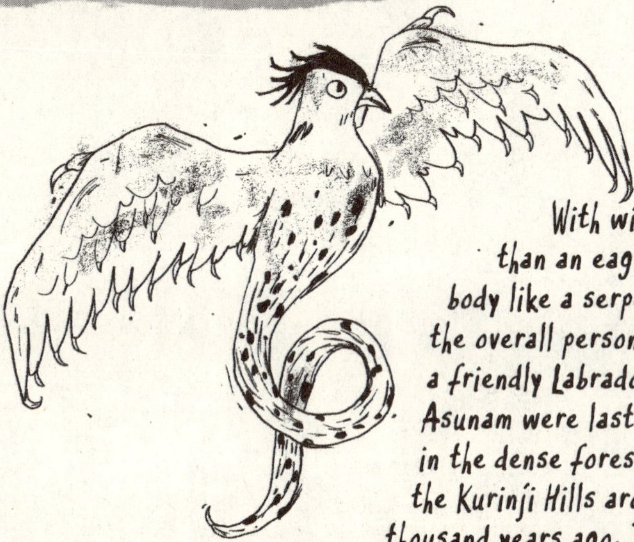

With wings wider than an eagle's, a body like a serpent's and the overall personality of a friendly Labrador, the Asunam were last spotted in the dense forests of the Kurinji Hills around a thousand years ago. They nest inside the darkest caves, and apparently only step out to listen to the chirping of birds and the rustling of leaves. The Asunam are shy creatures, and prefer their own company. But the most fascinating thing about them is their incredible fondness for music.

That brings us to why I'm lost in the forest, playing an ancient Tamil lyre. Before you ask, no, I didn't steal the yazh from a museum. I *borrowed* it. Only because I need it to draw an Asunam out. Besides, it wasn't as if anyone was using it. It was just sitting behind a glass case, untouched for years.

I had to borrow it because it's my only defence against a creature as formidable as the Asunam. Stronger than a horse, with claws sharper than a lion's, and the ability to stay in the air longer than any bird! I would be stupid to confront these creatures without a yazh to calm them. But the Asunam do have one other weakness – they are phonophobic. That means that they get scared and disoriented whenever they hear loud noises (the Asunam and I have that in common). If the stories I've heard are true and I manage to make this yazh produce melodious sounds, the Asunam will just gracefully fly out of their caves to listen. But if they are startled by sounds that are too loud for their ears, their hearts stop beating, and they fall from the skies, spiralling to their deaths.

The Asunam's undoing was their love for melodious music. When the early Tamils got wind of their weakness, they showed up in front of Asuman caves with yazhes and played the most harmonious tunes. Hypnotized by the music, the Asunam ambled out of their caves. And when they least expected it, hunters jumped out of the bushes and played a loud drumbeat – causing the poor creatures to die an instant death.

And that's how these majestic creatures were hunted into extinction. But I am still hopeful of finding one – perhaps a flock of tone-deaf Asunam cloistered themselves away somewhere, and perhaps I'll be the first human to see one, thousands of years later.

I just hope they're not the kind to hold grudges, with humans hunting them to extinction and all.

THE POHUVAL
the pohuval

20/5/2018
Thirūvālluvar, TN

It was supposed to be only one beast.

You see, I was going to look for the Asunam and then head right back home. I don't have very much money, and I miss being home. But I've been travelling through the villages of Tamil Nadu for about a month now, and during this time, I have unearthed more information about fascinating creatures than I'd ever hoped to find. I can't stop now – not when it seems like I've just begun.

Only last week, as I was tracking the Pohuval near Thiruvalluvar district, I came across an ancient burial ground from the megalithic period (around 2500 BCE to 200 CE). Gigantic stones were piled on one another to make house-like structures. I saw clay sarcophagi standing on a dozen legs, and large urns with bones inside, buried under the piled stones. But my most amazing discovery? That the ancient Tamils gave their dead a double burial. Apparently, they would first lay the corpses of the deceased out in the open, and when the body was reduced to just skin and bones, they would place it – curled up like a baby – inside an urn and cover it up with sand.

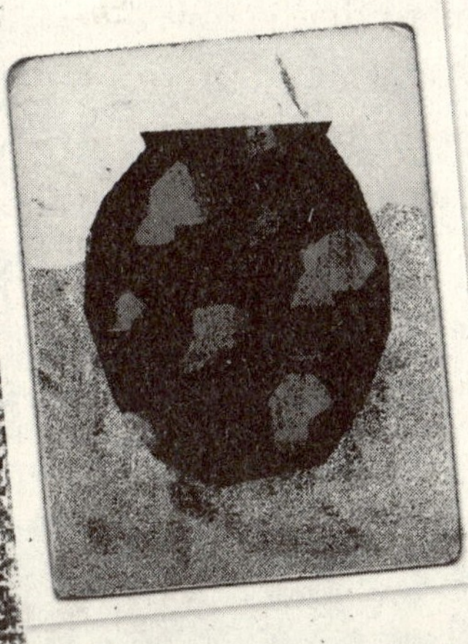

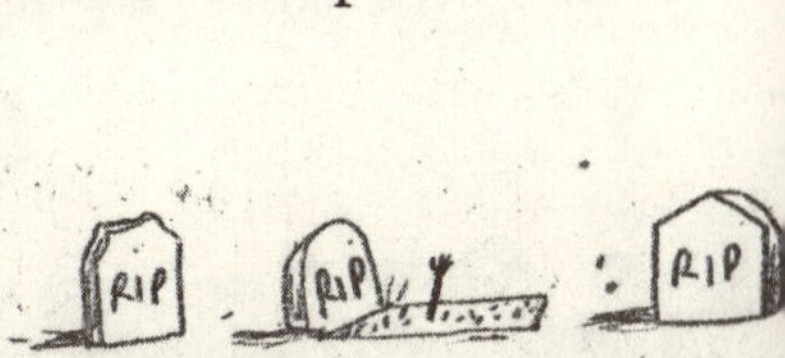

All around these burial grounds, they built stone structures called dolmens.

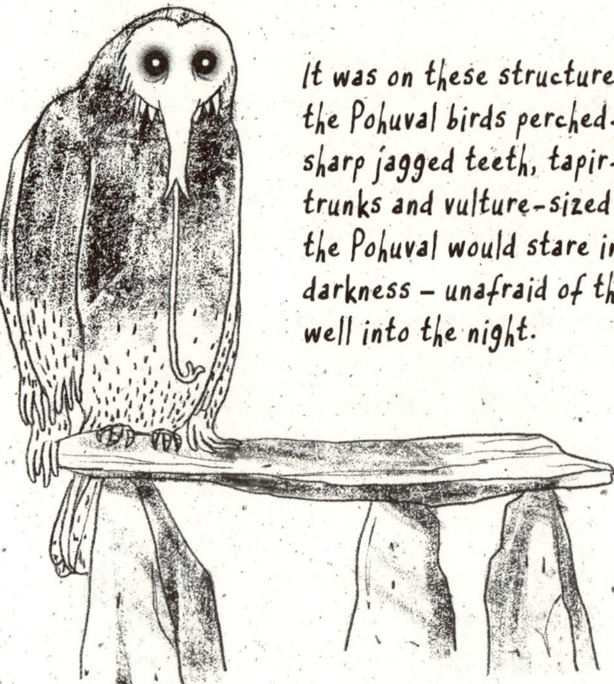

It was on these structures that the Pohuval birds perched. With sharp jagged teeth, tapir-like trunks and vulture-sized bodies, the Pohuval would stare into the darkness – unafraid of the dead – well into the night.

Graveyards have always freaked me out, the megalithic ones more than your run-of-the mill cemeteries. Because, according to lore, ancient burial grounds are often visited by demons who like to feast on the decaying corpses of humans as well as dance on the graves of the deceased. And honestly, I don't know what's worse – a horde of demons tearing me to shreds and feasting on my flesh while the Pohuval watches, or the demons being cordial and trying to dance with me.

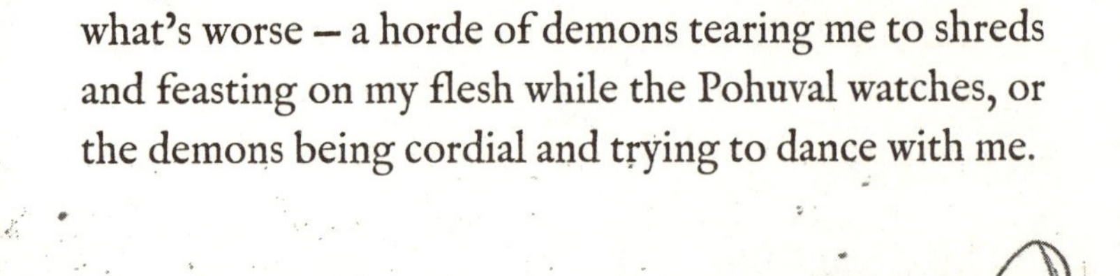

THE STRUTHOPODES

the struthopodes

21/5/2018

Thirūvālluvar, TN

VKP Lodge

I'm sorry if I came across as being a little too obsessed with death. That's what happens when I get excited – my mind wanders. If you have managed to get your hands on these pages and are still reading – despite the very nice note asking you not to – then I have two things to say to you. You are rude, uncivilized and have no manners. But, more importantly, you must know by now that my name is Thomas Iravathur, and that I'm travelling across the country in search of unusual beasts. I've always wanted to look for, catalogue and learn everything there is to know about these creatures hidden from the human eye. Now, I'm finally in a position where I can do it! Two years working in a dusty government library, one year spent mapping these beasts, and I'm ready to embrace my job as an assistant researcher.

Let me stop you before you get all judgmental and start sounding like my mother. I know my job might seem strange, but I'm not the first person who has made it their mission to track down so-called mythical creatures. Greek traders, Christian missionaries and English colonizers – they've all chased after creatures that no one else believed walked the earth. And they took what they did very seriously indeed.

Gaius Plinius Secundus, better known as Pliny the Elder, for instance, wrote about various Indian tribes, and creatures including the Struthopodes of south India. In his book of natural history, Pliny the Elder wrote:

'In the south of India, men have feet 18 *inches long and the women such small feet that they are called Struthopodes or sparrow-feet.'*

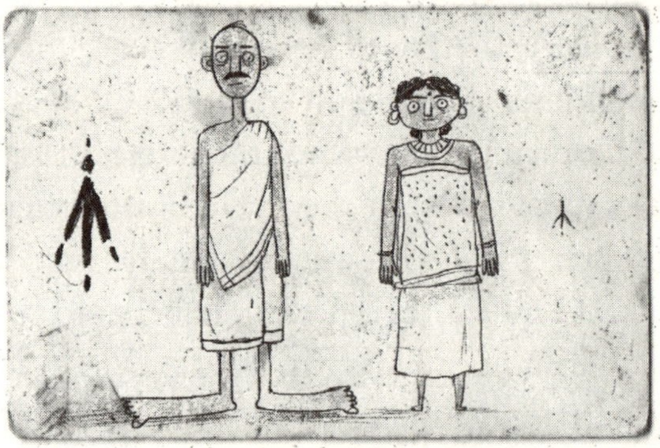

He described them as living in the dense forests, shielded from the rest of humankind. Intrigued, I kept an eye out for the tribe when I was looking for the Asunam, and when I ventured further into the jungle, looking for other creatures. But no matter how hard I looked, there were no ostrich- or sparrow-sized footprints side by side, although, according to Pliny, the women would often rest their feet on the men's while they walked. Or maybe this is all terribly outdated information. Perhaps things have changed over a couple of millennia, and it's now the women who carry the men around?

THE HORNED JACKAL
the horned jackal

23/5/2018
Thiruttani, TN

Some explorers just want to find a new species, but not I. I'm not doing it for fame or the chance to christen some unlucky creature after my ugly name. I love animals, and I want to discover more of them. It's as simple as that. Sir James Emerson Tennent, however, was nothing like me – he was in it for the fame. Tennent was a 19th-century British politician and a fellow of the Royal Society. He believed Horned Jackals walked the forests of India and Sri Lanka (called Ceylon then). He insisted that these creatures weren't a separate species; Horned Jackals were jackals who led their packs. He believed that they had a half-inch horn hiding in the fur on their heads, and he claimed to have found tiny narricombos (meaning

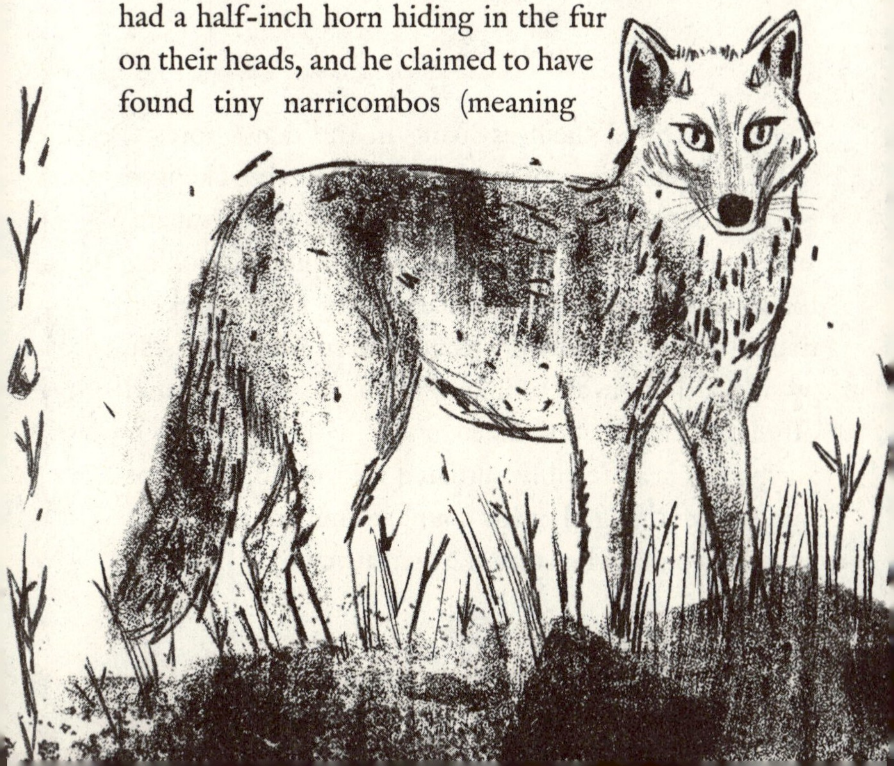

jackal horns in Tamil) projecting from their foreheads or behind their heads, in some cases.

Tennent also mentions in his book *Sketches of Natural History of Ceylon* that the horn was considered a lucky charm by both Tamils and Sinhalese, and was supposed to return to its owner regardless of how many times it was lost or stolen. He talks about an incident where a person who'd suffered numerous defeats in the courtroom finally managed to win a case after he carried a jackal's skull in. But this wasn't just some placebo that tricked him into thinking he was invincible in court. Instead, the person in question won a losing case only because the witness changed his statement and called it a day, thinking it was

Note to self: Must remember to carry a narricombo to court if ever implicated.

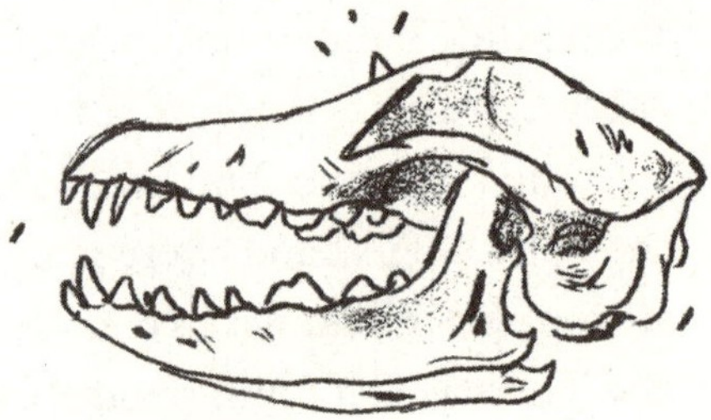

pointless to fight against the infinite power and fortune that the plaintiff's narricombo gave him!

I wonder if people in Sri Lanka still consider the horn a lucky charm that protects their wealth, and if crafty lawyers across the world are busy taking jackals for MRIs in the hope of getting their hands on a powerful horn.

THE PARAVAI NAGAM

the paravai nagam

27/5/2018
– Garudadri Express, TN

I outgrew religion a long time ago, but back when I was a child, my mother and I would walk to church every Sunday. We would go early in the morning and sit right at the back on the straw mats. My mother always preferred the mats to the off-white plastic chairs at the front of the church. The women sitting in the chairs asked too many questions about Appa, my father, and my mother didn't like talking about him, so she told everyone he worked in Dubai.

I liked sitting on those mats – there was enough room for me and my colouring book, and I liked colouring the sheets they handed out in Sunday school. I remember colouring this picture of Jesus standing with his palms stretched out, and Thomas, Jesus' disciple, checking if the holes on his hands were real. Well, I've heard a lot of stories about Thomas in church and Sunday school, but the Thomas I'm telling you about now sounds nothing like the one from my childhood.

The Acts of Thomas is a New Testament apocrypha (which means that the church does not accept it as legitimate) that describes the adventures of Thomas after he was sold into slavery by Jesus Christ, when Thomas refused to travel to India and spread the gospel. According to this, Thomas, who was fairly new to the subcontinent, talks about his encounter with what may have been a Paravai Nagam (a bird snake, or a south Indian dragon).

Thomas wrote, and I'm paraphrasing here:

'On the road, I found the dead body of a handsome youth. When I approached him, I was attacked by a huge black serpent. The serpent claimed to have killed the youth out of jealousy, because it found the youth with a woman it fancied. But once it learned that I was Jesus' twin (that's what Thomas fancied himself to be), it approached me with caution.'

Thomas adds that the beast identified itself as the very same serpent that caused Adam and Eve to be cast out of the garden of Eden, the same serpent responsible for the fallen angels, and the *same* creature that caused humans to sin and Judas, one of the original 12 disciples or apostles of Christ, to betray Jesus!

Thomas was not afraid of the dragon, though. He commanded it to suck out its venom from the deceased youth. Powerless against Thomas's words, the dragon drew out the poison from the boy and, as it did so, began to swell. It became larger and larger, until it exploded and died.

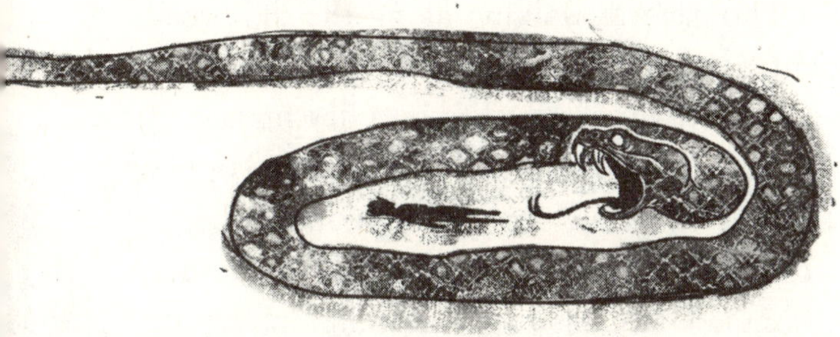

Someone should put that story in a colouring book!

THE TALKING DONKEY

the talking donkey

28/5/2018

Chennai, TN

I would have never thought about Thomas or the beasts he wrote about had I not travelled to Chennai. When you live deep in south India, in a tiny town that no one's heard about, travelling to Chennai gives you the most options by train (that's how unconnected my village is to the rest of India).

Since I arrived early in the morning with loads of time to spare, I figured I'd visit St. Thomas Mount, the place where he was killed.

I know his accounts are rejected by the church, and I know the church doesn't consider his gospel real. Nonetheless, *The Acts of Thomas*, the stories of his adventures in India, is a wildly popular book that has survived for hundreds of years as manuscripts in many, many languages.

My most favourite of all the creatures that he came across has to be the Talking Donkey.

So Thomas was walking along the dust roads of ancient Kerala, and just like that, he was approached by a donkey who claimed to be a descendant of the one that *Jesus* rode into Jerusalem. Recognizing Thomas as Jesus' twin, the donkey begged Thomas to ride on its back. Once the donkey carried Thomas to his destination, it just dropped dead.

Thomas's followers were upset and sad, and they begged him to bring the donkey back from the dead, but Thomas refused. He said that the donkey had fulfilled its purpose and that it was God's plan for him to die. Thomas wasn't completely heartless, though; he gave the donkey a decent send-off and buried it properly by the side of the road.

I wonder if they spread the donkey on a platform, waiting for it to decay before they could place it inside an urn and lower it into the ground. After all, Thomas was in Tamil Nadu around the same time that the locals buried their dead in urns and he may have taken to the practice. I don't know why, but it makes me shudder to think of the remains of a Talking Donkey, buried in an urn somewhere in south India, its body bent into a foetal position with utmost respect.

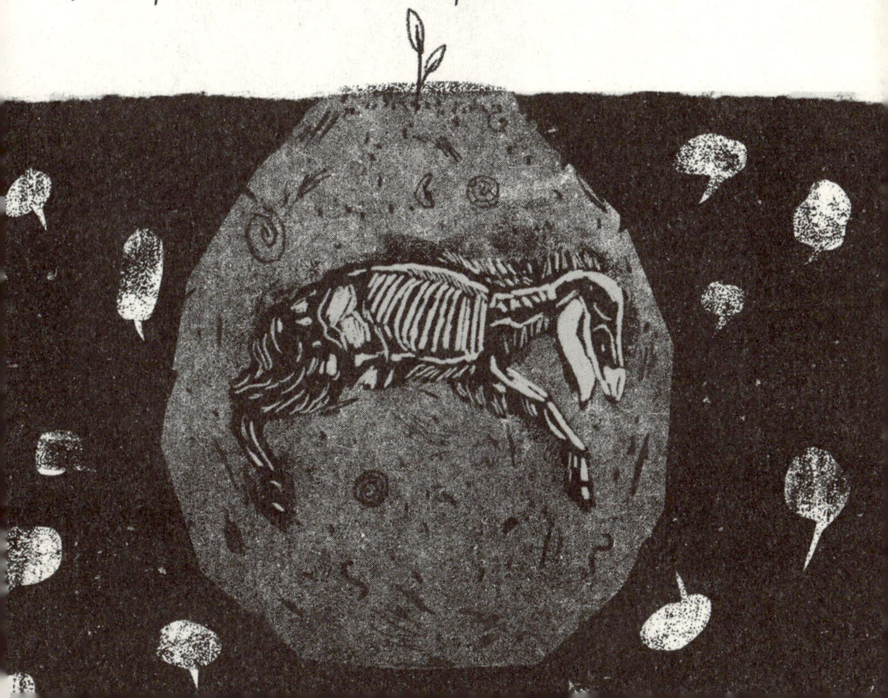

THE YALI
the yali

31/5/2018

Madurai Meenakshi
Amman Temple, TN

I did manage to squeeze in a beast before my trip to Chennai, and it was by far the biggest beast to have walked the shores of Tamil Nadu, or the entire world for that matter. My search for the Yali (if you're around Tamilians, take care to pronounce it 'aali') had me wandering across the state with no real plan or purpose. I travelled back and forth between Madurai and Tiruvannamalai, and came across sculptures of the beast in almost every temple I visited.

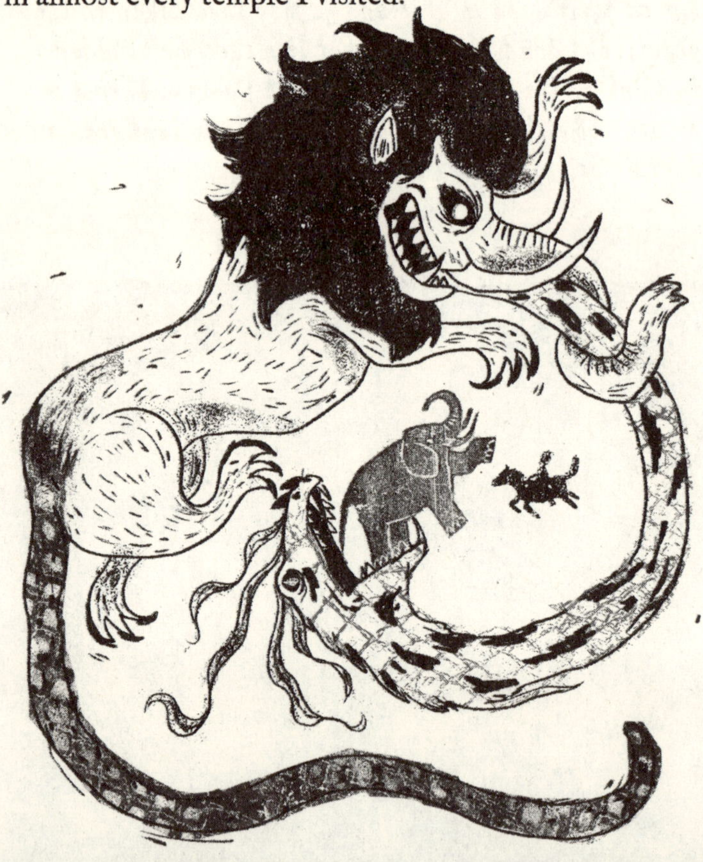

Wherever I went, the story was more or less the same. Yalis are ginormous beasts, large enough to flip an elephant on its head without breaking a sweat. They are so big that the ancient Tamil word 'aali' means 'wrath of nature'. I was told that they came in different forms and shapes: the Yannai Yali, with the head of an elephant, the most common one; the Magara Yali, with the head of a goat; and the Simma Yali, with the head of a lion. Locals believe that the Yali lived in the continent of Kumari Kandam, a landmass that connected India and Sri Lanka to Australia. The Yalis are supposed to have become extinct after a mega tsunami wiped them out, along with the continent they lived on.

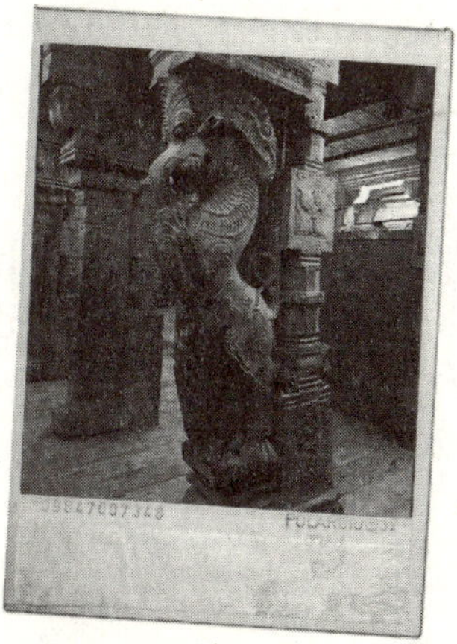

By far the best thing I found while researching the Yali was this statue! It's a bit disorienting to look at without context, but it actually depicts a passage from Sangam literature – a huge collection of the earliest Tamil writing – that describes the Yali as a gigantic creature in the process of devouring a dragon, which is moments away from swallowing an elephant whole, while the elephant is about to trample down an enemy general riding a horse.

You know how some people like to look at the stars to feel insignificant and small? Not me – I look at my picture of the Yali.

THE SARAMBAM
the sarambam

15/6/2018
Krauncha Giri
Bellary, KA

I've been to Karnataka once before, when I was eight or nine and we had a wedding to attend. I remember my father's family being there, and I recall leaving early – which was nice, because weddings are so boring. Nothing about my travel today feels the same, though; there are far too many trains, even double-decker ones, and some as luxurious as planes.

The Sarambam was an animal that lived along with lions and tigers in the mountains of what is now Karnataka. It would roam the forests, scaring other animals away and slaying any beast that dared stand in its path. With eight legs, and multiple eyes on the top of its heads, these creatures lived on raw flesh. Believe it or not, the Sarambam was also constantly hunted and consumed by humans as food at some point.

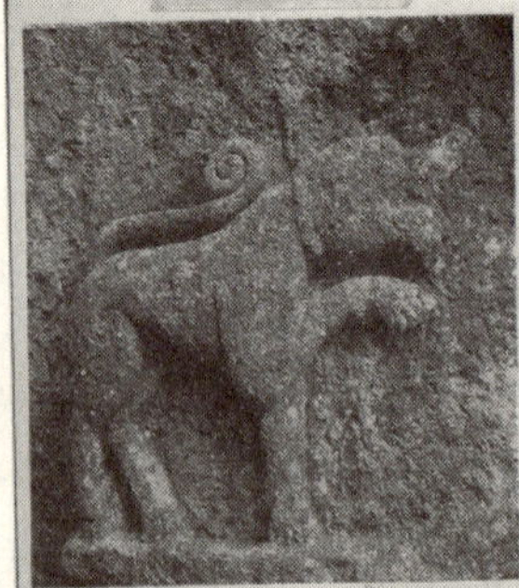

SARAMBAM IDOL

My wanderings in Karnataka soon brought me face to face – or rather face to face to face – with yet another very recognizable figure, the two-headed part-lion and part-bird, Sarambam. Best known as

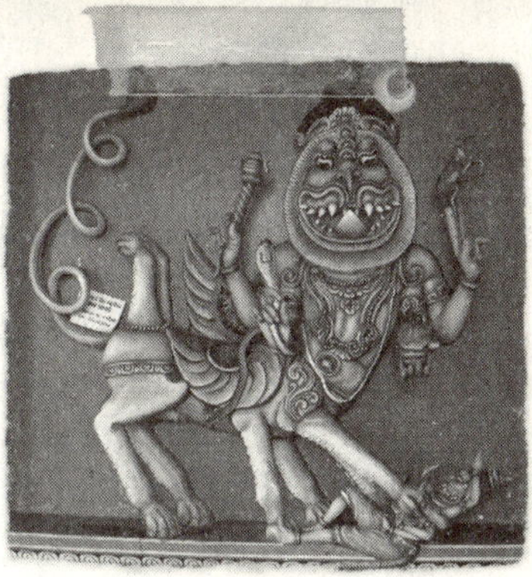

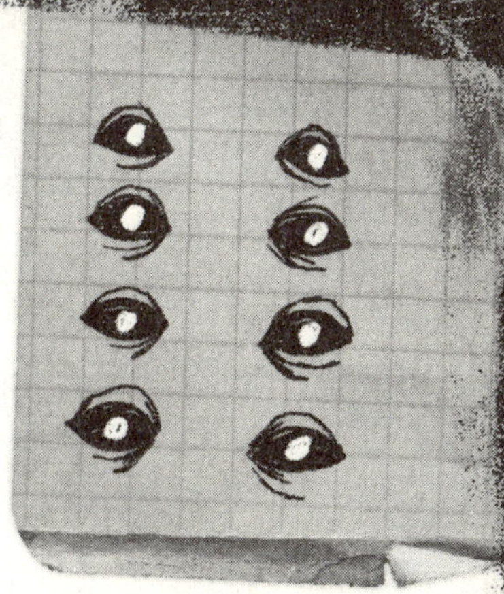

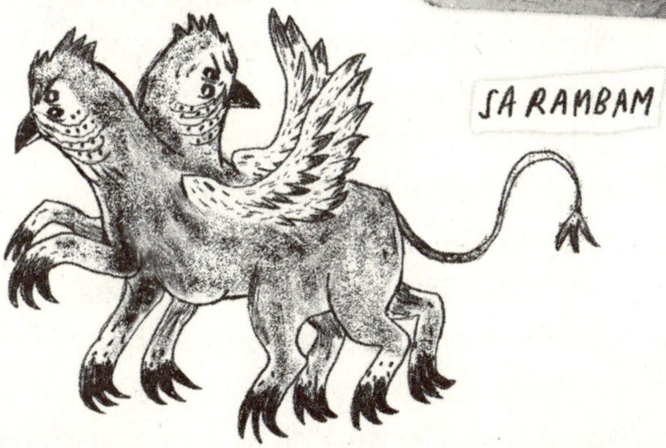

Narasimha, the form Vishnu assumed to defeat the asura Hiranyakashipu, the Sarambam has a lot going on outside of this avatar.

I am amazed by what we put into our mouths. What could possibly drive us to eat this kind of creature? The multiple eyes, the two faces, the trunk, the talons sharper than knives? But then again, what could have possibly driven us to drink out of an udder or bite into a sugar cane for the very first time? Part of evolution, they say...

Food for thought, huh?

There's nothing I like more than looking out of the window of a train – to see the varied landscapes of the country blend seamlessly into one another over the course of a trip, to watch the trees and people zoom by. What I like best are the often misspelt words scribbled on the sides of houses and railway stations alike. It has been an obsession of mine to try and read the text on the walls as the train whizzes by, and scribble these words in my journal, sometimes writing over important research.

If my mother were alive, she would scold me for not growing up – she might even slap my wrist for letting fun get in the way of serious research. But it's because of my spontaneous scribbling that I came across something fascinating. It started when I noticed the same characters etched on the walls of both houses and railway station washrooms. The text read ನಾಳೆ ಬಾ in Karnataka, and நாளை வா in Tamil Nadu. It was only after I asked my fellow passengers what the words 'naalai vaa' meant that they told me the story behind the phrase.

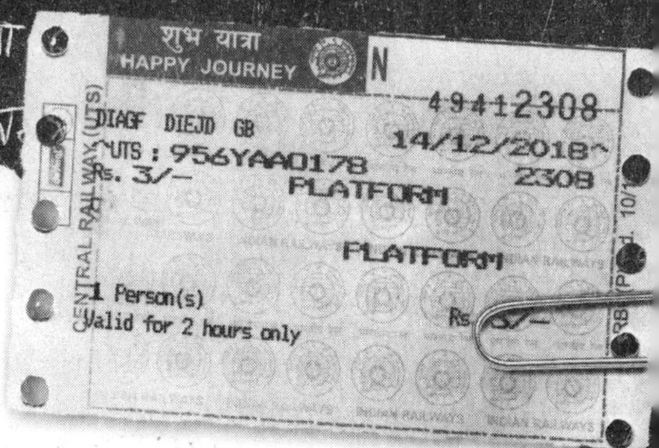

Legend has it that the spirit of a newlywed woman who died on a train travels along the south Indian railway lines in search of her husband. Embarking and disembarking, she visits only the smallest towns, knocking on strangers' doors and enquiring about her husband. 'The words "naalai vaa", meaning, "come tomorrow", are scribbled on doors as a precaution,' an elderly uncle with a hairline almost down to his eyebrows explained. 'You see, when the spirit sees it, she leaves and returns the next day, and the cycle goes on forever.'

I found it particularly cruel, but I guess it's just a silly urban legend.

'You should consider writing நாளை வா on the cover of your journal,' the uncle said.

'And send away my only reader?' I replied, and everyone laughed.

THE NOBUSUMA

the nobusuma

18/6/2018

Sholayar Reserve Forest, KL

I like Kerala more than all the other south Indian states put together. There's a whole lot to look at here, and the people are either as strange as me or stranger.

WATCH OUT

I ventured into the Sholayar Reserve Forest in central Kerala and found a forest officer, a flying squirrel on his shoulder, talking to a group of students. Looking at the creature, I was immediately reminded of the Japanese monster Nobusuma, and an article I'd read about how the myth could have originated from the Travancore flying squirrel.

Legend has it that the Nobusuma looks identical to a flying squirrel – just that it's a lot more dangerous! It's not created by magic, and doesn't owe its origin to gods or demons. These creatures are simply created by virtue of having lived a long life, meaning that a regular bat would evolve into a Nobusuma if it lived for an unusually long time. So what's frightening about them, then? Erm, the fact that they hide among the treetops, lying in wait for an unsuspecting human to pass by. When they spot one, they swoop down and latch on to their victim's neck, only letting go when the latter is drained of blood. The Nobusuma also feed on fire and berries, and I don't know why, but somehow this makes them *scarier*.

Here's the most interesting part about the Nobusuma, though – when they feed on enough blood or live an unusually long life, they transform or evolve into an even superior being called a Yamachichi. Unlike the Nobusuma, the Yamachichi look more like apes, with long anteater-like mouths that they use to draw out their victim's blood. The Yamachichi, however, aren't just found in forests; they follow their victims home and lie in wait. Once they know their victim is asleep, they sneak into the house and begin feeding. They suck the person dry, only waking them up when they're almost done. Most people die a few hours to a few days after that.

There is one way to defeat a Yamachichi. If a victim wakes up while the Yamachichi is feeding on their blood, the process reverses and the victim possesses the Yamachichi's life force and lives a long, long life.

And if the whole bat evolving into a Nobusuma and a Nobusuma evolving into a Yamachichi reminds you of something, then you're right. This is where Pokemon gets its inspiration from.

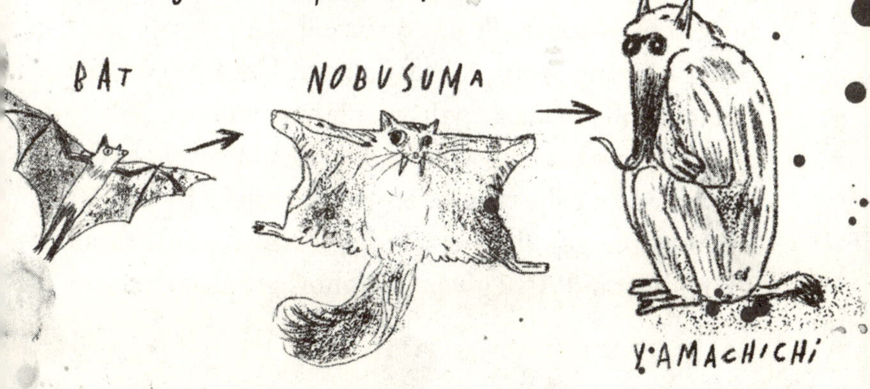

21/6/2018

Thiruvananthāpūram, KL

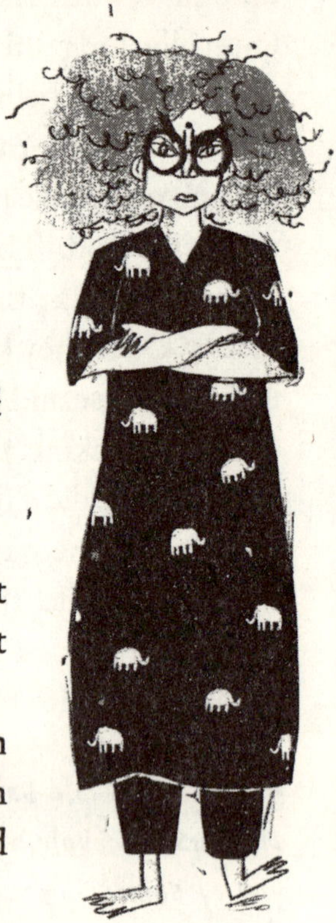

I first met Dr T. Cherian outside the Elephant Conservation Centre in Thiruvananthapuram, Kerala. Her hair was curly and dishevelled, her feet were bare, and she wore a long flowing kurta. She was glaring daggers at the man standing in front of her. As far as first impressions go, she looked positively cuckoo.

'Madam, for the last time, we won't meet with you because you don't have enough evidence.'

'What do you mean?' Cherian snapped. 'I've been walking through those forests for years, and I've lived with the Kani people for months!'

'Yes, ma'am, but you don't understand – you don't have sufficient proof – or any proof, for that matter. Until you do, the Kalanna will remain a myth and nothing more.'

Cherian was a tiny woman, five feet in height at the very most, but she seemed to grow at least a foot taller when anger got the best of her. 'No, I don't think *you* understand! I've given you photographs, I've sent you eyewitness accounts. I've given you more than enough proof.'

'Pictures of a *single* elephant – it might have been malnourished, or a juvenile.'

'Have you seen a baby elephant? They throw tantrums and fall on their faces – they are idiots! The picture I sent you was of a full-grown Kalanna, a dwarf subspecies of the Indian elephant, foraging for food on its own and scaring away other herbivores. Do you really think a silly elephant calf can do *all* that? Of course not, the picture I sent you was of an adult.'

'Madam, what is your problem with baby elephants? Everyone loves them, especially ones with fuzz on their heads.'

'That's not the point!'

'Okay, ma'am...' The man from the conservationist society looked tired. He backed away from the angry woman gradually and sprinted out the front door when she paused to reach for her bag.

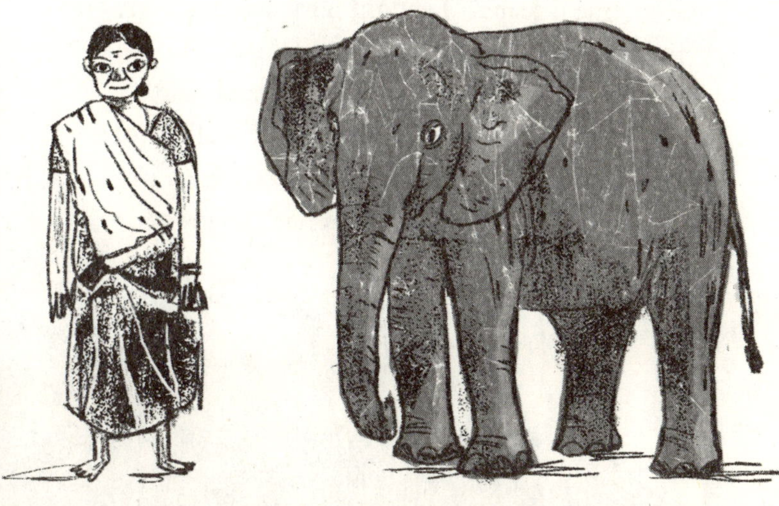

'What are those pictures,' I asked sheepishly.

Dr Cherian was acerbic and curt, but when she spoke about the Kalanna, something changed in her. Her eyes lit up, and for those brief moments she seemed friendly and approachable.

'They're called Kalanna – stone elephants – because they're almost always spotted in rocky terrains. They're about as tall as a juvenile Asian elephant, are no more than five feet tall, but are much faster than the average Indian elephant. They have bigger ears, longer tails, and they're frequently spotted by the Kani tribe.'

'And yet, no one's managed to take a picture of a herd?'

This seemed to upset her. 'I have nothing to prove to you or anyone else, and neither does the tribe. If it weren't for the potential conservation funding, I would have stopped trying to convince people ages ago. Maybe it's for the best that they live peacefully in anonymity,' she snarled. 'Not that I expect someone like you to understand.'

'Someone like me?' I caught her glancing at my book stuffed with notes about different beasts.

'Someone who chases after fairies for a living.'

It must be strange, I thought as I walked off, dedicating your life to proving the existence of just one beast. Mini elephants – what's so great about them anyway?

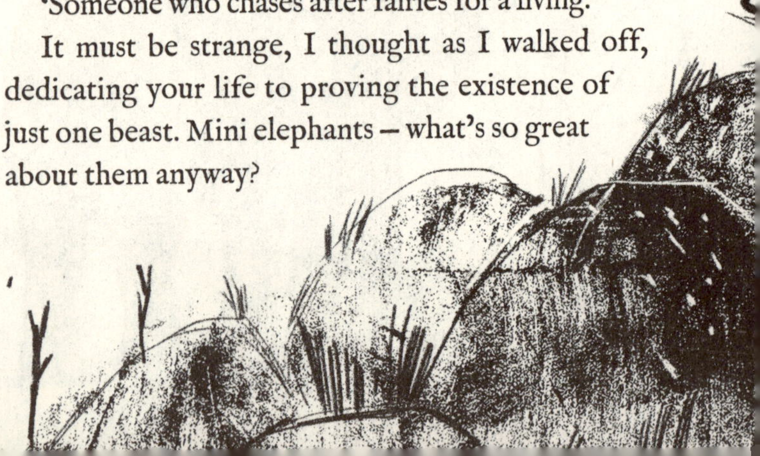

27/06/2018

Bus ride to Palakkad

Despite our rocky start, Cherian and I ran into each other off and on, and got along surprisingly well. She often accompanied me on my travels across Kerala, and regaled me with the strangest myths and tales about monsters.

'I've never really understood why the Yakshi have such a bad reputation.' Cherian had a problem separating the conversations she had in her mind with those she had with people. This made her go off on unrelated tangents, often with little warning. 'I think it's because of the media – they're obsessed with portraying strong women badly!'

'I don't know about that – south Indian vampires aren't the most lovable characters if you ask me!' I replied, leaning closer to her, much to the dismay of the others sitting in the women's section of the bus. 'Take Sreedevi, the woman we call Kanjirottu Yakshi. She was cunning and manipulative, and her obsession with the palanquin bearer Raaman drove her to do some truly disgusting things. When they were children, Raaman would carry her brother and her everywhere, and when Raaman and her brother became friends, she became resentful. She was jealous of her own brother – can you imagine! – and of Raaman's wife, whom she killed by the way.'

'Yes, yes, we all know how the story goes! Her brother rats her out, Raaman strangles her under the pretence of finally falling in love with her, and then she dies, bitter and alone,' Cherian said, adjusting her spectacles. 'But there's something to be said about her sheer willpower. Not everyone is capable of simply *willing* themselves back from the dead to be reborn as a Yakshi, terrorizing men, all the while nursing a broken heart, courtesy of Raaman. She did end up getting her way – she was reunited with him.'

'Just for a year! And only on the condition that she agreed to be confined to a temple after the year was up,' I replied, sliding into the vacant seat beside her. 'That hardly counts as a good deal.'

Cherian gave this some thought. 'All this does is prove my point, that there are kind Yakshis, there are Yakshis who guard treasure, there are Yakshis who are warriors, and Yakshis who are gentle water spirits. Yet, the first thing you think of when you hear the word Yakshi in Kerala are shameless vampires who want to prey on men. The patriarchy is obsessed with playing the victim, not to mention using this as an excuse to bring down strong women.'

'Yakshis that are kind and just? Really?' I raised an eyebrow.

'Yes, kind and just!' she said, leaning forward. 'Take Purushadevi, the daughter of the queen of Pennarasunadu, which was, I will have you know, a kingdom of only women. She was attacked by the neighbouring kings, all because she fortified the kingdom's walls after her pregnancy. The women of Pennarasunadu fought bravely, but they were no match for two kingdoms that had ganged up against them.

'Seeing the war and destruction around her, Purushadevi, a Yakshi, cut open her stomach and threw her unborn child at the invading kings. Ashamed at realizing how low they had fallen, the attacking kings took their own lives as penance. So, there you have it, a good Yakshi who put an end to violence.'

'How did the princess get pregnant in a kingdom of just women?'

'Is that all you understood from this? Are you serious?' Cherian was furious. 'It's an allegorical tale of the violence men inflict on women. And it took the drastic act of having a foetus thrown on them for the kings to come to their senses. Do you not see how that's a problem?'

At that moment, there were many things I wanted to tell Cherian. I wanted to tell her that she was right, but that she couldn't have it both ways – they were either a kingdom of warriors or a kingdom of women and children. I wanted to tell her that I had points of my own, and I wanted to make another joke. But, instead, I said nothing, I stood there knowing full well that she was right, and that anything I said would be wrong.

30/06/2018
Palakkad, KL

We didn't really look for beasts while in Palakkad. We loitered around the fort, took pictures with a statue of a Yakshi near the Malampuzha Dam and trekked all the way to the rock gardens, refusing to leave until we absolutely had to.

Now I'm a complete wreck, somehow. I don't have an appetite, my lungs feel heavy and I don't feel like writing. It's strange the way certain people can have a lasting impression on you, even if you've only met them for a very short time. It's a shame Cherian and I parted ways this afternoon, but we did manage to cram in a lot on our last day together. Last night, we dug up all the information we could find on the occult practice of odi vidya, the dark magic that the Odiyan practised to gain their supernatural abilities.

The Odiyan myth became well known around the 1950s, and accounts of their black magic and supernatural abilities spread like wildfire across Kerala. The Odiyan were believed to have the ability to take any form of their choosing, often turning into a bull, a dog or a wild cat. The Odiyan also possessed superhuman strength, stamina that knew no bounds and the ability to jump to great heights. They were believed to work as contract killers and could, in theory, be hired by the masses to assassinate their upper-caste oppressors.

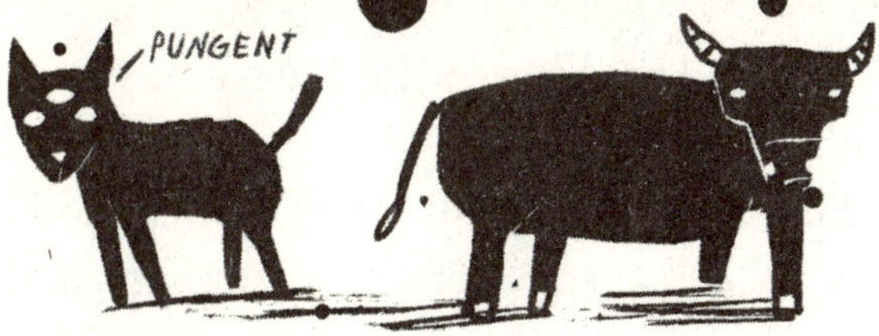

There were many wild stories and superstitions about the Odiyan, and it was believed that the source of their power came from a black-oil that they applied on their ears. The oil – since it was extracted from a foetus – was thought to possess dark magical powers that made their shape-shifting possible. These beliefs were popular in a time when there wasn't any electricity in the smaller towns, providing the perfect cover for the Odiyan to strike. They would change into an animal of their choice, and this transformation would always result in a deformity – a dog with a third eye, a bull with a missing limb. This would encourage their victims to take a closer look at them. As they walked close to the Odiyan, they would smell the pungent liquid applied behind their ears, realizing at once that they were in grave danger.

'You know what?' Cherian said. 'If you asked me, I'd say much of this myth was exaggerated – gruesome stories made up by the downtrodden to try and keep upper-caste tyrants in line. The myth and mystery shrouding them worked in their favour. The ghastlier the stories got, the more scared the "lords of the land" became.' Cherian paused. 'Isn't there a story about the way they got the oil that they used behind their ears?'

I was glad her bus was late and secretly hoped that it wouldn't turn up.

'There is, but I'm not sure you want to hear it,' I replied. Cherian stared at me, narrowing her eyebrows. I sighed.

'The Odiyan would target young women who were pregnant for the first time. They would mark their victim early in the day and return later in the night to draw her out of her house using a special spell. Their victim would sleepwalk out, and the Odiyan would steal their unborn baby before sending them, still asleep, into their homes with an open belly.'

Cherian nodded. 'They probably just made up a lot of those stories, you know. Life was tough with upper-caste people constantly bullying them, so I guess the Odiyan could have exaggerated the stories to scare away the tormentors. You know, as a survival tactic.'

When we were done discussing the Odiyan, I worked up the courage to ask Cherian if she would like to join me on my journey, but she declined my invitation. The Kalanna was the only creature on her mind, and I could never be content obsessing about just one beast.

Cherian and I said our goodbyes, and by late afternoon, we had parted ways. But just as she left, she said something that seemed completely out of character. 'I'm sorry about calling your job unimportant. Fairy chasers like you? You unravel stories and unearth our history – things that we would have otherwise lost.'

My mother once told me that I get completely taken with anyone who's willing to show me the slightest bit of compassion. I hope she isn't right.

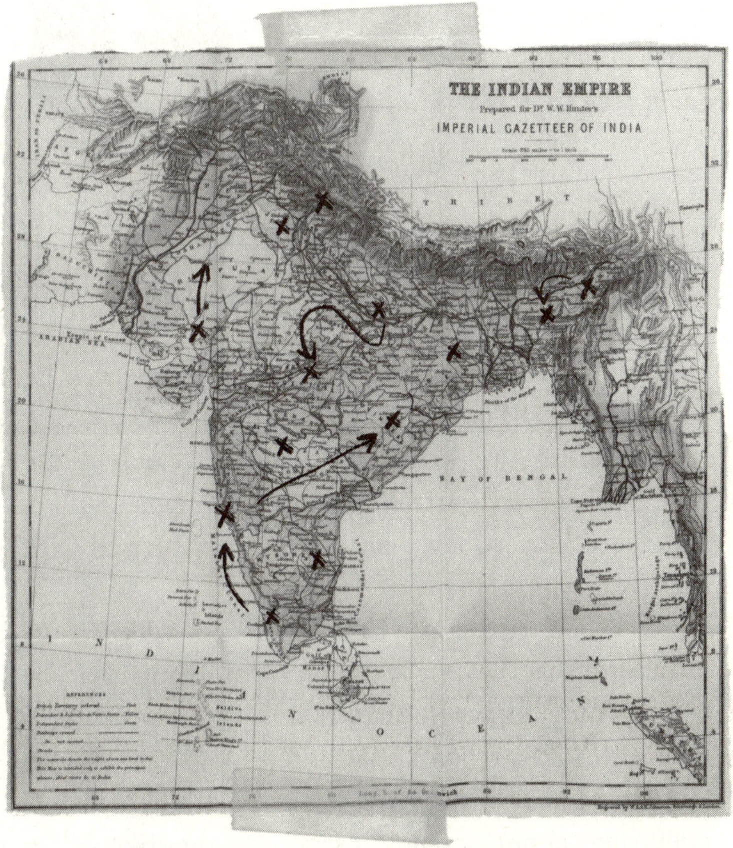

With hundreds of undiscovered creatures spread across our country, I have my work cut out for me. The question is, where do I go next?

THE WERECAT

the werecat

30/09/2018

Villages along the River Savitri, MH

Tyger Tyger, burning bright,
In the forests of the night;
What immortal hand or eye,
Could frame thy fearful symmetry?

– William Blake

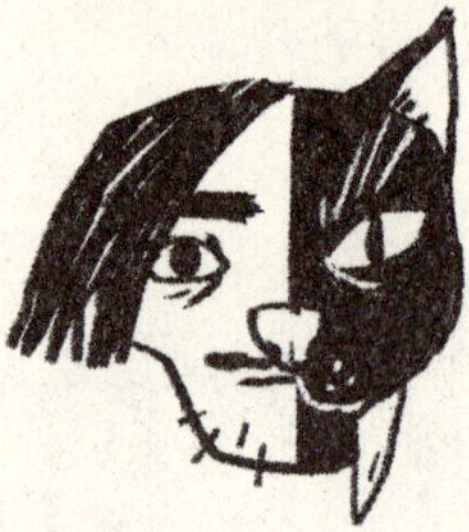

Ravi as a person alternated between 'creep-you-out' and 'curdle-your-blood'. He hardly ever said a word, tended to walk right behind you soundlessly, and he constantly proclaimed, to the world at large, that he was, in fact, half man and half cat.

'There are two kinds of Werecats; one type are feral monsters that attack livestock and humans alike, and the other are level-headed humans blessed with cat-like strength,' he said.

Ravi had somehow convinced the villagers of Kemburli that he was a Werecat, swearing that he wasn't going to harm them, but that he was there to help instead. So when I travelled through the villages along the banks of the River Savitri, south of Mumbai, enquiring about strange creatures, the people of Kemburli proudly proclaimed that they had their very own resident beast – the Werecat Ravi.

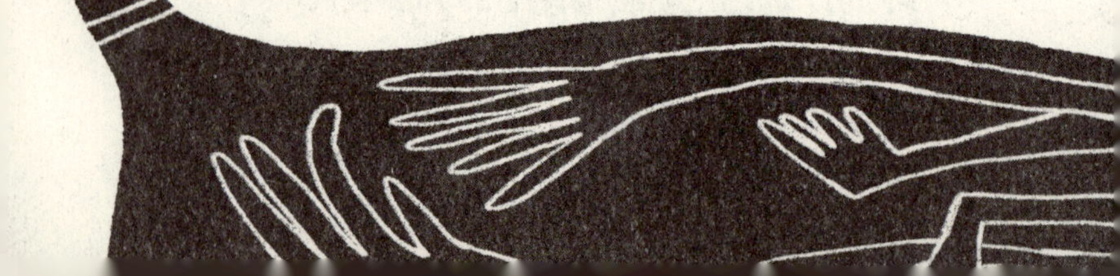

I didn't believe him for a second, but when I found myself alone in a forest, with no clue about how to get out safely, my mind began playing tricks on me. I was almost willing to give him the benefit of the doubt.

'So how does one become a Werecat?' I asked. 'Do you need to be bitten by another Werecat? What's the process?'

'Of course not!' He looked very insulted. 'There are several ways to become a Werecat and getting bitten by one is *not* one of them,' he said. 'You transform into a Werecat if you've lived a life of evil and ask for forgiveness only at the last possible minute. This *always* turns you into a beast. You can also be cursed into becoming a Werecat, or you can transform into one by boiling and drinking the blood of a dead tiger.' After a small pause, he added, 'It is also possible to pay someone to use black magic and turn you into one, but I wouldn't recommend that.'

'Why not?' I asked.

'People claiming to perform black magic? They're all just frauds! They hunt tigers and chop off their paws, claiming that wearing a tiger paw coated in gold brings wealth and good luck. Do you know just how many big cats they've killed?' He didn't wait for me to respond.

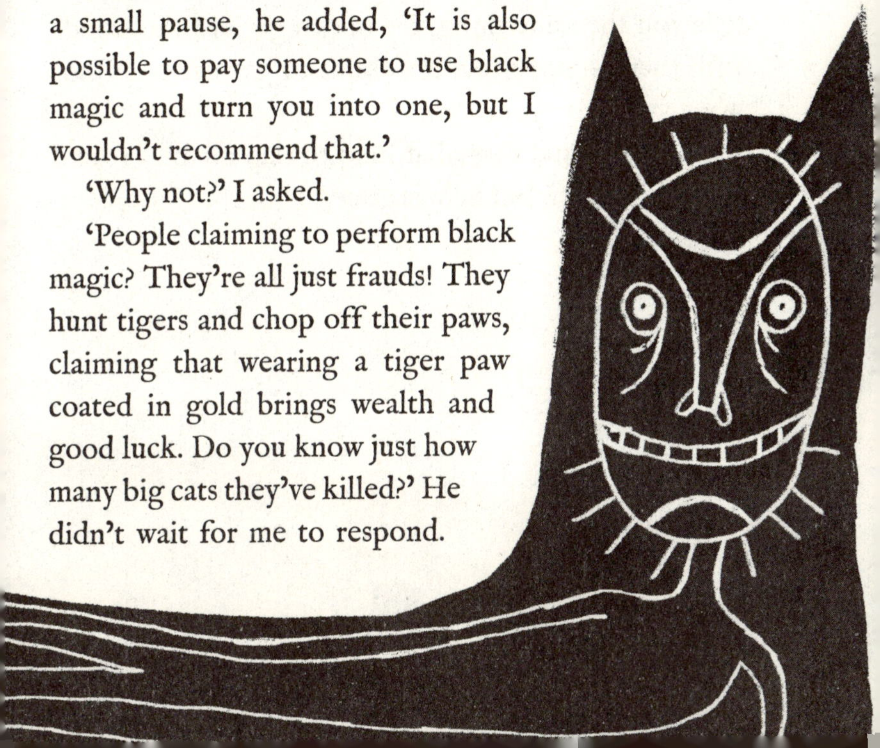

'Far too many!'

'I'm sorry, I didn't know,' I replied.

'Some day, they'll cross my path, and when that happens, I'll tear them into ribbons. Huh! You know, I never talk this much – it's probably the most I've spoken my entire life. There's something strange about you, the way you get people to open up.'

Werecat Ravi muttered something under his breath, and then he sighed. 'Keep walking for five minutes, the nearest village is that way – ek dum straight.'

'Aren't you going to take me to the other Werecat –'

He cut me off. 'You look like a smart guy, so let me give you some free advice. Never accept mithai from strangers. But more importantly, when someone tells you they're a Werecat, and when the rest of the village tells you the same thing, try not to go into the woods with them – not when it's about to get dark and not when you're on your own.'

I laughed and turned around to slap my new friend on the shoulder, but he was gone.

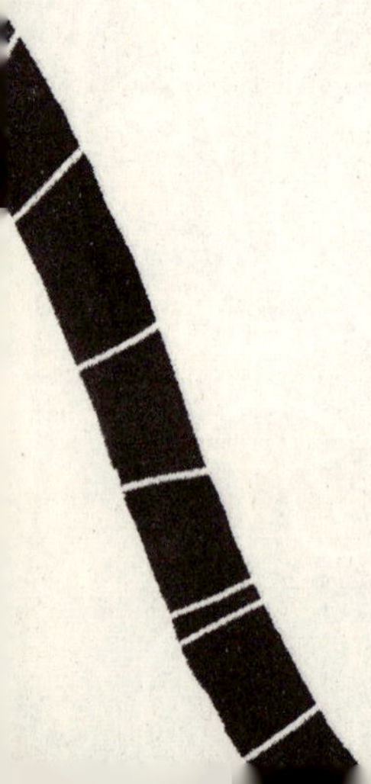

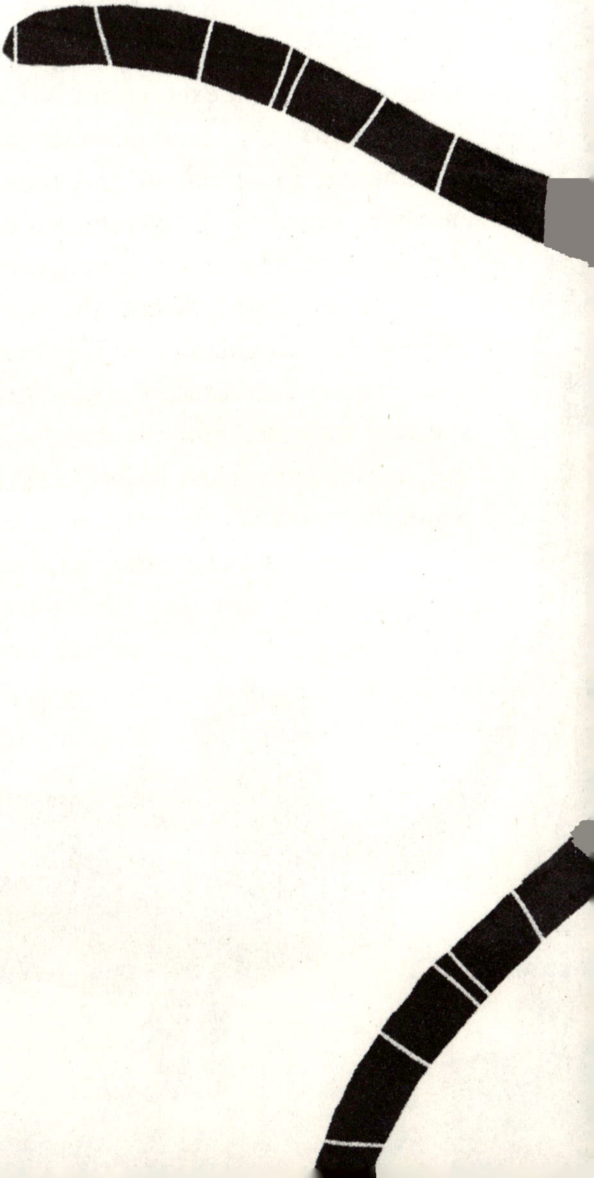

THE KARKADANN

the karkadann

28/09/2018

Villages along the River Savitri

I had travelled by sea to get to the west, and looking back, it wasn't the best idea, but I don't want to talk about that. I wandered the streets of Mumbai, dazed and confused, and exactly one week after my arrival, I decided to move further west, towards the deserts of Gujarat, in search of the Karkadann. You may not have heard of these creatures before, but you've definitely heard of their cousin, the Unicorn.

Make no mistake, despite the horn protruding from its head, the Karkadann is no Unicorn. Described by the 10th-century Persian scholar Abu Rayhan al-Biruni as a creature with the build of a dark, scaly buffalo, a short tail, eyes hanging close to its cheeks and the horn bent upwards from the top of its nose, these creatures are ferocious. In fact, they were considered so fierce that they were thought to attack any animal they saw while it was grazing, unprovoked.

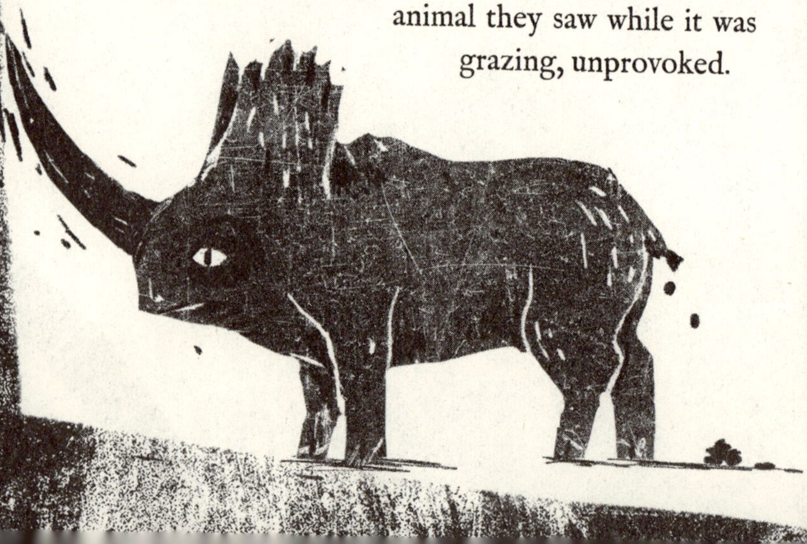

The Karkadann also makes an appearance in *The One Thousand and One Nights* in one of Sindbad the Sailor's voyages, where they're believed to be sworn enemies of the elephant. According to the story, after spotting an elephant, the Karkadann would sharpen its horn against a tree and charge right at the elephant, piercing its soft underbelly. But since it used so much force, the Karkadann's horn would invariably get stuck, and the elephant would fall on it and kill it in the process! If it did manage to survive, the fat of the elephant melting under the sun would blind the Karkadann, and leave it immobile and vulnerable to the gigantic Roc Bird carrying it off along with the elephant to feed its young.

The Karkadann's horn is believed to possess healing properties, and merely holding it is said to help cure constipation. But I'm not interested in its magical properties, nor do I really think it can cure lameness and epilepsy. That last bit is almost definitely made up. But the thing that really interests me about the Karkadann is not the creature itself, but the fact that fossils of the Elasmotherium, an animal almost identical to the Karkadann, were found in eastern China and southern Russia. So maybe these creatures did find their way to India, and if they did, perhaps there are other 'mythical' creatures out there, waiting for me to bring them to light.

Note to self: Do not pick up the Karkadann horn on a full stomach.

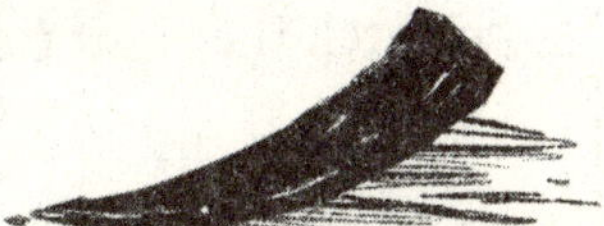

ROMPO

rompo

5/8/2018

Kachale Village, Raigad
Fort Natural Reserve

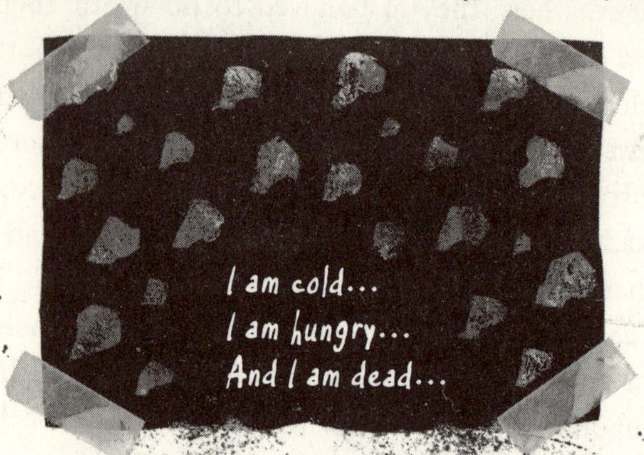

It was alarming to count the number of people who would ignore a dead body lying within the boundaries of their village and simply go about their day, without a care in the world. Perhaps, they thought I was a scamster, or maybe they didn't want to touch me because they didn't quite know my caste. Or, perhaps, I was overthinking this – they really had no reason to notice me. I was just a stranger who'd waltzed into their village and pretended to be dead, a stranger whose only way of whiling away the time was to count the number of people who walked away nonchalantly.

So why was my stomach pressed to the cold ground, my face prickly with impressions from the sand pressing against my cheek? Well, because you need the right bait to catch the right fish, don't you?

You see, I was lying in wait for the Rompo. What's that, you ask? The best way to describe it would be to close your eyes and think of a ferret. Now add a bit of possum, drop in a bit of gremlin and throw a bucket of water at it. And that's sort of what a Rompo looks like. Even though they're ferret sized, with slender bodies no longer than two to three feet, the Rompo can be quite vicious. These creatures are often described as having rabbit-like faces, human ears, a horse's mane, and arms and legs that resemble a cross between those of a stout badger and a bear cub.

The Rompo comes out only at night and loves to feed on human corpses. It tends to circle around a dead body multiple times and purrs gently as it begins to feed. I made sure not to move around too much, because when a Rompo smells someone alive, it gets nervous. When it gets jumpy, it changes its colour to match its surroundings, and take it from me, you will never spot a Rompo once it blends in with the landscape, no matter how long you decide to play dead.

Something I learned the hard way.

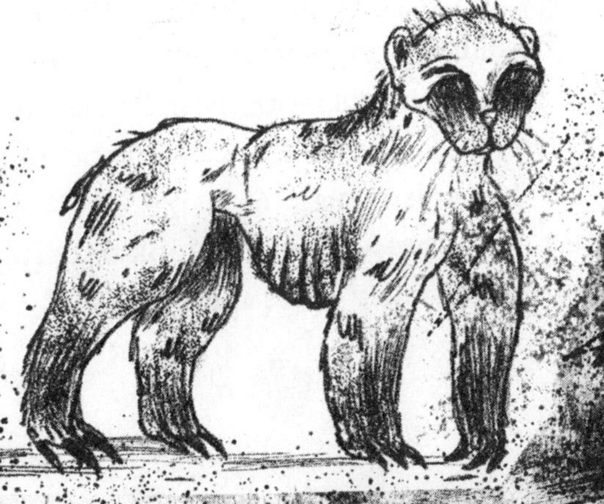

THE MANTICORE

the manticore

8/10/2018

Purna Wildlife Sanctuary, MH-GJ

What should you do when you come upon a Manticore?

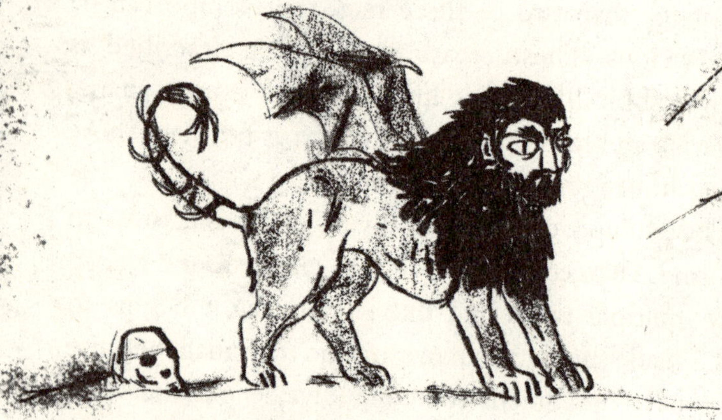

The answer to that question is simple – nothing. Because there's nothing you *can* do when face to face with a Manticore.

Manticores are said to be creatures from Greek mythology, but if you believe that, you're buying into one of the oldest examples of cultural appropriation. These creatures have their origins in Persian lore, where they're described as beasts that can only be found in the depths of the Indian jungles.

So just what does a Manticore look like? Remember that one bearded uncle who's at every family gathering?

Just paste his face on the body of a lion, add some bat wings and a scorpion's tail, and there you have it! These creatures possess the speed and agility of a lion, they can fly like bats, yet they almost never use their claws or wings to hunt. Instead, a Manticore relies on its tail and the venomous, porcupine-like spikes that they launch into the air to shoot down their prey and paralyse it. The Manticore prowls the jungles of western India and is said to have a great fondness for human flesh. It hides behind bushes so that only its bearded face can be seen, and if its victim ventures close enough to take a look, it's already too late.

However, there is one way to protect yourself from a Manticore. Despite having the face of a human, these creatures can't speak our language – they can only produce noises much like the sound of a trumpet. So if you ever find yourself in a jungle, and hear the sound of a trumpet accompanied by distant imagery of bearded men in the bushes, run as fast as you can, because if a Manticore spots you, it will eat you whole – skin, bones and clothes – leaving no more than a splatter of blood.

The desert is a strange place to visit alone. To me, it feels like purgatory, like a never-ending beach with the promise of the sea one dune over. I have been here all day, with nothing but a map and a compass, and some water in a dirty plastic bottle. I fear that I may get lost if I dare venture further.

Yet, I push on, lured by the promise of the sea lapping at my toes, cursed by the pursuit of trying to spot just one fantastic beast, lurking on the other side of the dune yonder.

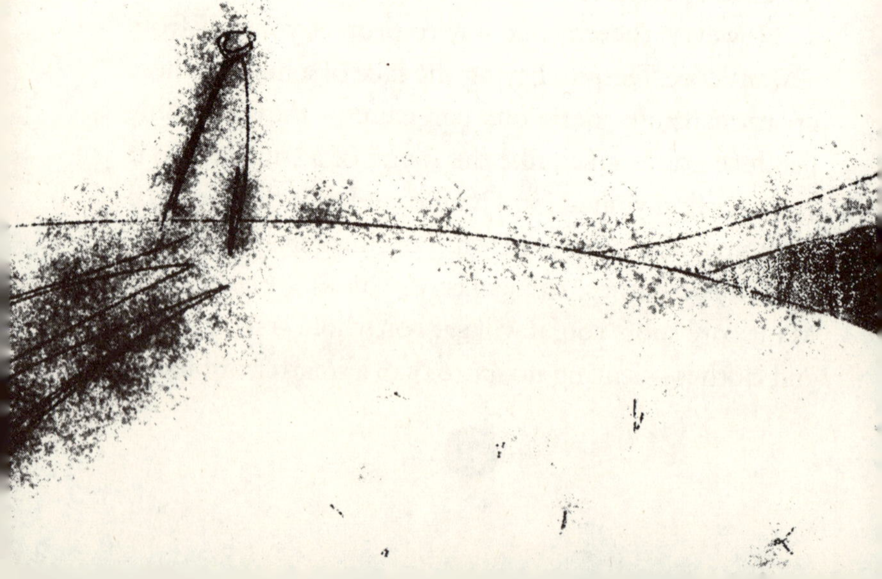

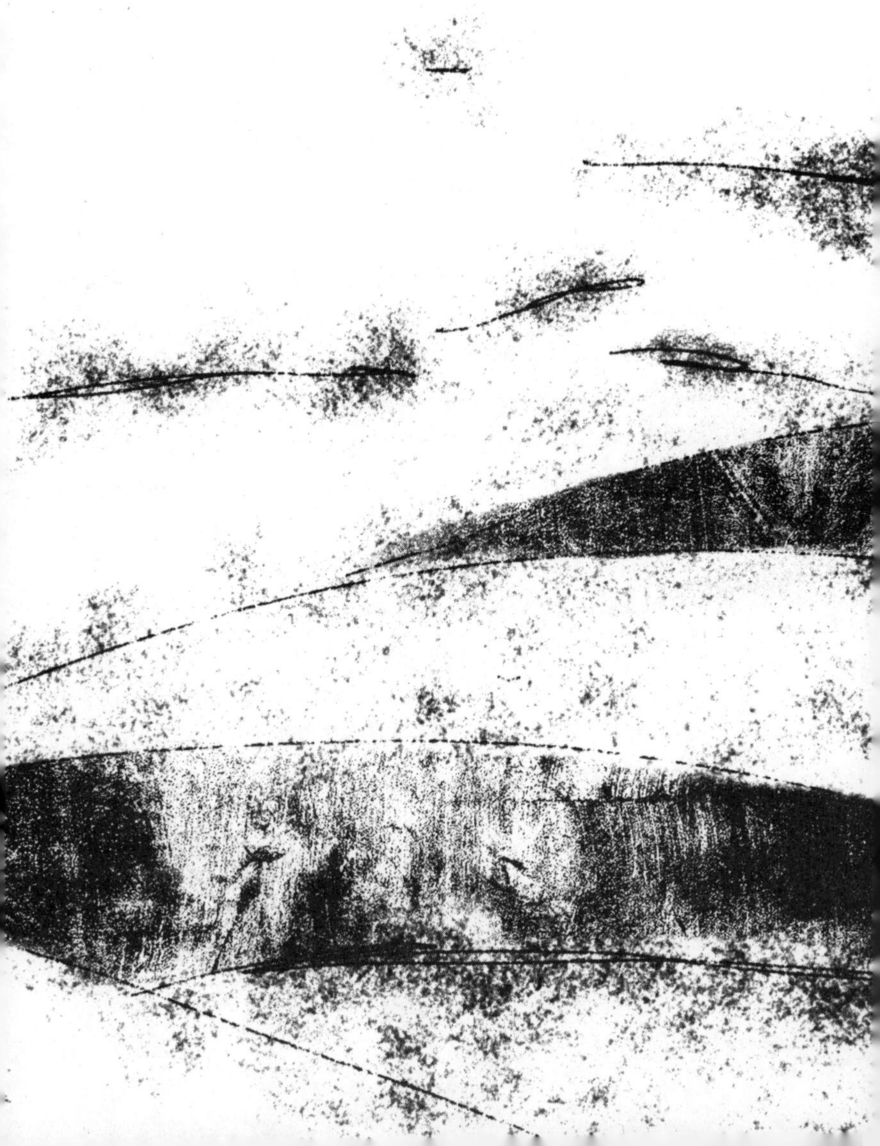

THE MYRMEX INDIKOS
the myrmex indikos

10/10/2018
- Unknown, Kachchh, GJ

Most people who have crossed the deserts in search of the Myrmex Indikos have done so to find the gold dug out of the sand by these creatures. But not me. I don't care about gold or wealth (though, to be completely honest, I *could* use some money to pay for my travels right now). I just want to meet these fascinating beasts, tell their stories, and maybe snap a picture or two, even if, come to think of it, I'm completely unprepared to meet them.

Herodotus, a Greek historian and geographer, wrote in his book of histories around the fifth century CE that the Myrmex were fox-sized ants who lived in the deserts of India, guarding large deposits of gold. They lived under the earth and shifted large amounts of golden sand from their burrows to the surface. When robbers ventured into the desert to steal this gold, they would prepare for days.

Note: While on the subject of ants, look out for the Myrmecoleon if you can. They are supposed to be the offspring of ants and lions, so their occurrence in nature is, well, rare. They don't live very long, often starving to death within weeks of their birth. The ant body can't digest the food that its lion head eats, and its lion head can't eat the food that the ant body can digest. The logical statement, therefore, is that 'the Myrmecoleon perishes for lack of food'.

The first and most obvious rule that I'm breaking is that I'm going alone. In the past, the tribes that looted the Myrmex's gold often travelled in large parties, each person taking three camels with them – two male and three female. The robbers would ride on the female camels, while the male camels were made to follow behind. They would pick the hottest day of the year to raid the Myrmex as it was common knowledge that the giant ants would be deep in their burrows, their gold left out in the open. The tribesmen would then zip across the Myrmex's land, pillaging gold as fast as they could.

It only takes a few moments for the Myrmex to realize that they've been robbed, sniff the thieves out and chase after them. These ants are unparalleled in speed, and those raiding their gold, especially those weighed down by greed, were almost certain to get caught if they didn't rush. The raiders would ride as swiftly as they could, and if it seemed like the ants were catching up, they would cut loose the male camels for the Myrmex to devour. The reason they chose to ride the female camels was because they were much faster – they had their young on their minds and would return to them at all costs.

So, you see, I was hopelessly underprepared. But maybe the Myrmex would be kind when they sniffed out my true intentions. Perhaps they might even reward me with some of their gold.

Maybe I'm just plain stupid.

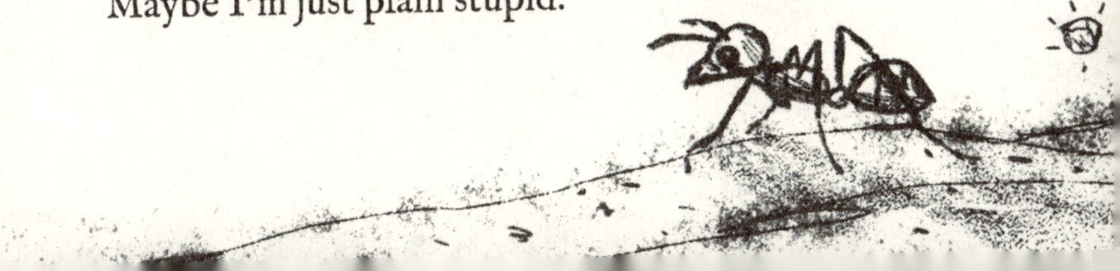

THE GRIFFIN
the griffin

13/10/2018

Unknown Location,
Kachchh, GJ

All my life, I've been made to believe that Griffins belong to the stories from the West. I've read fantasy stories about them in English, I've seen them on European flags, and even spotted them as logos of sports teams. But, like most lost creatures, Griffins might also have origins in India. They reigned over a domain that stretched between the Persian plains and East India. I use the word 'reign' because they were considered the rulers of all creatures, probably because they were part lion (king of the beasts) and part eagle (king of the birds).

Griffins were frequently found in ancient India and would nest on top of mountains, decorating their nests

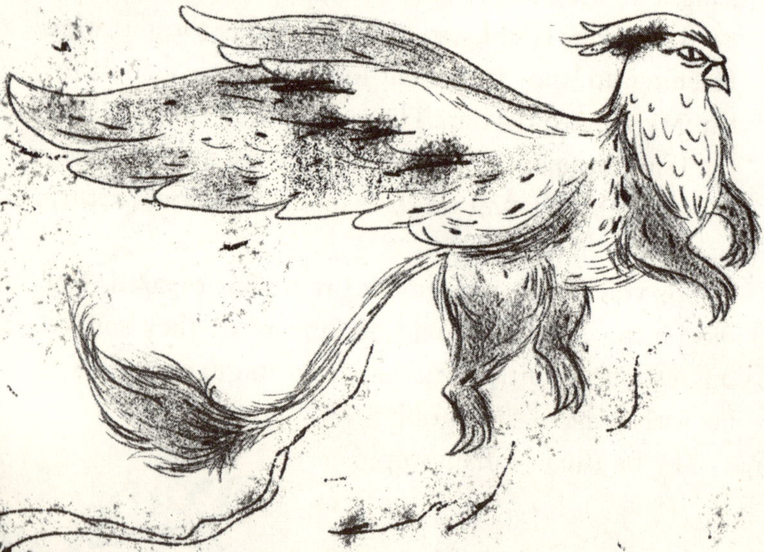

with gold and other precious metals. They were also guardians of treasures, and seeing as how they were very territorial, Griffins were known to frequently kill bandits who tried to make away with their gold.

They were also believed to possess various powers. Their golden feathers, for instance, could cure blindness, and their claws and eggs brought prosperity and wealth. Although these creatures didn't pose much of a threat to humans – apart, of course, from the occasional hiker who wandered too close to their nests – they did pose a threat to livestock like sheep and goats. Yet people tended not to make too much of a fuss about missing animals because the Griffins always made sure to leave golden feathers as payment.

The Griffins of Asia, however, are a bit different from the ones in Europe. Unlike their European cousins, Indian Griffins are considered to be more lion-like, with less eagle in them. Indian Griffins aren't the best flyers – they are sort of like peacocks. Like peacocks, they can only fly short distances comfortably. But make no mistake, they are still powerful enough to kill elephants and dragons.

Note: Sometimes, Griffins mate with horses to produce half-horse and half-griffin creatures called Hippogriffs.

I hate travelling; from stand-offish villagers to broken-down buses, there are many known, as well as *hundreds* of unknown, challenges and annoyances along the way. But sometimes, once in a blue moon, everything goes exactly according to plan, and occasionally it goes better than expected.

I had planned on taking trains all the way from the south to the west of India, but with limited seats and my increasing impatience, I decided to travel by sea. The plan was simple – I would meet the ship in the sea when it stopped to transport weary sailors back to land, and it would take me to Mumbai. What I hadn't accounted for, however, was the hassle of being ferried to it. But here's the part where everything goes better than planned. I was able to get a place aboard a fishing boat that promised to take me to my ship in exchange for a few days' labour. I didn't have to pay a rupee! It was awesome.

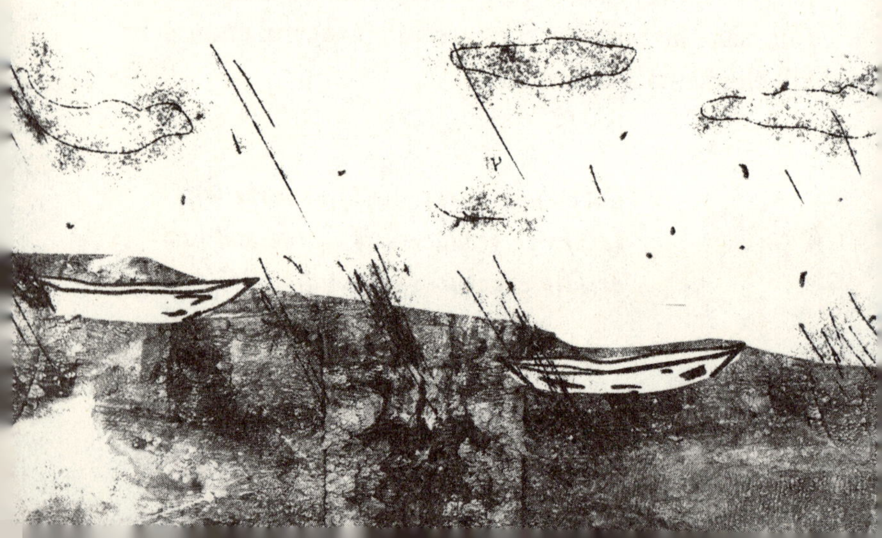

05/07/2018
Kochi Port, KL
(Day 1)

THE MAKARA
the makara

As I got ready to board the boat, I couldn't help but think of the sailors who had stood on the banks of this very port over a thousand years ago. My ancestors were probably not much older then than I am now, and they were ready to set sail on this life-threatening journey. The sea must have been a terrifying place back then, with legions of unidentified legends lurking beneath the surface, and bloodthirsty pirates, greedy traders and belligerent navies above.

Makaras, though, weren't something sailors feared – instead, they revered them. Often depicted as a mixture of creatures – most commonly, with the face of an elephant, the paws of a lion and the body of a crocodile – the image of the Makara would be engraved on ships and vessels, possibly a talisman for a safe passage. According to the Vedas, the Makara is described as the vehicle of the god Varuna. Over the years, the Makara has found its way into the gates and stone carvings of

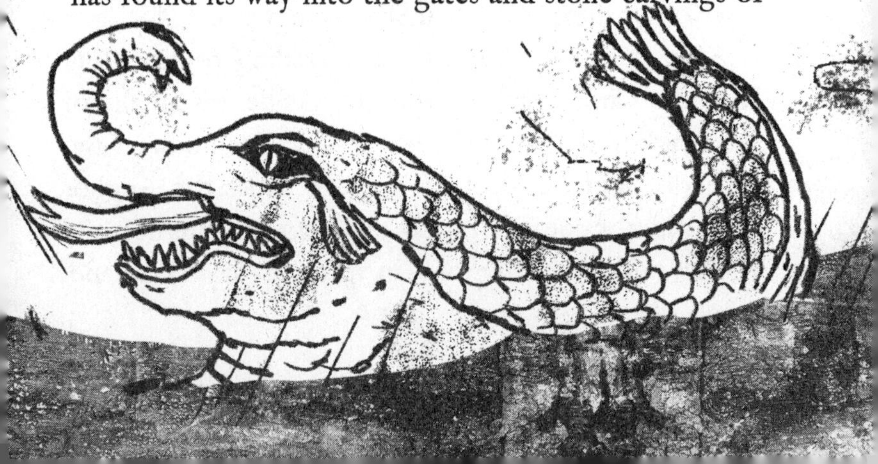

many temples across the Indian subcontinent and South-East Asia, each sporting a different depiction.

On the very first day of my voyage, I pictured my ancestors – the Chola dynasty – on the shores, ready to set sail for the Malaysian peninsula. After establishing their dominance in south India, they were looking east.

Their control over seaports along the Indian Ocean was the driving force of their success. But the stronghold they'd maintained so far was in serious jeopardy. As shipbuilders became better at their jobs, ships became stronger. Soon enough, large boats only needed to dock in one port, as opposed to two or three ports as they did before. Since the ports along south-east India and South-East Asia were the largest and most important ports of the time, the two kingdoms – Chola in south India and Srivijaya in Malaysia – each needed to make sure that ships chose their ports over the other's. The ambitions of the Chola dynasty were met with stiff resistance from the Srivijaya Empire of present-day Malaysia and Indonesia, with the king going so far as to employ sea gypsies or pirates to attack Chola ships and force other ships to dock in Srivijayan ports.

After constant interference in trading routes, King Rajendra Chola was forced to act. As he was an ally of the Angkor dynasty of present-day Cambodia, King Rajendra sent his fleet of ships to assist the Angkor king when a conflict broke out between Angkor and Tambralinga, a kingdom in present-day Thailand.

Rajendra Chola split his force into two parts, a main invading fleet and an auxiliary fleet, and met the Srivijaya ships in the Malacca Strait in the year 1025 CE.

What the Srivijayan king did not know, however, was that only the auxiliary Chola ships were sent to the strait, reserving the bulk of the attacking force to go around the island and land in the Srivijaya capital. It was a feat considered impossible, especially during the monsoon, when the seas were simply too choppy to navigate. But the Chola vessels were among the most technologically advanced in the world at the time, and equipped with compasses and even flamethrowers! The Chola force caught the Srivijaya Empire off guard, and after sacking the capital city, they sailed towards the Malacca Strait, surrounding the Srivijaya naval forces from both sides. The Chola vessels were then able to sail to Tambralinga and secure a victory for their Angkor allies.

I don't know if it's just a curious coincidence that the Makara lived in the very same waters that the Chola ships travelled, or if the Chola Empire had something to do with introducing the beast to South-East Asia. Because in the temples of India and parts of south-eastern Asia, across Tibet, Malaysia, Thailand and Cambodia, different versions of the Makara are found – Makaras with the body of a seal and the head of an elephant, with fish scales and the jaw of a crocodile, with an elephant trunk and the tails of peacocks – all of them equally majestic and terrifying.

SUVANNAMACCHA

suvannamaccha

06/07/2018

Sri Lānkan Waters

(Day 2)

Many people are prone to seasickness or being gloomy when they sail the seas, but not I. I like the gentle rocking of the boat, the swell of the ocean, the smell of the breeze. But, most of all, I love the dreams that the sea gives me.

I'm thinking about the dream I had about my ancestors and how their influence travelled across the seas. It has got me wondering if I could spot a Kadal Kanni (a mermaid). I would particularly like to meet Ravan's mermaid daughter, Suvannamaccha. I'm not sure if she's around anymore, but perhaps I'll get lucky and chance upon other mermaids from her tribe. As for Ravan's daughter, I just have to make do with her story.

The mermaid princess Suvannamaccha appears in the Angkor and other South-East Asian versions of the Ramayana. Her story begins when

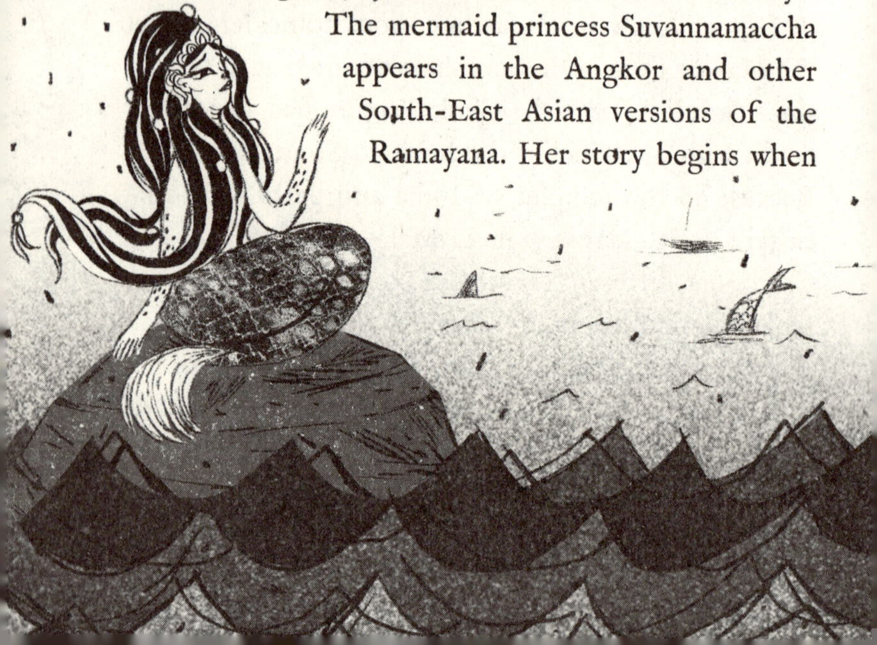

Hanuman noticed that the rocks tossed into the sea by the vanars, when they built the bridge to Lanka, disappeared into thin air. He found out that the boulders were being carried away by mermaids the moment they touched water. Enraged, he sought out their leader and charged at the princess Suvannamaccha, who evaded his attacks with ease. As the two fought, they began to fall in love with each other. Hanuman told the princess about Sita's abduction, and Suvannamaccha, smitten with the son of the wind god, agreed to stop stealing the stones and put back the ones they'd taken earlier.

So, you see, Hanuman had finally met his match, and could not have defeated Suvannamaccha had she not fallen in love with him. The misfortunes of war caused them to part ways, but Suvannamaccha's story does not end there...

Note: There are over 300 versions of the Ramayana, with different ones appearing across Myanmar, Indonesia, Cambodia, Laos, the Philippines, Sri Lanka, Nepal, Thailand, Singapore, Malaysia, Japan, Mongolia, Vietnam and China, besides India, of course! Unlike the Indian version of the Ramayana, the South-East Asian versions use clothes, weapons, landmasses and natural disasters from their own cultures, some of them even introducing new characters and plots.

...Because in the Ramakien, the Thai version of the Ramayana, Ram and Lakshman were abducted by Maiyarap, Ravan's rakshasa cousin and the king of the underworld. Maiyarap disguised himself as a vanar and used his magical sleeping powder to put Hanuman and all the other vanars to sleep. He then nabbed Ram and Lakshman, and locked them in a cage to have them cooked the next day.

A few hours later, Hanuman woke up from his slumber, enraged, found the gateway to the underworld in the form of a nine-petalled lotus and shrank himself down in size to fit through its stem. Hanuman plunged into the depths of the netherworld and, once there, he went on a rampage, killing a thousand demon guards, an elephant and hundreds of chicken-sized mosquitoes. Hanuman advanced along the underworld, until he was accosted by a vanar warrior with the tail of a fish.

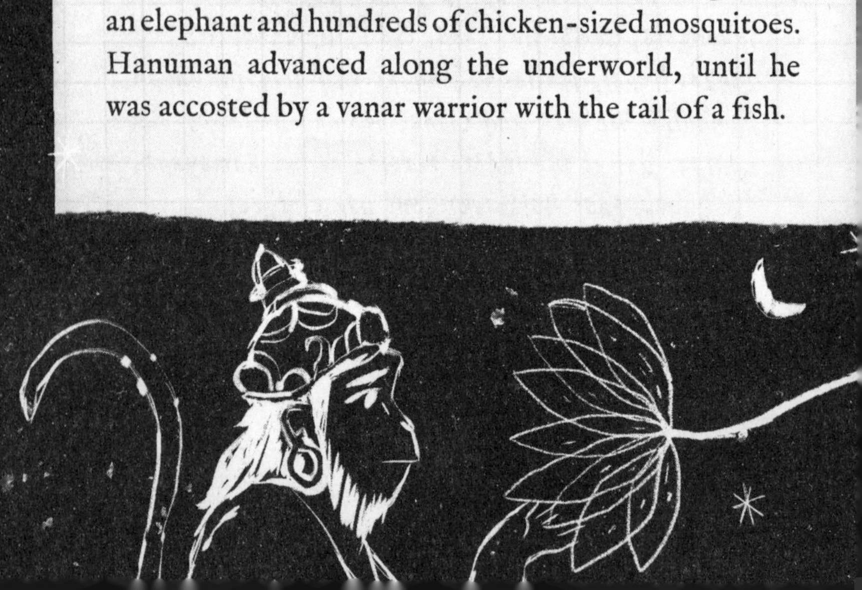

The two warriors fought fiercely, trading blows and dodging each other's attacks with equal dexterity. Surprised by the skills of the fish-tailed warrior, Hanuman asked the fighter's name, and was proud to learn that his opponent was none other than Macchanu, his son with Suvannamaccha.

Macchanu, however, didn't believe Hanuman, and insisted that his mother had always told him that his father was a cosmic creature. Hanuman responded by smiling, and when he opened his mouth, he exhaled the moon and the stars, and they filled the skies of the underworld.

Macchanu finally believed that the warrior in front of him was his father. Although conflicted about betraying his foster father, Maiyarap, Macchanu finally relented and revealed the way to find Ram. Hanuman smuggled himself into Maiyarap's kingdom, defeated Maiyarap, and freed Ram and Lakshman from their cage.

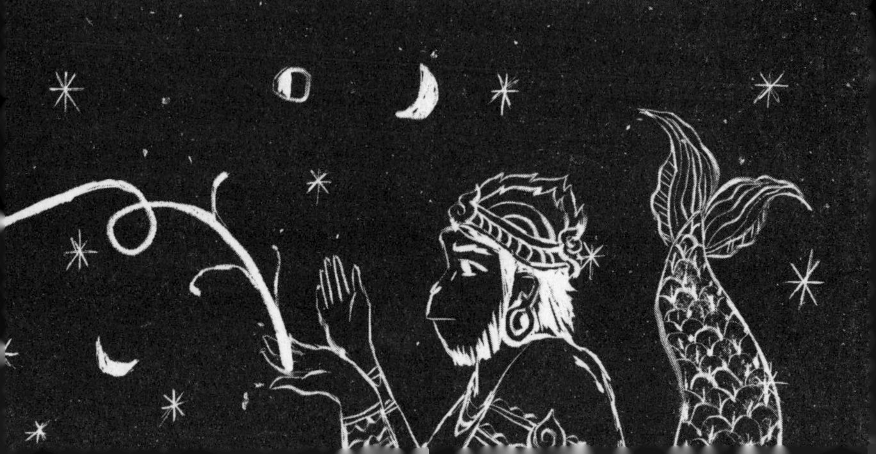

07/07/2018

Sri Lankan Waters
(Day 3)

I had no idea that fishermen stayed out in the sea for days. I had no clue that it required so much work, and I hadn't the faintest idea of the sacrifices involved. The men I've got to know over the past couple of days spend weeks, sometimes as long as 20 days, out at sea. They sail over parts of the ocean that are anywhere between 2,000 and 6,000 feet in depth, and they fish throughout the day and night with hardly any rest!

The first thing I learnt about fishing in the sea was that it takes close to nine hours to reel in the net. The nets are spread across several hundreds of feet and require a crew of at least 10 people, working in shifts of an hour each, to pull them in. The net is fastened to a pulley with two people pulling it in and one person keeping watch. This is done so that the fishermen can drag the bigger fish in and keep them from falling into the sea when they hit the boat. A group of people then drag the net away and untangle the fish from it. Most fish stuck in the nets end up dead, but the ones that are alive really put up a fight! Work goes on like clockwork, and the more fish we catch, the faster time flies.

It's hard to make time for sleep on the boat, let alone an extra hour or two to ourselves. Most of us spend our free time playing cards below the deck in the boat driver's room – the driest room on the boat and quite cosy.

Today is my third day on the boat, and I was woken up early in the morning by the sound of the engines revving up.

'What's going on?' I asked.

The boat driver didn't respond. There was something about the way he looked ahead, his eyebrows narrowed, mouth slightly open. He looked confused beyond measure.

'What is it?' I asked once more.

This time, he tapped on the radar, muttering a few words under his breath.

'But there's nothing under us,' I said, glancing at the radar.

'Exactly, not a thing!' he said, powering the engine once again.

This time, the boat dragged a couple of feet, coughing and wheezing puffs of ash-grey smoke. It was almost as though we were playing tug of war with the sea. I looked at the radar once more, and all at once it struck me!

'I know what's going on!' I gasped. 'It's the Echeneis...the Remora...'

I ran to the deck of the boat, hoping to catch a glimpse of them, but of course I couldn't see them. If the accounts of Pliny the Elder and of Isidore of Seville were true, then I should have known that I couldn't see them, not unless I dived below the hull.

According to the ancient Greeks, the Echeneis or Remora were tiny fish with disc-shaped suction mechanisms on their heads and bodies. They were found in the Indian Ocean and would latch on to the hulls of boats and ships. The Echeneis would appear in large numbers and were powerful enough to slow down or even hold back a ship!

It *had* to be them. I would have jumped into the sea to check for myself had I known how to swim. I alerted the crew, and soon enough, one of the better swimmers, the one who could hold his breath the longest, dove under the boat. I grabbed him as soon as he surfaced, asking him what he had seen underwater, but his reply was disappointing.

'Just some fish,' he said. 'Maybe it's an issue with the engine.'

'The fish! What did they look like?' I pressed.

'Small – not something I've seen before, but small,' he replied.

I ran back to the boat driver's room, and when he powered the boat this time, it jerked for a moment and then smoothly cut across the water, unburdened by the Echeneis. The crew has chalked it down to an engine malfunction, but I know what it really was.

It's such a shame I don't know how to swim.

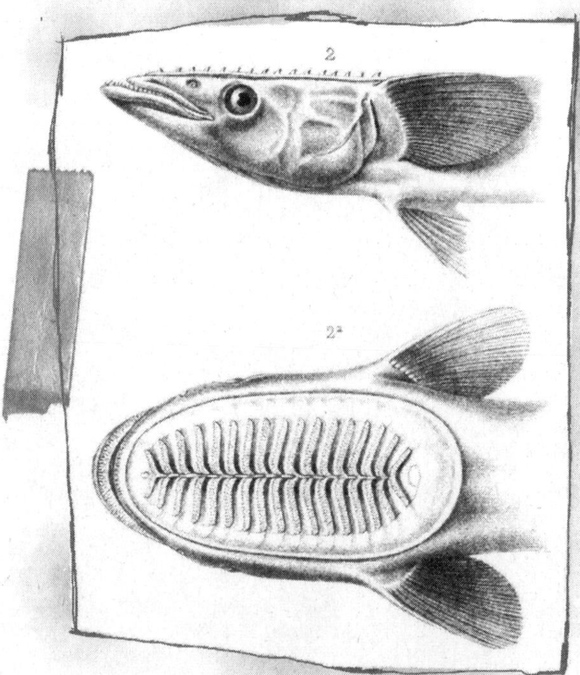

I am finally ready to talk about my journey from the south to the west. However, I wish never to speak of it again, and of the experiences I lived through on the fishing boat I called home for a week.

The ocean holds many secrets, and though I am happy that I was able to unravel a few, I am grateful that they didn't cost me my life.

TIMINGILA
timingila

10/07/2018
Arābian Sea

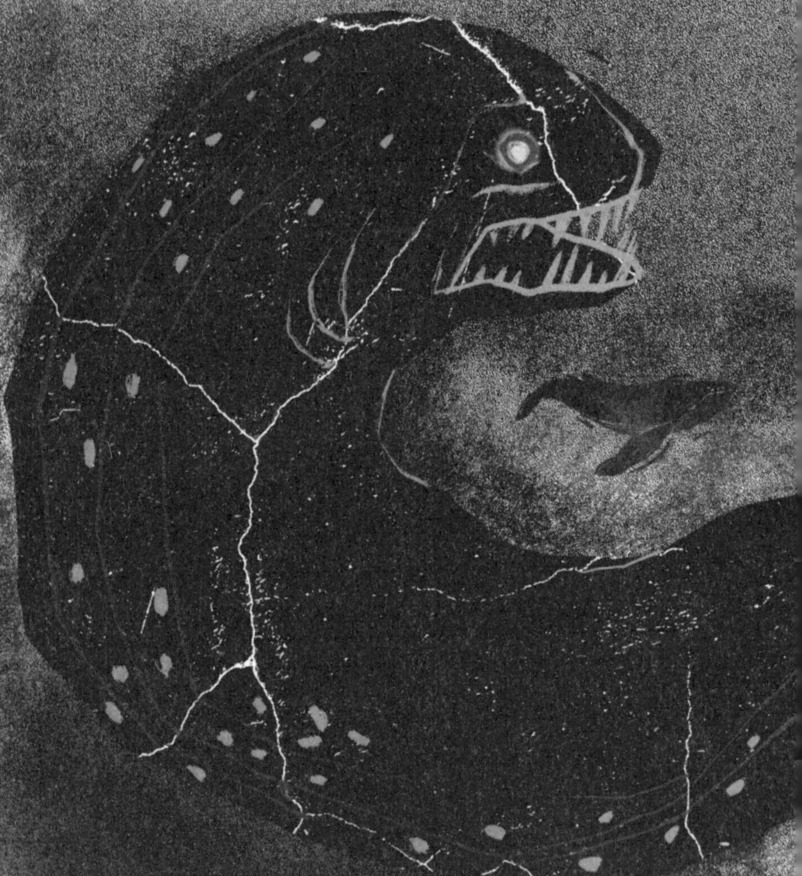

Sinusoidal waves swerved and curved,
striking the ship's swollen sides.

Snakes of water struck with force,
startling the ship's safe insides.

I'm a shipwreck, spirit sunken,
body tossed from side to side.

Not by storm or sea or stone,
but by the Timingila's silent scorn.

The largest creatures on Earth, the Timingila can move the seas. Tsunamis engulf the shores when Timingila swim close enough to land; storm clouds appear when they surface to exhale hot air against the cold sea breeze; and Earth shakes when they rest their heads on the seabed.

The Timingila are so large that they can swallow a pod of blue whales in a single gulp.

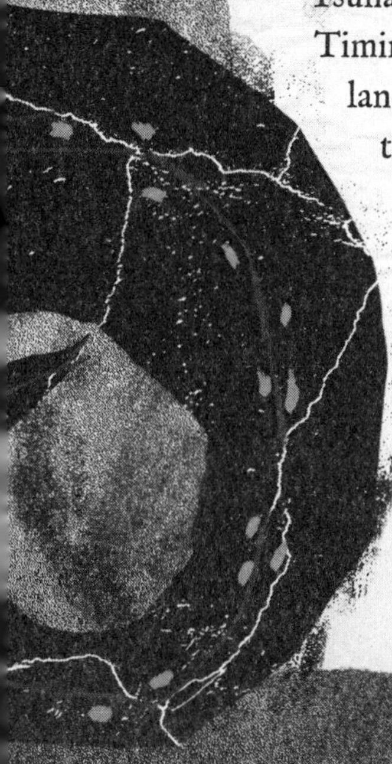

THE KETEA INDIKOS

the ketea indikos

11/07/2018

Arabian Sea

(Day 7)

The waters between India and Sri Lanka were once said to be infested with all sorts of monsters. The Timingila, for instance, reigned here. But in addition to the bigger, scarier monsters, there were also those creatures that didn't pose any threat to humans.

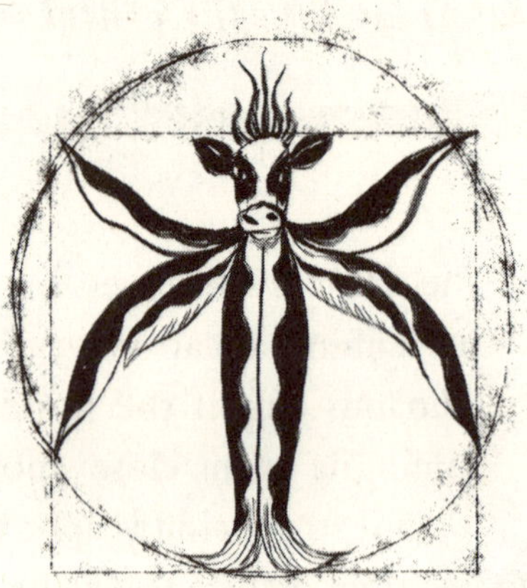

The term 'kete' or 'ketea' is a blanket term used for these monsters. They're sea creatures with the bodies of fishes and the heads of cows, wolves, lions, dogs or pretty much any animal under the sun you could think of, including humans. Only, the human Ketea, despite bearing a resemblance to mermaids, are more beastly to look at, with spikes and spines instead of hair.

Ketea are mostly harmless – as a matter of fact, they

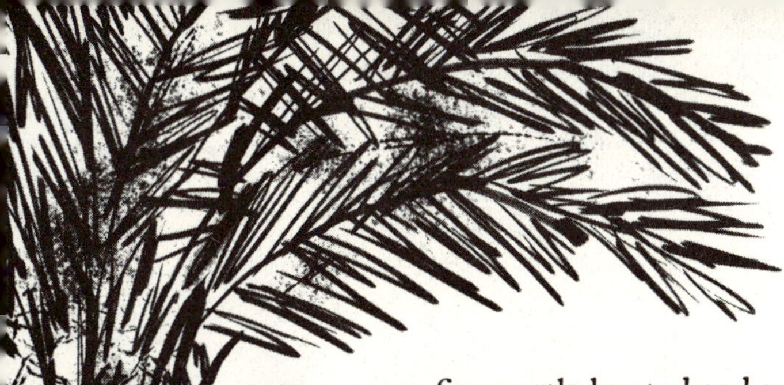

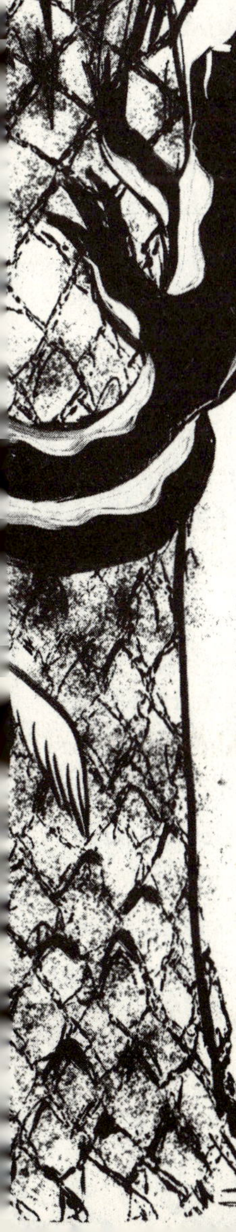

were frequently hunted and caught along with fish by the ancient Sri Lankans. The tail of a Ketea loops and coils many times over, and its legs end in sharp claws or feet. The Ketea remain inside the sea for the better part of the day, but when morning turns to night, they leave their watery homes to graze in the fields by the sea.

According to the Roman historian Aelian, the Ketea enjoy eating the ripe fruits of the date palm, and they knock them off the tree by whipping their prehensile tails against it, or by coiling their tails and shaking the tree until all the fruits fall down. They loiter around on land as long as it is dark, but when the sun begins to rise, they plunge back into the sea, disappearing deep into the water. I've spent many sleepless nights looking for them, sometimes hearing loud splashes in the water when I turn on my torchlight.

11/07/2018

Coasts of Mumbai
Day 7

I did a lot of digging when it came to undiscovered animals and where they live. But with the Farasi Bahari, I was completely unprepared.

Like certain kinds of Ketea, the Farasi Bahari are horses that live in the sea, but they're more horse than fish, and they're very picky about when they leave the water. They only step onto land on certain nights, and there's usually no logic or reason for why they pick a particular night.

These creatures have green scales that make them shine like emeralds in the moonlight. They may look like horses, but they are swifter than the fastest horse on land. In fact, they are so fast that horse breeders tend to let their mares loose by the sea at night, hoping a Farasi Bahari will mate with them. You see, legend has it that a horse born of a Farasi Bahari and a mare will be tireless and never fall short of breath, mainly because they are born without lungs! But as enticing as it is for breeders to allow their mares to roam free, they also risk their animals following the Farasi Bahari into the sea or being dragged in by other predators. Should a horse breeder wait around to keep an eye on their mares, the Farasi Bahari will simply turn and run back into the sea.

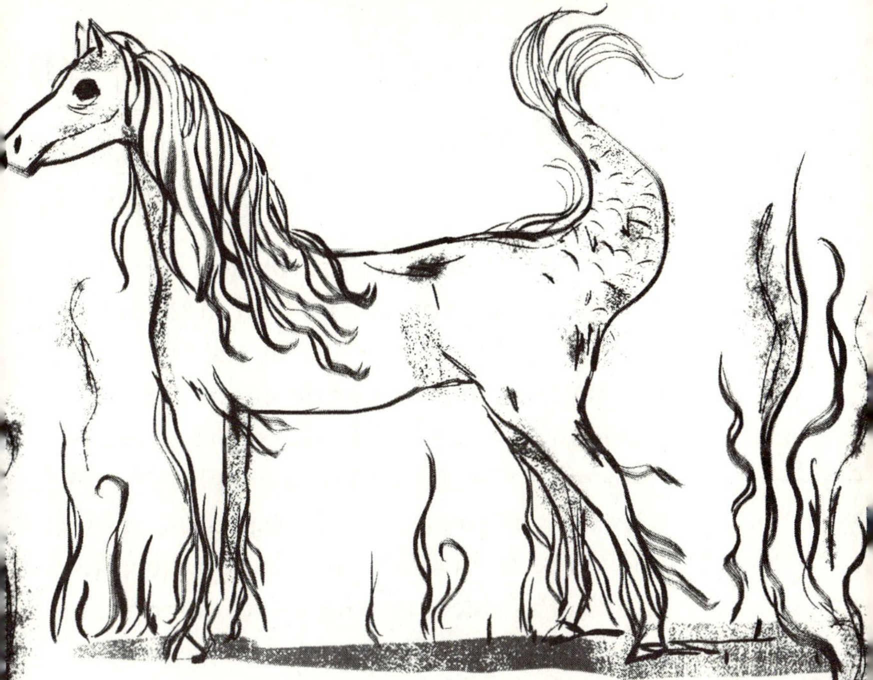

Oh, and it is practically impossible to trick this creature. Breeders, and enthusiasts such as me, have often found out the hard way – these creatures hate the stench of humans and they can, in fact, smell humans from hundreds of metres away.

I don't like colognes and perfumes (they give me the worst headaches), but it might be advisable to cover yourselves in a strong fragrance if you want to try and spot a Farasi Bahari, or perhaps you could try a bucket of fish guts, just in case they find the scent closer to home.

THE PHOENIX

the phoenix

14/10/2018

-- Unknown, Kachchh, GJ

This is awkward... I don't have the slightest idea where I am. I mean, I'm pretty sure I'm still in the west – Gujarat, most likely. I travelled here by sea, I visited the deserts of Kachchh in search of the Myrmex Indikos, and I even made my way out of a desert to find my way to a nearby town. But this is where things begin to get murky. I was ready to move on to Rajasthan, and was lucky enough to hitch a ride on a truck heading that way. Then all of a sudden, a few hours into our trip, I was awoken and kicked out of it for no reason whatsoever.

Was it my snoring? I don't think I snore, not too loudly anyway. Or maybe the driver felt I was being ungrateful – good conversation is currency while hitchhiking after all. Perhaps, I forgot to thank him for the meal at the dhaba, or maybe he wanted me to pitch in and clean the vehicle. Or it could be the fact that I just sat there, smiling. Before I dozed off, that is. Now that I think about it, he must have been lonely driving across the country. Maybe he wanted to exchange a few words, and there I was, asleep on the uncomfortable bench behind him.

It sucks to be stranded in the middle of nowhere. It's scorching hot and the sun doesn't look like it's setting any time soon. But, on the bright side, I'm under the very same skies that the Phoenix flew across all those years ago.

Okay, I know this is a stretch, and I know that the Phoenix mostly flew over Egypt and Arabia. But who is to say that it didn't take the wrong turn and end up flying over western and central India?

Widely regarded as eagle sized, the Phoenix – meaning reddish-purple in Greek – got its name because of its gold, red and purple feathers. But the most interesting thing about it is that the world couldn't have more than one Phoenix at any given point. The average lifespan of a Phoenix was about 500 years, though some accounts seem to suggest that it lived the length of the Egyptian Sothic calendar, which is 1,461 years!

So how did they go extinct? It could be because there was only ever one of them around; maybe they got lonely? Or it could be because of their very complicated birthing ritual. You see, once a Phoenix got old, it made one final trip to Heliopolis – the City of the Sun – in Egypt, where it gathered cinnamon and other aromatic twigs to build a nest at the top of the Temple of the Sun. The rays from the sun would set the bird's nest ablaze and the Phoenix died in the flames, only to have a newborn chick emerge from the ashes and fly back to Arabia to start its life anew.

The very first thing that the Phoenix chick did was to fly away and gather as much myrrh as it could find. The chick would roll the myrrh into a ball and carry it back to the nest, where it hollowed out the ball and created an opening to store its predecessor's ashes. The chick then sealed the opening and carried the ball to the Temple of Ra, the Sun God, thereby completing the previous Phoenix's life cycle.

I've always thought of a Phoenix as being immortal, but they're not. They just got really good at parthenogenesis (the ability to reproduce without a mate). The sun is still blazing above my head and, unlike a Phoenix, I have little hope of regeneration. It would be such a shame if I collapsed here and burned to death, but it wouldn't be the worst if a mini me emerged from my ashes and migrated back home.

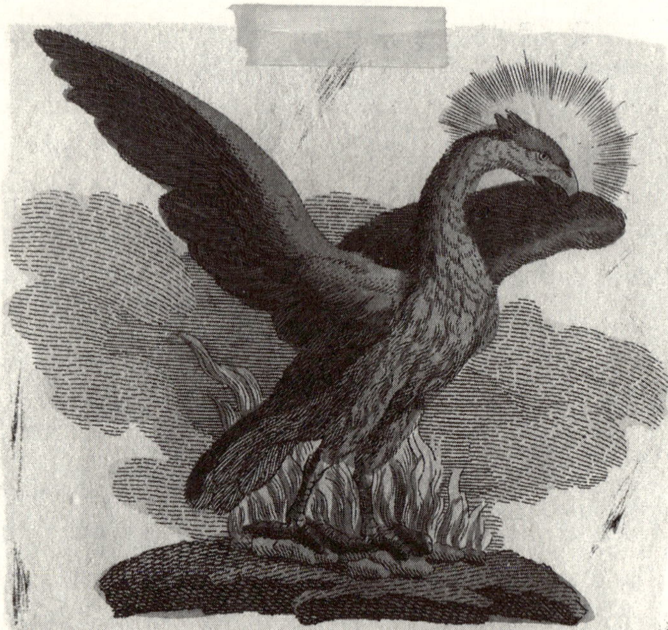

Imperij tueantur opes, ceu munera Diuûm:
Participes alios vt simul esse velint:
Præsertim sanctæ pietatis, & artis alumnos
Ingenuæ: per quos regna, domusq; vigent.
Diuitis hæc auri virtus est vna: benigna,
Qui prosunt alijs, mente iuuare bonos.

Vnica semper auis.

EMBLEMA XXXVI.

Ad Christophorum Herdesianum Iurisconsultum.

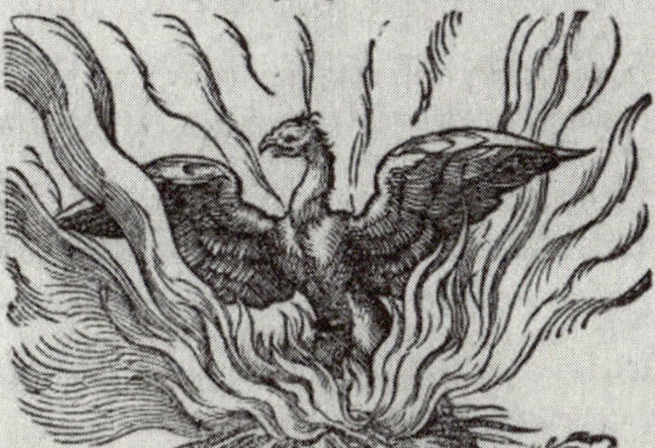

Quæ thuris lacrymis, & succo viuit amomi:
Fert cunas Phœnix, busta paterna, suas.

Vnica

THE AMPHISBAENA TORTOISE

the amphisbaena tortoise

14/10/2018

Unknown, Kachchh, GJ

Things are not looking good. I'm writing this entry waiting by the side of the road, and judging by the three cars that drove past me in the last hour, I can say for sure that I'm stranded in the middle of nowhere. I guess now is as good a time as any to fill in my most embarrassing entry, when I behaved like a fool and a complete brat. In my defence, I'd just encountered a rare and mysterious creature, the likes of which I was pretty sure I'd never see again, at the Kochi fish auction house right before I left for Maharashtra.

At first glance, the creature looked a lot like a tortoise. It was small and unremarkable, and covered with barnacles. Its shell was a boring shade of brown, its feet were smooth and free from cuts and wrinkles, but there was something strange about the way it moved. The poor creature looked lost and disoriented. Perhaps, it was weary from capture? Or maybe it was the shouting and bargaining that filled the auction house.

'Why did you bring it here?' a man asked. He had on a black shirt, sported a big, bushy moustache and looked as though he'd just returned from the sea. 'We're going to be in a lot of trouble if someone finds this!' He picked the tortoise up in one swift move and raised it high above his head.

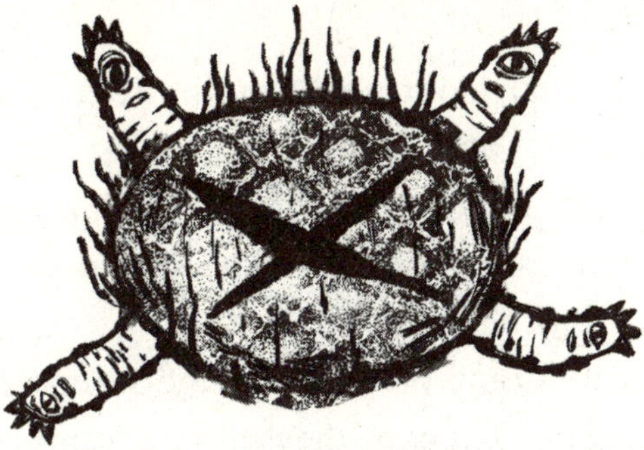

And that's when I saw it: the X-shaped marking on its back, the extra feet below its shell, the grotesque way its eyes and mouths were arranged.

'One thousand for the tortoise!' I yelled, but the man with the tortoise ignored me.

'Two thousand!' I cried, bidding against myself.

'Three thousand!' I tried again, desperate.

Still, the man ignored me. He began walking towards the sea briskly, and before I could run after him to stop him, he set the creature free.

'Why did you do that?' I kicked over a basket of fish and stepped on a crab, causing everyone in the auction house to stare. I was so livid that I was ready to attack the man, despite his being at least twice my size. The man didn't say a word; instead, he pointed to a board with pictures of starfish, shells, corals, tortoises and other aquatic life forms they were forbidden to catch.

'But that wasn't a tortoise!' I wanted to yell. In the brief moments that I'd glanced at the animal, I was able to tell that it was an Amphisbaena Tortoise. The ends of the X mark on its back led to its four eyes, below which were four mouths, all leading to a single throat and stomach. There was no mistaking it; it was an Amphisbaena Tortoise, and I had it within arm's reach. I should've picked it up the moment I saw it!

According to Greek travellers, the Amphisbaena Tortoise could only be found in the seven isles of the Indian Ocean. Though they're small and seemingly commonplace, their blood has powerful healing properties. It is said to be able to cure cuts in an instant, and even glue together severed limbs if the cut is still fresh!

I calmed down eventually, and when I did, I was thoroughly ashamed of myself and the way I'd acted. Perhaps, it wasn't an Amphisbaena Tortoise to begin with... maybe it was just a regular old tortoise with a mutation. I really hope it was, because I can't imagine coming *this* close to catching an Amphisbaena, only to have it pried away from me by a rule-abiding gorilla. Life is so unfair.

Note: Not to be confused with the Two-headed Amphisbaena Serpent from Libya.

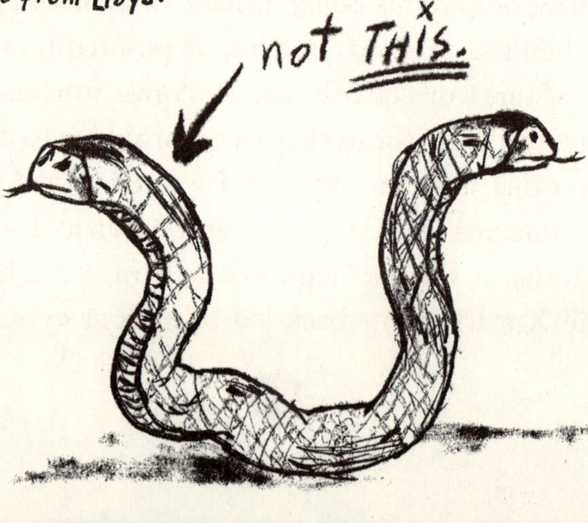

15/10/2018

En-route to MP

My saviour wasn't a man in a cape, he didn't wear his underwear on the outside and he didn't put on a mask to fight for justice. Instead, he took the avatar of a frail old man moving several very noisy boxes across the border. His van had a sticker of the 'I Move You' moving company plastered along the side, and when he said he was driving to Indore, I had exactly 10 seconds to make a decision: take my chances out here in the middle of nowhere and pray for someone heading towards Rajasthan, or alter my plans and head to Madhya Pradesh.

Judging by how I got to ride in a car with air conditioning, I think I made the right call. It had been ages since I'd been in an air-conditioned car, or air conditioning of any kind for that matter, and I couldn't risk being booted out again. So, unlike last time on that truck, I started talking to my new friend. I told him about my travels, and I told him about the so-called mythical beasts I was cataloguing. And oddly enough, he didn't look at me like I was a madman.

'So, what do you mean by mythical creatures?' he finally asked.

'Creatures whose existence hasn't been verified, but is accepted culturally,' I said.

'Like the Matsya?' he replied. 'Do you know the story behind it?'

It wasn't like I didn't know the story, it's just that no one had given me all the details growing up. I told him that.

He began:

'The story starts with Manu, the first man, finding a tiny golden fish in the river. The fish begged Manu to save its life from a predator, so he took it home and placed it in a pot. But the very next day, when Manu checked on the fish, he realized that it had managed to outgrow the pot. Manu then transferred the fish to a well, a pond, and finally a lake. But no matter how many times he relocated the fish, it always outgrew its home. He decided that the fish should be transferred to the sea, but when he saw the fish outgrow even the sea and sprout a horn, he grew suspicious and asked the fish who it really was. He learned that the fish was Vishnu, and was commanded to build a big boat and fill it with all the animals of the world, the seeds of all the plants of the world, and the seven sages. Vishnu told Manu about

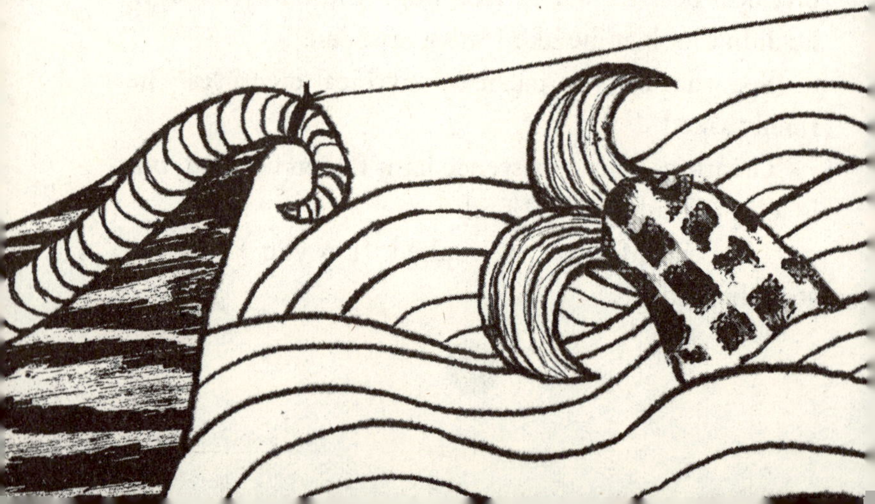

the flood that was about to destroy the world. When the day of the flood finally arrived, Matsya asked Manu to tie the boat to its horn, and ushered them to safety.'

'Let me guess: then, they started the world all over again?' I asked.

'That's right, they created it from scratch, with Brahma's help. How did you know that?'

'It's just like the story of Noah, or the flood from the epic of Gilgamesh,' I replied. 'There are plenty of stories like these. It's almost as though all the religions of the world copied off each other.'

'And this makes you doubt the existence of God?' he asked.

'Yes, it does,' I said, after a minute.

'That's strange,' the old man replied, 'because knowing that the same story exists around the world just makes *me* believe in God.'

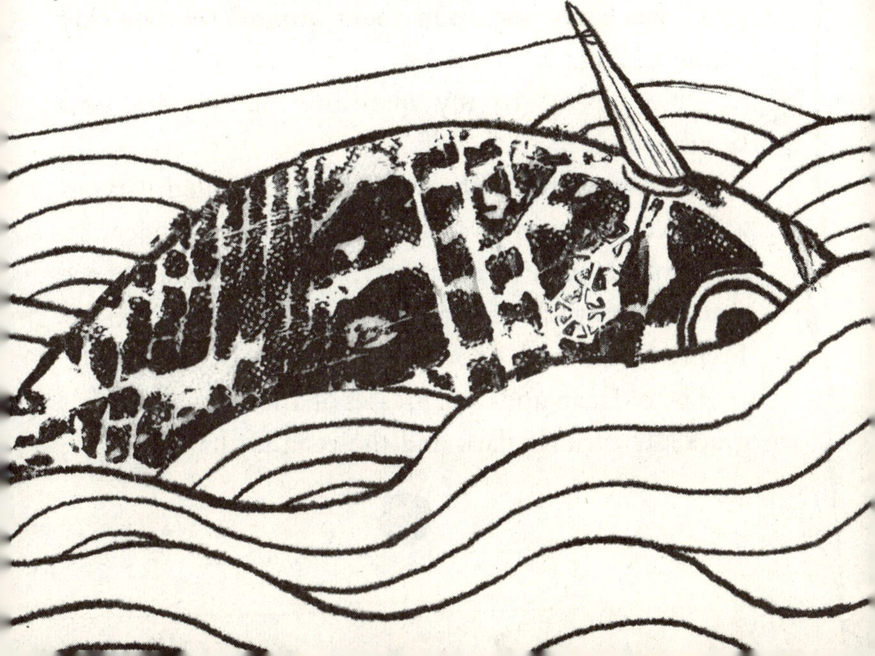

15/10/2018

En route to MP

'So you believe in tortoises with healing powers but not God. Huh.'

It's hard writing in a moving car, more so with Pankaj, my saviour, asking abrupt questions after long, sullen silences. He drives for kilometres without making the slightest sound. Then, when you least expect it, he springs a question on you.

At one point, he asked me what my parents thought about my job; before that, it was a string of questions about why I wasn't married yet; and before *that*, he was genuinely curious about how they got the marble in a Banta bottle to reseal the bottle. (I happened to know the answer to this one: they placed the bottles in these small machines and spun them around very quickly while adding gas to it.)

'No answer to my question?' he presses, this time around.

'Well, people didn't believe in the duck-billed platypus a couple of centuries ago, but explorers and scientists were able to prove its existence. So there's a small chance that I can prove that at least one of these creatures exists,' I reply. 'With God, I don't think I ever can.'

The old man nods and presses on the accelerator. It's gradually turning dark and the road is almost empty, except for a few oncoming trucks that occasionally blind us with their headlights. I've learned the hard way that staying silent can get you kicked out of the car, and so I force myself to ask the old man a question.

'So is the Matsya your favourite? Or do you know of other creatures?'

'The Navagunjara – that's my favourite beast,' he laughs. 'You must have seen it in paintings. It's the most wondrous creature on Earth! Imagine a single beast made up of nine different creatures; the head of a rooster, the neck of a peacock, the hips of a lion, the hump of an ox, the four limbs consisting of an elephant leg, a tiger leg, an antelope leg and the hand of a human holding up a lotus...' He scratched his head. 'Wait, I'm missing one. The head of a rooster, the neck of a peacock, the hips of a lion...'

'Tail of a snake!' I reply.

'Ah, that's it!' he cackles. 'Imagine coming across such a magnificent beast; I would be shocked out of my wits. Arjun from the Mahabharata certainly was – exiled in a forest, meditating in solitude, and the first thing he saw when he opened his eyes was this strange beast. He reached for his bow and arrow to shoot it, but then the beast raised its human hand and gave him a flower.' He paused. 'Goes to show how much we fear the unknown, doesn't it?'

I nod in agreement. We drive in silence for a while, and then a few kilometres later, the old man shakes his head and mutters, 'You believe that the Navagunjara could be real, but you're not convinced that it's an avatar of Krishna? Right?'

I don't respond.

'I think I've figured you out,' he says. 'You go to all these lengths, trying to unearth these fantastic creatures, but you refuse to go the extra few steps and look for God. Maybe you'll change your mind someday, or maybe you won't, but I'm glad to have met you and to have had this conversation with you.'

I smile at the old man and look out the window long enough that the letters on the signboards gradually coil and morph into a different language. I must have fallen asleep right after, because when I next open my eyes, we are already driving into Indore.

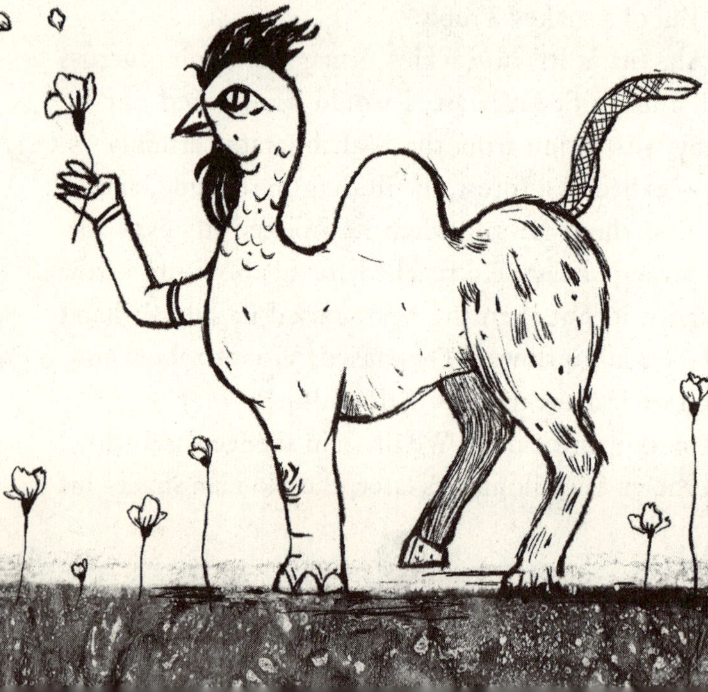

THE HIPPOS MONOKERAS

the hippos monokeras

17/10/2018

Indore, MP

I'm really glad I ended up in Indore because I just found out that the Hippos Monokeras roamed the forests around these parts. Who knew, right? Well, I should have, considering I'm the only beast researcher in the country.

It's all because I went back to look at my research on the Karkadann. You see, the Karkadann aren't the only unicorns that are supposed to have wandered the landscape of central and western India. The Greeks and Romans spoke about another unicorn, the Monokeras – meaning 'single horn' – which was said to live in the central and northern regions of India. As a matter of fact, the creatures were known to visit the lands surrounding present-day Indore.

The Greek writer Photius describes the Monokeras as white-skinned animals that are larger than horses. They have dark red heads, blue eyes and a two-foot long horn protruding from their foreheads. Photius wrote that the creatures' horns are white near the base, black in the middle and flaming red at the tip. The

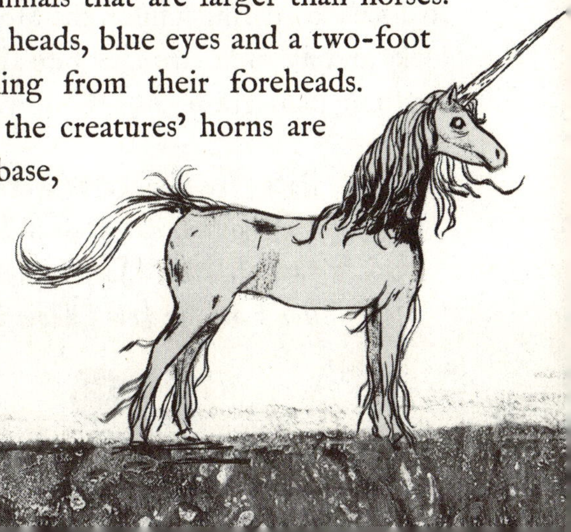

Monokeras are light on their feet, swifter than horses (and even cheetahs!), and considered impossible to catch, except when they are with their young.

Back around the first century CE, the only way to catch the Monokeras was by surrounding them with many people while they took their young to feed. Unwilling to abandon their young, the Monokeras would charge at their attackers, kicking, biting, impaling and killing several horses and men in the process. But if there were enough men with spears, and if they were fortunate enough to strike one of the creatures in the head, they could put an end to it and harvest its horn. Those who drank from cups made of these horns were said to become immune to epilepsy, convulsions and even poison! Photius, however, was certain that it was impossible to ever catch these creatures alive.

The Roman author Aelian wrote that it would be foolish to try and capture a Monokeras because, when threatened, they strike their enemy's ribs with their horn, disembowelling them. And if that's not enough to dissuade a daring hunter, the Monokeras has a strong kick, and an even stronger bite that can tear away at anything in its grasp.

Note: The Monokeras were only hunted for their horns, not as food because their flesh tasted bitter. Sort of like a garden slug. Don't ask me how I know that.

18/10/2018

Indore, MP

THE CHAKORA

the chakora

Fine, I may have eaten a slug or two when I was a kid.

Okay, fine, it was two weeks ago, and I had a perfectly good reason for it.

Pah...you got me. I did it because I was curious. What is this, the Spanish Inquisition? But now that I've tasted a slug, *you* won't have to. I can tell you for a fact that it's their slime that makes them bitter. (A great way to keep hungry birds off your back, if you ask me.)

In any case, if I were a slug and if I came across a Chakora, I'd have one less thing to worry about. Because Chakoras aren't interested in slugs, or bugs, or food for that matter. Instead, they live on *moonlight*.

Ask any birdwatcher, and they'll tell you that the Chakora looks a lot like the greater coucal, a crow-sized bird with copper-brown wings, a long black tail and a track record of being terrible at flying. Though these two birds look awfully similar, a few things set them apart. For starters, the greater coucal spends most of its time hopping from branch to branch in search of fruits, or foraging for worms and insects on the ground. Not the Chakora. These birds are a lot more complicated than their simpleton cousins, not to mention more dramatic. Chakoras conserve energy during the day, just so they can stay up all night and stare at the moon with their mouths open.

Why, you ask? Because Chakoras are in *love* with the moon. They spend their nights shedding tears of longing and serenading the moon with the most beautiful songs, knowing full well that they can never be together. The bittersweet pain of love and longing makes their lives worth living. On a full-moon night, the sight of the object of their adoration fills them with melancholy and happiness.

See, I told you they were dramatic.

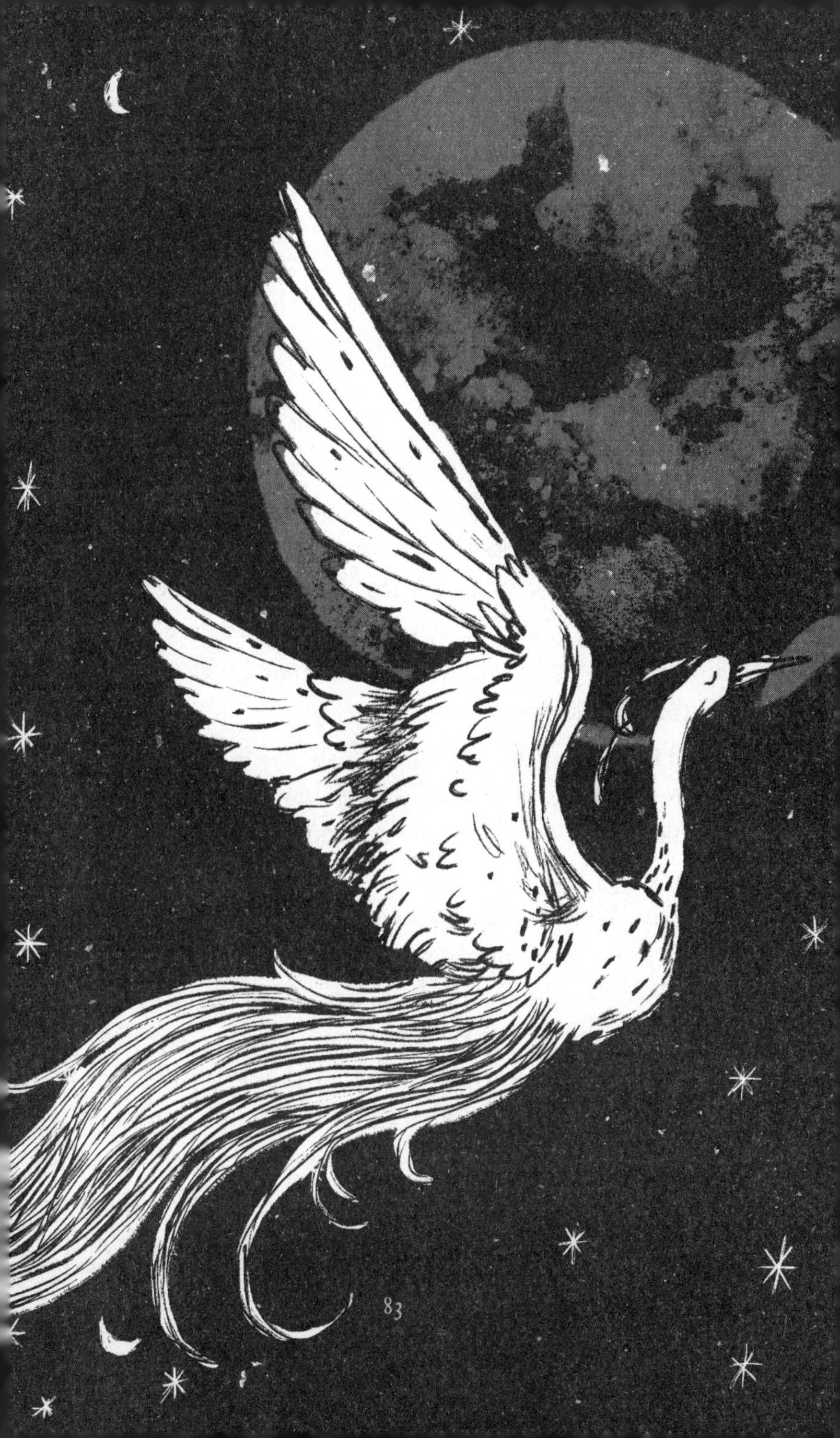

THE CHATAKA
the chataka

19/10/2018
– Indore, MP

Spotting magical birds, especially the smaller ones, can go either way. You can be enchanted by the most remarkable bird and find out later that it was nothing more than a ratty pigeon, or you can spend an entire afternoon in the company of sparrows only to find out later that they were the stuff of legends. We tend to keep our imaginations in check, and we only allow our minds to see what we think we already know. So who knows, maybe the birds in front of me are just Jacobin cuckoos, or maybe they're actually Chatakas. It's hard to tell as the two birds are virtually indistinguishable, with their dark bodies, white crest and distinct markings on their wings.

Well, I've got a foolproof tip to tell them apart. If you ever come across a tiny black-and-white bird drinking out of a pond or a puddle, or just about any source of water on land, you're looking at a Jacobin cuckoo. Unlike their doppelgangers, the Chataka find water on Earth impure and polluted, and would never stoop so low as to drink it. The Chataka only drink rainwater falling from the skies. In the absence of rain, they are known to travel all the way to clouds – sometimes enduring fierce thunder and lightning – just so that they can have a drink of water.

Now, that's what I call dedication. Or maybe they're just a bunch of little divas who think they're better than us.

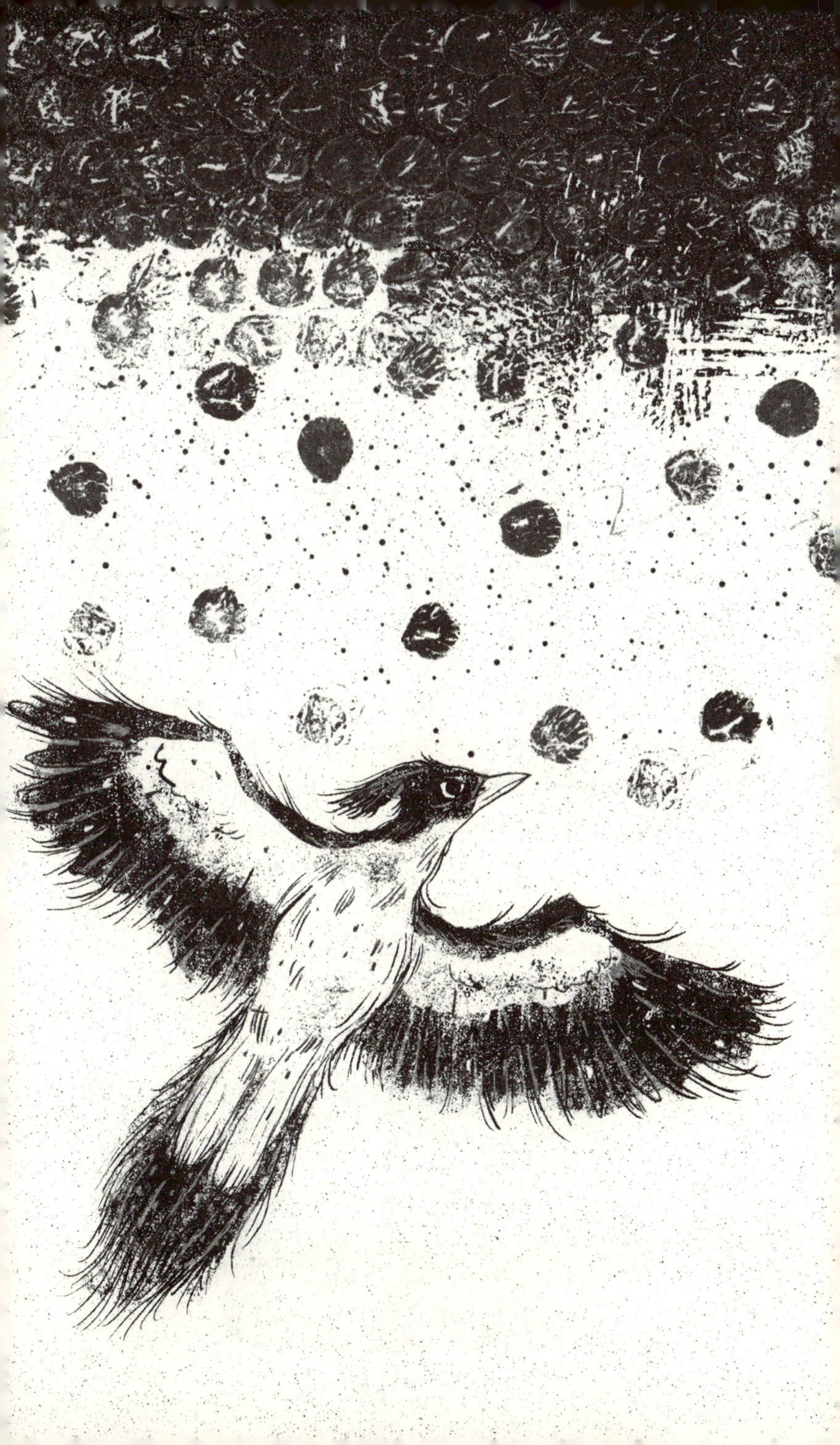

THE SIVATHERE

the sivathere

23/10/2018

Outskirts of Indore, MP

There are plenty of forests and wildlife reserves within a day's drive from Indore, and considering how common the Sivathere were 8,000 years ago, it really didn't matter in which direction I went. After all, these giraffes, now extinct, walked the length of India, spanning all the way from the foothills of the Himalayas to the tip of south India. So I trusted my instincts and travelled south towards Betul district, which rests almost entirely in the Satpura Range.

It was there that I came across the Ambadevi rock shelters, the oldest known site of recorded human life in central India. Just 60 kilometres north of the Amravati district of Maharashtra, the Ambadevi shelters in the Satpura Hills housed prehistoric human settlers 25,000 years ago. Within the rock shelters are caves with hundreds of wall paintings as old as 20,000 years. The paintings are mostly red, with a few splashes of green,

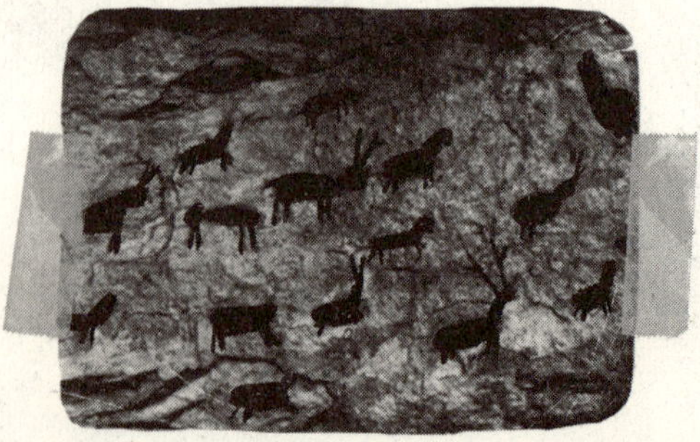

white, black and yellow, and depict numerous known and unknown animals, including the Sivathere.

What's fascinating is that cave paintings of the Sivathere have been found in parts of Africa and Australia as well, depicting the animal exactly the way the paintings in southern Madhya Pradesh depicted them.

The Sivathere were prehistoric giraffes that were believed to have weighed as much as an elephant, although judging by their bones, and their 10-foot-tall bodies, it was more likely that they weighed between 1,000 to 1,600 kilograms. These gentle giants lived alongside humans years and years ago, and are believed to have been hunted to extinction. But here's where things get really interesting: there are villagers and people around the world who swear that the creature still exists, wandering the densest forests of India and Africa, isolated from the rest of the world.

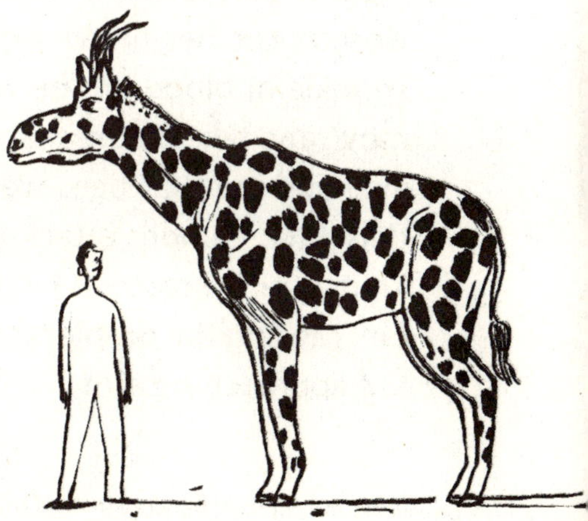

Note: As a kicker, I was also able to find the paintings housed inside the caves. Seeing the memories of our ancestors live on, challenging even time, I can't believe how far we've come.

The past few weeks have been great. I took a break from tracking down beasts and walked the narrowest roads of Chhattisgarh and Odisha, keeping my ears open to stories that the smallest villages had to offer.

I learnt that red ants were born after a young woman cut her finger while husking rice. The sprinkle of blood on the white rice made them move and take on the shape of an ant. Someone also told me that bees were born when Earth's daughter – under attack from a neighbouring king – spilled castor oil in front of a winnowing fan, causing the droplets to take flight and sting the approaching army.

Then I heard that mosquitoes were created without blood and they bite us because they rely on us to fill their bodies; and that spiders were born when a woman dropped a hair while swatting a mosquito, and now the hair builds webs to catch and eat the mosquitoes out of spite; and that crocodiles were born after tired women jumped into lakes while drawing water.

My weeks were filled with the strangest stories, and yet nothing compares to the tales of Indian dragons that I heard during my travels in Chhattisgarh.

THE DRAKON INDIKOS

the drakon indikos

23/10/2018

Rural Chhattisgarh

Everything that we know about Indian Dragons was penned by the Greeks close to 2,000 years ago. As evidence, there are similarities between their description of Dragons and the indigenous carvings of the beast scattered across the country. Both local and Greek writers of yesteryear went on at length about Dragons and elephants being enemies. Drawings of Dragons fighting elephants have been found in mediaeval manuscripts, and epic battles between the two were chiselled into rocks as statues.

According to Bartholomaeus Anglicus, who was a 13th-century scholar from France, the two were constantly at each other's throats. Dragons liked to kill elephants because an elephant's body was often cold, and feeding on elephant blood quenched the Dragon's thirst and cooled its body. Aelian, the Roman teacher and writer, wrote that Dragons would hide on top of trees, waiting for elephants to tug on branches and feed. When the moment was right, the Dragon would lunge at the elephant and gouge out its eyes before coiling around it and choking it to death. The two were such sworn enemies that often they died together in battle, with the elephant collapsing on the Dragon and crushing it.

Aelian adds that humans benefitted from the rivalry between the two beasts. They would wait patiently in the bushes, and when they were sure that the two creatures had killed each other, they would rush to claim the spoils – ivory, Dragon hide, and treasures that the Dragon had gathered.

He also wrote that close to 2,000 years ago, India was filled with Dragons. Supposedly, they occupied marshes, mountains and plains, and were about as common as big cats or bears. Like big cats and bears, Dragons came in different shapes and sizes.

Marsh Dragons

The Marsh Dragons were the least remarkable of the lot. They were sluggish and lethargic, measured about 45 feet in length, and were pitch black with very few scales and no crest. They weren't very social and kept to themselves for the most part.

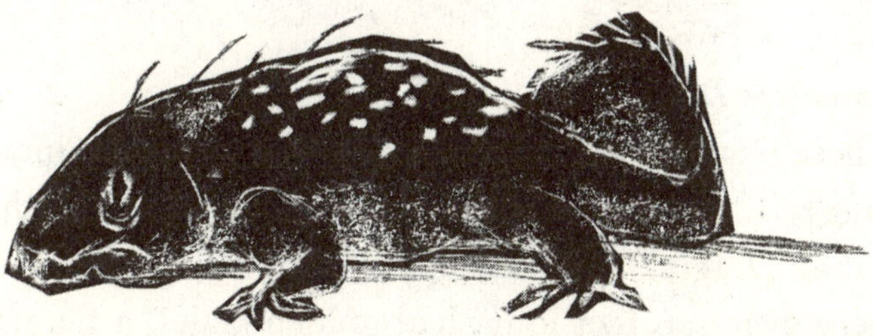

Plains Dragons

The Plains Dragons lived along the foothills and would sometimes migrate up to the mountaintops to get away from humans. They fed on smaller animals and grew as large as 120 feet. Despite their size, they were swifter than the fastest animal, allowing nothing to escape. These Dragons had large crests on their chests, serrated backs, bearded faces, eyes the colour of murky firestones, and scales that made their bodies glitter and glimmer under the sun. They turned a shade of blood-red as they grew older.

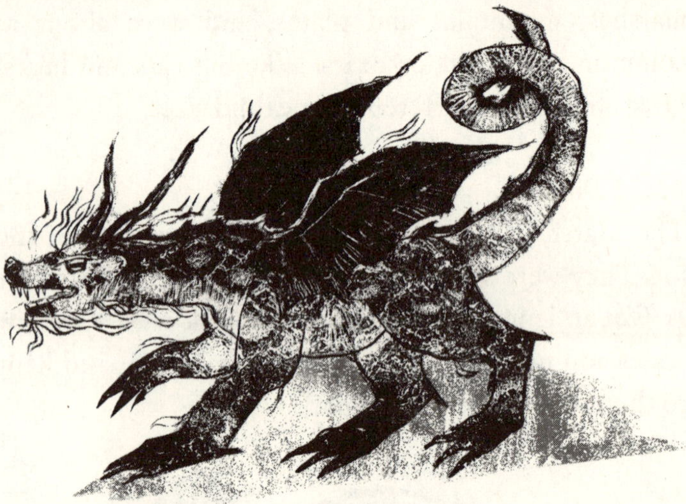

Mountain Dragons

These Dragons nested on the ridges of a long mountain range. They were solitary creatures, which meant that a lone Dragon would occupy a ridge of its own. They were over 200 feet long, had golden scales, a flaming red crest, bushy beards, sunken eyes and eyebrows like a forest fire. The mountaintops would thunder when they burrowed into the earth. They would hunt elephants the way eagles hunt rabbits.

These creatures were so powerful that the only way to defeat them was through magic. Ancient Indians would charm the Dragons with spells to make them fall asleep. Since the Mountain Dragons had a habit of sticking their necks out of their burrows while they slept, they would be vulnerable for just a few minutes. Ancient Indians would see this as an opportunity and rush at the Dragon, hacking into its neck. When the Mountain Dragon's head was severed, the men who slayed it would enter its burrow, hauling more gems than they could carry. But

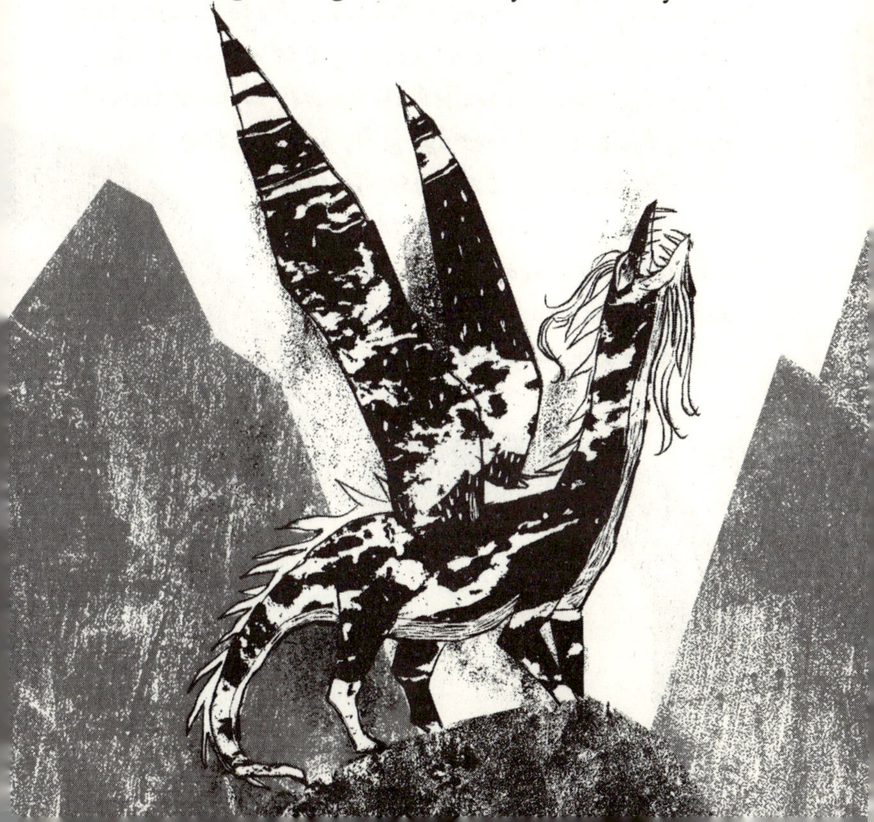

humans weren't always successful in slaying the Dragon. Sometimes, it would wake up and carry the humans over the mountains, dropping them to their deaths.

Aelian also talks about a city under the mountain, Parax, and the Indians who live there. He says that the men and women from Parax were trained from an early age to hunt Dragons, and that they consumed the hearts and livers of the beasts they killed, all so that they could understand their language and their ways.

Note: Onesicritus of Astypalaia wrote that during Alexander the Great's conquest, he wanted to visit an Indian king who was rumoured to have a Plains Dragon measuring 120 feet and a Mountain Dragon measuring 210 feet! But Alexander never got to see them. This is like the time I travelled all the way to Kodaikanal to watch the sun set over the hills, but all I saw was clouds of fog. I suppose the reason I won't be spotting any Dragons is because they probably got sick of us and flew back to their own realm a couple of thousand years ago.

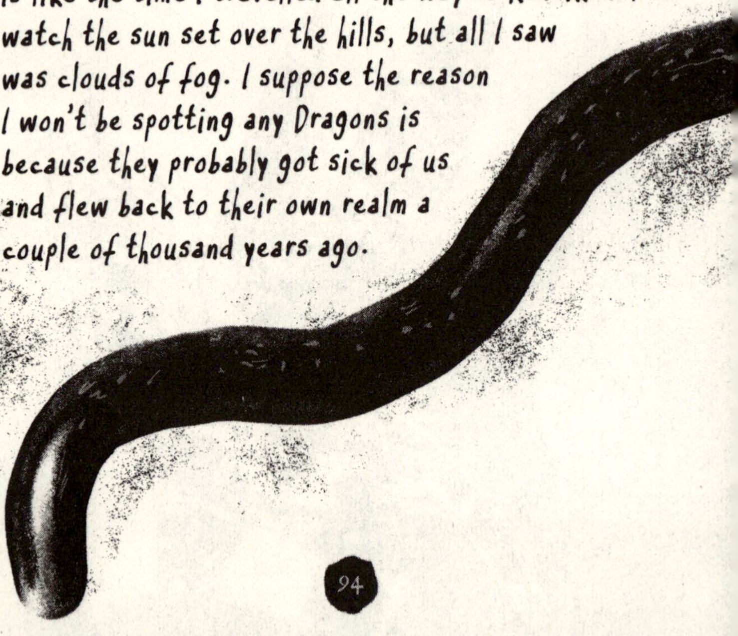

23/10/2018

Rural Chhattisgarh

THE NAGAS

the nagas

If you spot a human with a snake around their neck, a serpent that appears smarter than the average snake, or a human-snake hybrid hiding in the shadows, chances are you've just stumbled across a Naga. Neither gods nor humans, most Nagas live in Nagalok, in beautiful palaces under the earth. The Nagas can shape-shift into humans of their choosing. There's no need to be alarmed; they won't harm you unless you try and hurt them first. Besides, who knows – maybe you're best friends with a Naga and just don't know it yet.

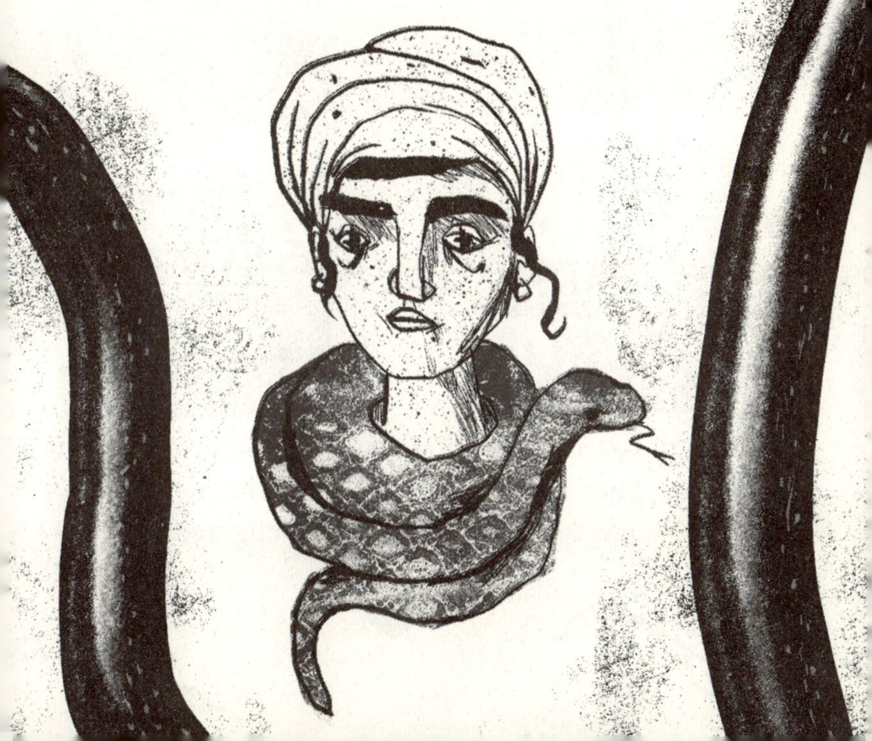

Five Nagas I'd like to can be friends with:

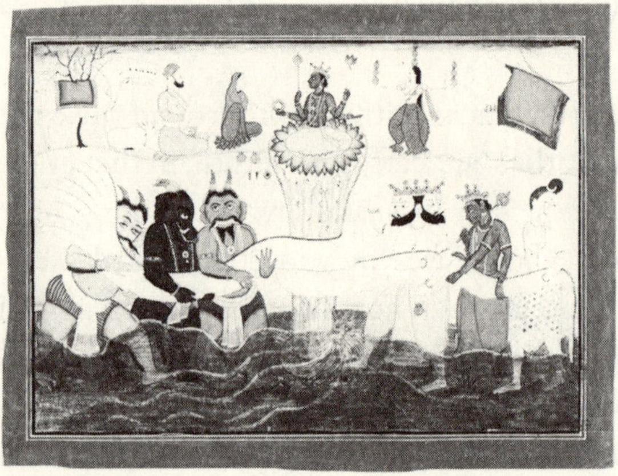

VASUKI: He was used as a churning rope to churn the cosmic ocean of milk. Also likes hanging around Shiva's neck.

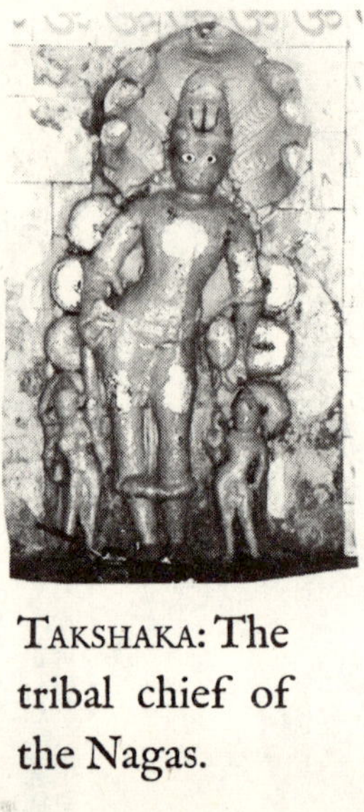

TAKSHAKA: The tribal chief of the Nagas.

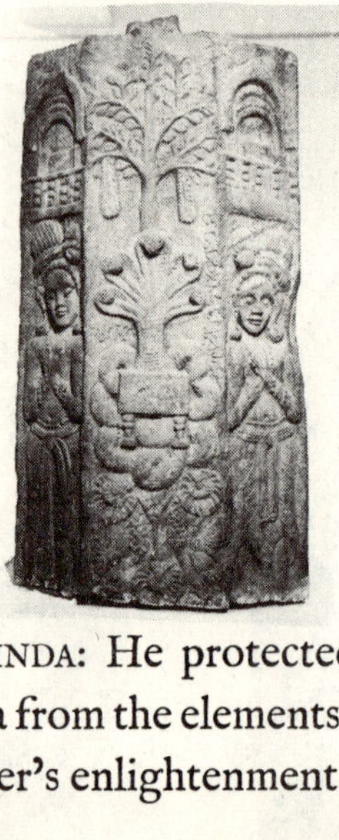

MUCILINDA: He protected the Buddha from the elements after the latter's enlightenment.

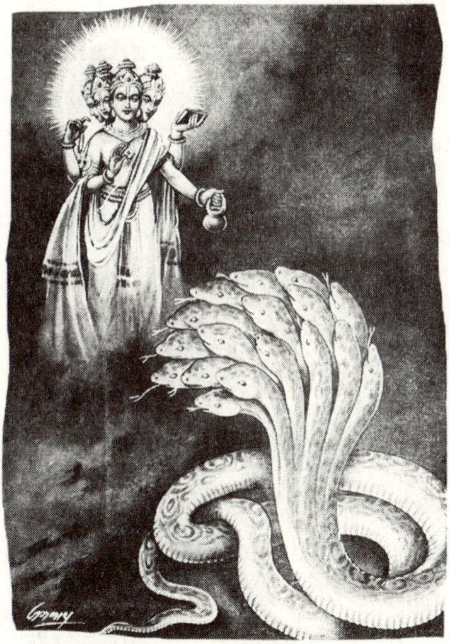

SHESHA: He has multiple heads and holds all the planets of the universe in his hood. Time moves and creation takes place when he uncoils. The universe is destroyed when he coils back.

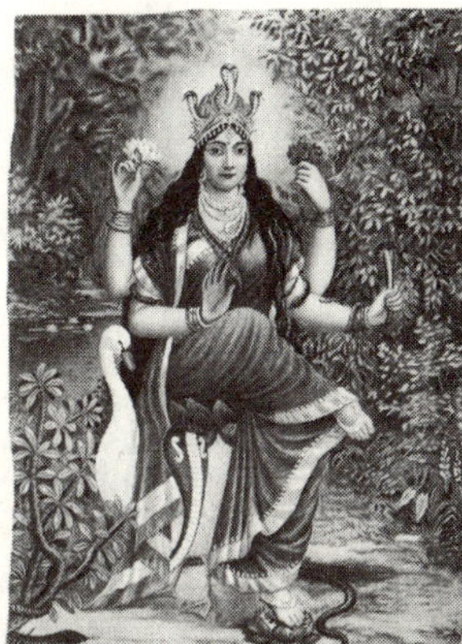

MANASA: The goddess of snakes.

THE SHAHMARAN

the shahmaran

25/10/2018

-- Rural MP

I've been obsessed with the Nagas these past few days. I've been drawing them on scraps of paper, dreaming about them before I go to bed. I think it's because I used to read Naga comics as a kid.

Okay, fine, I still read them, but only when I find them in a second-hand bookstore. The Nagas had somehow slipped my mind, but the moment I found a dusty comic book in my hotel lobby, I knew I would *have* to add a snake beast to my list, so here goes.

There are several similarities between the Nagas and the half-woman, half-snake Shahmaran from a Middle Eastern legend. Both half-human, half-snake creatures live under the earth. The main difference between the two, however, is how tragic Shahmaran's life was. Sure, the Nagas had pretty awful lives too, but not as unfortunate as Shahmaran's.

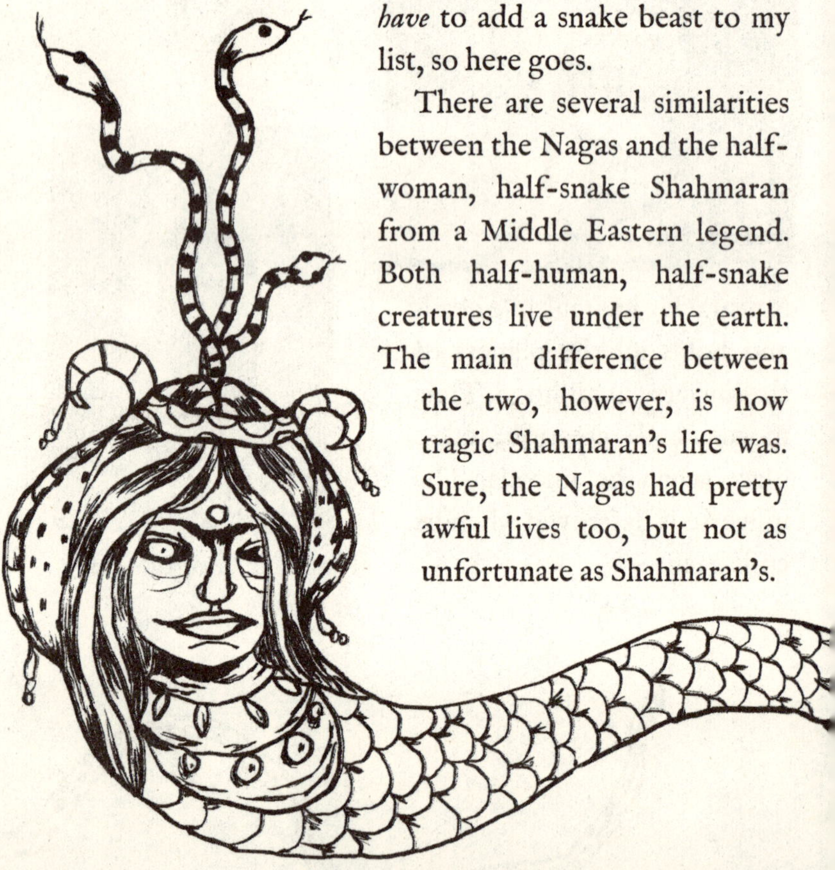

According to legend, Shahmaran was discovered by a poor farmer named Tahmasp when he found a small crevice at the bottom of a well. Tahmasp squeezed into the crevice and fell asleep the moment he set foot in the realm under the earth. When he woke up, he was surprised to find hundreds of snakes staring at him. One among them was their queen, Shahmaran.

Tahmasp and Shahmaran exchanged stories about their worlds, and soon fell in love. They lived together happily for years, but when Tahmasp missed his family and the world above him deeply, he left, promising Shahmaran to never breathe a word about the subterranean world. He also promised never to enter a public bath. You see, Tahmasp had lived with the snakes for such a long time that he'd started showing some of their characteristics. His skin would glisten like a snake's whenever he touched water, and anyone who saw him like that would know his secret.

Years later, the king who ruled over Tahmasp's land became ill. He was told that the only way to cure his disease was by eating Shahmaran's flesh. The king's advisers knew that the skin of the people who'd come in contact with the snakes shimmered in water, and so they ordered everyone to get into the public bath in the presence of guards. Tahmasp tried to hide, but was eventually caught out. He tried hard to keep Shahmaran's whereabouts hidden from the king, but gave in after he was tortured.

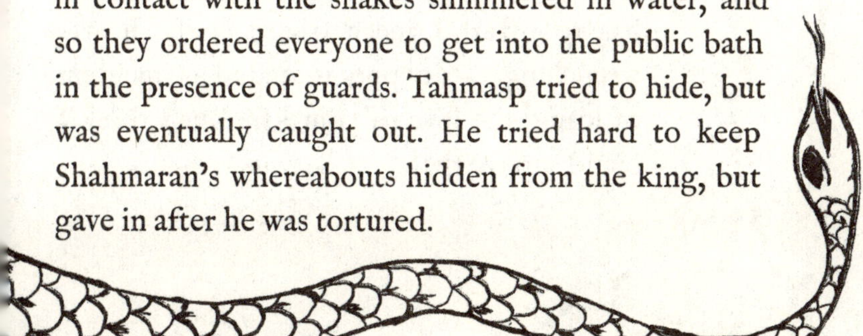

Shahmaran was brought to a bathhouse for her execution. Just moments before her death, she cried out to the king: 'If you eat my tail, you will gain all the knowledge in the world, and if you drink my blood you will become all-powerful, but the person who eats my heart will die at once!'

Heartbroken at Shahmaran's death, Tahmasp grabbed the heart and ate it, while the king and his general ate her tail and drank her blood.

Plot twist!

The king and his general died instantly, while Tahmasp was filled with wisdom. He became a doctor and wandered the world, treating people in need. But it is said that word of Shahmaran's death reached the snakes, and that they bear a grudge against humans to this day.

Call it confirmation bias, but this situation sounds like a win-win to me. To have found a mythical creature and to know all the world has to offer! I mean, there is the heart-wrenching – no pun intended – incident of losing the love of your life. But I think I could survive that...

HE INDIAN MOUSE_EATING PLANT

he indian mouse-eating plant

26/10/2018

Nainpur Forest,
Range, MP

One must be really, really careful when roaming the forests of India. Take, for instance, the Mathikettan Solai - meaning 'the forest that ruins minds.' It's located a few kilometres west of Kodaikanal, and rumour has it that anyone who ventures into it is walking towards certain death. On the off chance that they do make it out alive, they usually come out having lost their minds and memories. It's true! Mathikettan Solai has claimed the lives of 12 explorers that we know of. Why, there's even a signboard from the forest department that says so!

While the forest officials maintain that people don't make it out alive because the murky jungle disorients them, causing them to wander aimlessly under the dense canopies till they die of exhaustion, there are those who believe that the forest plays tricks on the mind, gradually driving its victims insane. It does this through a plant that nobody has ever seen. Legend has it that when flowers of this plant bloom and hit the ground, they release a sweet scent that makes the human mind forget all about itself, leaving the person to roam the woods aimlessly or walk off the jagged mountain ridges.

I ought to take my own advice every now and then.

Still, can you really blame me? The promise of finding the Ausadhirdipyamanas (a plant used to heal battle wounds) or the Sanjeevani (a magical herb that can cure pretty much everything, including death) is far too tempting! The one that I'm most optimistic about has to be the Indian Mouse-eating Plant, from around these parts in Madhya Pradesh, which was said to have been on display in London's Horticultural Hall until 1924. It's still considered a cryptid, an animal or plant whose existence is not confirmed by science. The Indian Mouse-eating Plant releases an odour to attract mice to the hole at its centre. When the mouse falls inside the hole, it's killed by the plant's antennas and liquefied by its digestive juices.

The reason this plant fills me with hope is because scientists discovered a rat-eating carnivorous plant, *Nepenthes attenboroughii*, in the Philippines in 2007. The plant differs in description from the Indian Mouse-eating Plant – the one found in the Philippines traps rats after they fall into its long pipes, which are filled with liquid. The rats eventually drown.

It just goes to show that anything can happen, and that maybe what I'm doing isn't a child's dream after all.

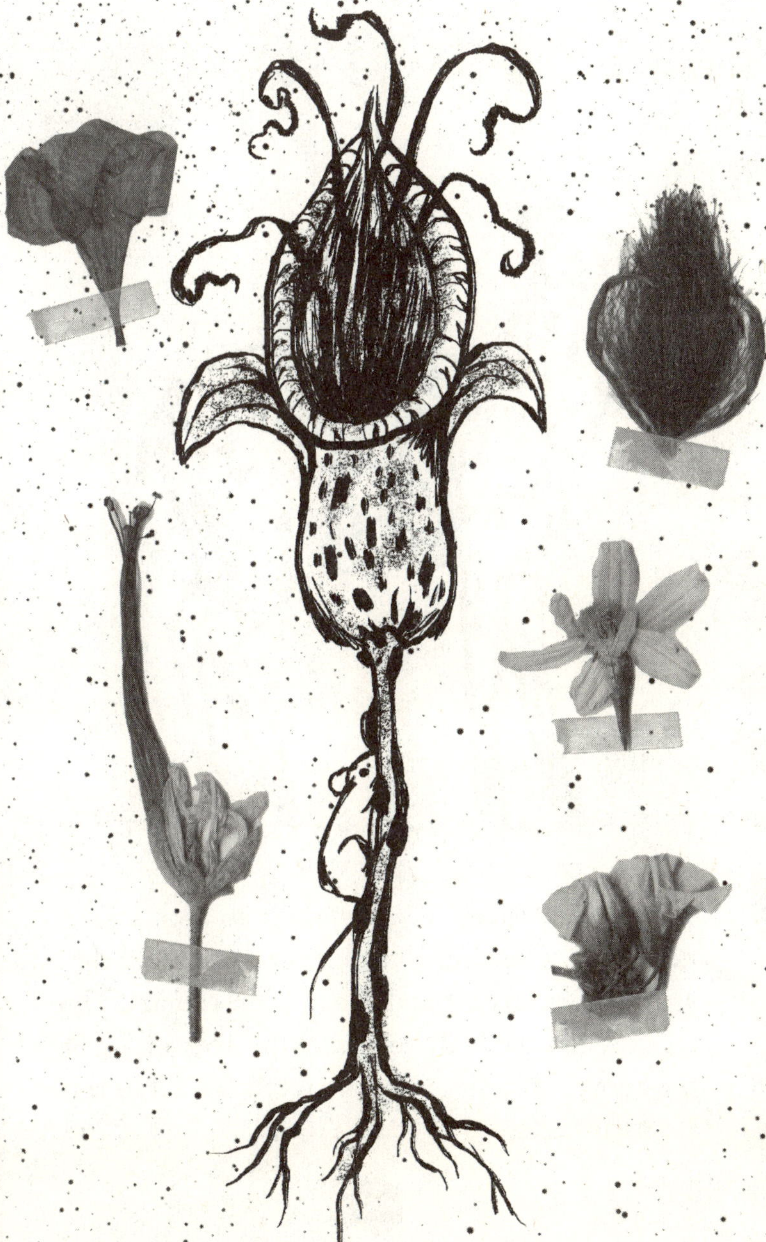

THE CROCOTTA

the crocotta

29/10/2018

Rāsilpur, MP

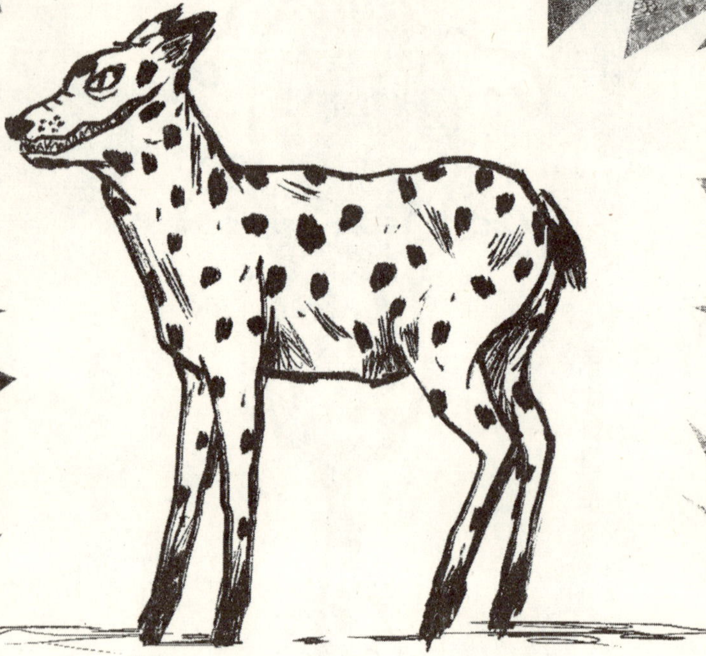

I don't really need to *go* anywhere to look for my next beast. The Crocotta are so abundant that they are supposed to be found all across the country. This creature has the body of a stag, the neck of a lion, the hooves of cattle, and sharp teeth that fill its jaws from ear to ear.

Pliny, the Roman author and naturalist, wrote that these creatures could be found in forests across north and central India, and that they're capable of biting through just about any living being and digesting them in an instant. The Crocotta also possesses the power to change its colour and sex at will, and it's been known to dig up the remains of humans and other creatures to snack on. However, what's most alarming about these creatures is their unique ability to mimic the voice of humans, often posing as them to lure out pet dogs and eat them.

Aelian recorded that the Crocotta were as clever as they were vicious, and would hide in dense bushes, listening to farmers calling one another by name. The Crocotta would learn the workers' names, and call out just one name, luring them deeper and deeper into the bushes with their mimicry. And when the beasts knew that they had got the victim all to themselves, they ripped the farmer to shreds and fed on them whole.

I'm always ready to believe in a fantastic creature's existence. The reason they haven't been found is because we haven't looked hard enough, that's all. Yet there's something about the Crocotta that makes me think that they're just hyenas. Maybe they were mistaken as supernatural beings that could mimic humans because of their laugh. Maybe they don't exist after all. But then again, I could be entirely wrong. Maybe the Crocotta are right around the corner, lurking in the bushes, eager to learn my name.

THE MUSCALIET

the muscaliet

29/10/2018

Panna National Park, MP

I've been in Indore for a little too long, and I think it's about time that I get on with my travels. What better way to ease into my quest than by looking for the smallest mammal on my list? (Okay, second smallest – the rat-sized elephant is probably a tad smaller.)

Honestly, I don't really know much about the Muscaliet, and neither did the Greek travellers who wrote about them ages ago. It was initially thought to be a fox-sized rat. Aristotle mentioned it a few times and claimed that Alexander the Great had discovered it during his battles in India. But other accounts of the animal, specifically those of Pierre de Beauvais and other little-known Greek writers, suggest that it has a body smaller than a rabbit's, a tail larger and bushier than a squirrel's, and claws so sharp that they'd give the fiercest wolverines a run for their money. The Muscaliet spends most of its time up in trees, jumping around. Those who have had a chance to look at one up close have described it as having weasel-like ears, pointy mole noses, and teeth sticking out on both sides, like tiny tusks.

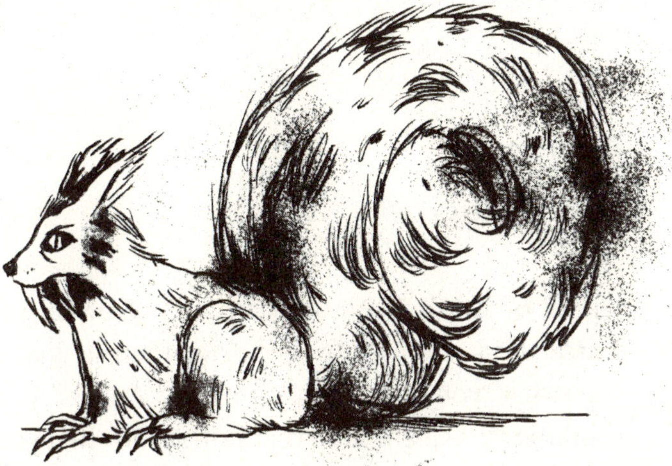

There's nothing all that remarkable about these mammals, except for the excessive heat that their bodies emit. The Muscaliet's body temperature is so high that they can cause trees to wither and die when they burrow to live among the roots!

Well, all that aside, these creatures are proving very difficult to track, given their size. Besides, the only thing mentioned about their whereabouts is that they live in the land of the three talking trees that predicted the death of Alexander the Great.

Talking trees? And there were three of them? How did I miss this chapter when I was in school?

THE NITTAEWO

the nittaewo

30/10/2018

Unknown, MP

Think of Bigfoot. No, a Sasquatch! Now shrink it and make it about a foot shorter than us humans, and what you get is a Nittaewo. And if you're thinking, 'But, Thomas, that just sounds like you're describing my hairy, socially awkward uncle,' then I have just two things to say to you:

1. I can't believe you're still reading my journal, despite my *nicely* asking you not to.
2. You're right; they do sound awfully like humans.

The Nittaewo used to live in the jungles of Sri Lanka, and they've been described by some as short, hairy, dagger-clawed proto-humans who migrated from central India to Sri Lanka thousands and thousands of years ago. People have long searched for the Nittaewo, believing them to be a predecessor to *homo sapiens*, but without fossils and historic debris to prove their existence, they are considered cryptid. There are, however, accounts that may have been about the Nittaewo provided by – you guessed it – Pliny the Elder, who described them as 'beast men'.

Despite their appearance, the Nittaewo were quite harmless. They lived in caves and on the branches of trees, and were said to be a nuisance to the early humans of Sri Lanka, presumably because the two tribes fought and stole from each other a lot. The humans were afraid of the Nittaewo and their strong claws, and avoided them at all costs. That is, until they found out where the Nittaewo lived. Armed with spears and fire, the humans sacked Nittaewo settlements, killing them by the hundreds and forcing the last among them into caves. Then, they sealed the caves and set them ablaze, killing the Nittaewo once and for all.

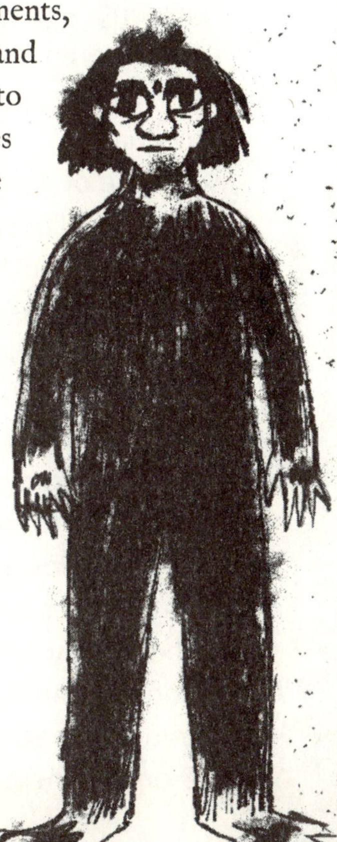

I wonder if we would behave differently if we found the Nittaewo today. I mean, surely, we're not going to charge into their caves, sacking and burning their homes, right? But then again, considering our current response behaviour to people and situations, and how mean we've become over the years – thanks, Evolution! – maybe it's wiser for the Nittaewo to stay hidden.

I've always wanted to visit Khajuraho, and since it's on the way to my next stop, Allahabad – I'm sorry, *Prayagraj* – I figured it would be the perfect time to visit.

'I was right! Everything about this place filled me with wonder: the weather, the people, the greenery, and finally, the temples. But what brought me here is the statues! While there are thousands of them, depicting everything from everyday life to the erotic, there was one statue in particular that drew me in – the hunting of Shardul. Okay, that's probably not what it's actually called, but in my defence it's a sculpture of a couple of men trying to chase down the mythical beast Shardul.

'For anyone finding it difficult to focus, we're looking for the gargantuan beast with the body of a lion, and the head of an elephant, a parrot, or a horse.' Our guide, Premji, was a veteran. He had probably hosted his tour a thousand times, yet his enthusiasm suggested that he was only just finding out about the facts he shared with his group. 'The Shardul represents many things – our wishes and desires…' he paused to stare intently at the carving in the wall. 'And those two men represent humanity trying to control our base desires. The one in front is about to be swallowed whole by the beast, and the one at the back is moments away from being trampled.' Premji smirked. 'At the end of the day, we are all slaves to our wants. But don't let those two get you down. Perhaps you'll have better luck with taming your Sharduls.'

The rest of the tour flew by. Premji answered questions, evaded potholes, crossed busy junctions and delivered his monologue masterfully. The reason I even brought up the tour guide is because he ended our trail by showing us a statue of a woman with scorpions resting on her thighs. I was instantly reminded of my time in Karnataka, where I'd gone looking for a mythical scorpion, but had instead found a scorpion goddess. I wasn't completely disappointed, because I'd reached Kandkur village in northern Karnataka during Nagara Panchami, where instead of worshipping snakes like the rest of the country, people from the village climb up a hill and catch venomous scorpions to play with. It was an astounding sight to watch kids and oldies gather scorpions by the dozens, some placing them on their arms, or even inside their mouths!

I spent the rest of the day looking for more scorpions – on arms, legs, backs and butts, and when I grew tired of walking, I sketched the temple as best I could. And as the sun went down, I knew that I had to continue my journey north.

03/11/2018

Northern MP border

I enjoy drinking chai out of an earthen cup. There is something satisfying about crushing the cup under your shoe when you're done, returning it to the earth. I'm on my way to the newly named Prayagraj. I think I'm only about four hours away now. All along, the road is dotted with tea shops with pictures of Hindu gods and goddesses pasted on the rickety facade or hanging from the top of the counter.

There are a lot of similarities between the Greek and the Hindu pantheon. Like Zeus and Indra, for instance – they're both rulers of the gods, they wield thunderbolts as weapons and they live on the top of mountains. Then you have Hades and Yama, rulers of the underworld, responsible for shepherding the dead,

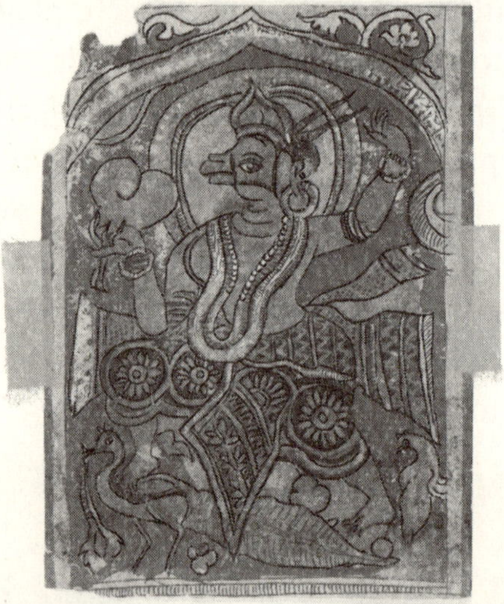

and owning similar pets. Cupid and Kamedeva, Apollo and Suryadev, Athena and Saraswati...the list goes on.

My favourite similarity has to be between two lesser-known gods from Hindu and Greek mythologies, Naigamesha and Pan. The reason I like them so much is that both are often connected to fertility. According to the Jain text *Kalpa Sutra*, Naigamesha was tasked by Indra, the king of the gods, to shift the embryo of Mahavira from the womb of Devananda (a Brahmin woman) to that of Trishala (a Kshatriya woman). People who want children pray to Naigamesha, and he is almost always accompanied by children in his sculptures.

Pan, like his doppelganger, is also associated with fertility, but he can be a little mean. Pan is known to scare people and animals alike, causing stress, anxiety and panic to those who meet him. And no, that wasn't a pun; the word 'panic' comes from the Greek god Pan, and it literally means 'caused by Pan'.

Still, despite their similarities, and despite the fact that they're both half-goat, half-human gods, the two look starkly different. The Greek god Pan has a human head and a goat's body, while Naigamesha has a goat's head and a human body – it's like they are inversions of each other.

Statues of Naigamesha have been found from as early as the second century BCE, and he is depicted with short horns that curve backwards, a long beard and sleepy eyes. Naigamesha is also frequently sculpted with children latching on to him, not entirely unlike the laughing Buddha.

THE HELMIS INDIKOS
the helmis indikos

04/11/2018
— Uptron Chauraha, Prayagraj

It's been years since I last visited this city, and yet I remember it like the back of my hand. I know the hub for the cheapest rickshaws, the place for the best samosas and the fastest route to get from Civil Lines to Teliarganj. I know all the shortcuts, and I know that I'd have to walk through the narrow, winding streets of Govindpur to get to the most secluded part of the riverbank.

Ctesias wrote in his fourth-century BCE book, *Indica*, that the rivers of India – particularly the Indus that flows into Pakistan, and the rivers of the north – were so unfriendly to life that the only creatures that could live in them were the Indian Worms. An Indian Worm is about 11 feet in length and so thick that a child couldn't wrap their arms around its body if they tried. These creatures have two 8-inch teeth, one on the lower jaw and one on the upper, that are so powerful that the beast can crush rocks and bones with ease. It feeds on wood and tree trunks, and lives at the bottom of the river, hiding during the day and hunting at night. Their skin is about two fingers thick, and they are known to take their victims by surprise. These creatures are hard to spot because they are covered in mud, which makes it easy for them to attack horses, cattle, or even humans. They drag their prey back into

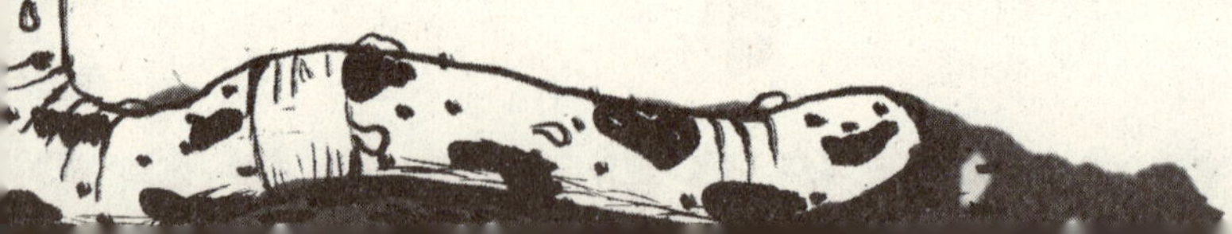

the river, devouring everything but their intestines.

So how exactly did humans fight these creatures back in the day? They went fishing! People who hunted the Indian Worm would make fishing lines out of metal chains or strong ropes, and hook an entire lamb or a kid to catch them. And when a worm took the bait, it needed at least 30 men to fight the creature and reel it in. They would hurl spears, stab it with their swords and beat it with wooden clubs to kill it.

Here's where things get interesting. Once the worm was reeled in, it would be hung to dry under the sun for 30 days. A leather vessel made from the creature's skin would be placed under the beast to collect all the fat and oil, and on the thirtieth day, the oil would be presented to the king of the land.

Aelian wrote that the oil collected from the beast was special because it could be used to light a fire without a spark! The oil could be used to burn people by simply pouring it on them. More often than not, kings would go into battle armed with vats of this special oil. They would spill the oil down on the enemies or sling the containers over the gates of the forts under siege, causing entire armies to burst into flame, burning metal, leather and flesh alike. Can you imagine the number of wars that would be fought over the Helmis Indikos should governments and dictators learn about their existence?

THE GIANT LOCUST
the giant locust

04/11/2018

Naini, Prayagraj

The whole of the Gangetic Plain sounds like a death trap. Or, at least, it did to the Greek writers of the first century; if the worms in the lake didn't get you, you were likely to die of starvation caused by hordes of Giant Locusts.

Imagine thousands of locusts hatching out of wave upon wave of egg clusters, with each egg giving rise to a locust almost the size of a dog! Imagine the strongest snake you can think of. A single locust could kill it by gripping the snake's throat with its teeth or use its legs to tear into the reptile's body. These creatures were so strong that the legs of a dead Giant Locust were often broken off and used as saws.

According to Pliny, these Giant Locusts took to the skies in hordes. Their flapping wings sounded like galloping horses. They flew hungry for days, and when they spotted a farm or a village they would descend and strip it clean of food in seconds – sometimes even eating the doors of homes! Pliny also writes that these creatures were very hard to kill since they flew in swarms, and were only known to die by accident – when they were carried away by stormy winds and thrown far into the sea.

Somehow, this is the beast that scares me the most. Sure, a Yali or a Manticore can kill you in the most

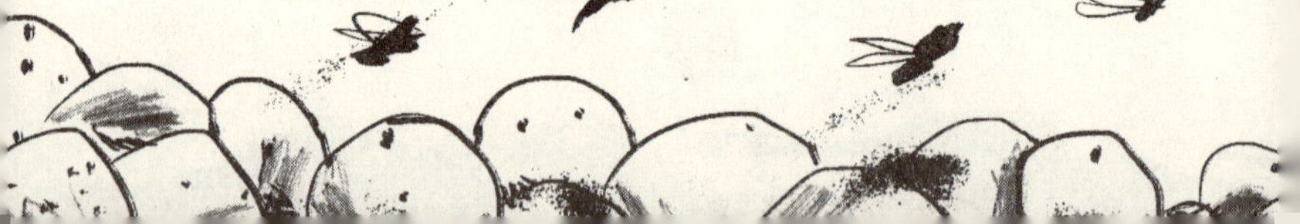

horrendous way, but a horde of Giant Locusts whose only purpose in life is to feed...they can put an end to our entire species.

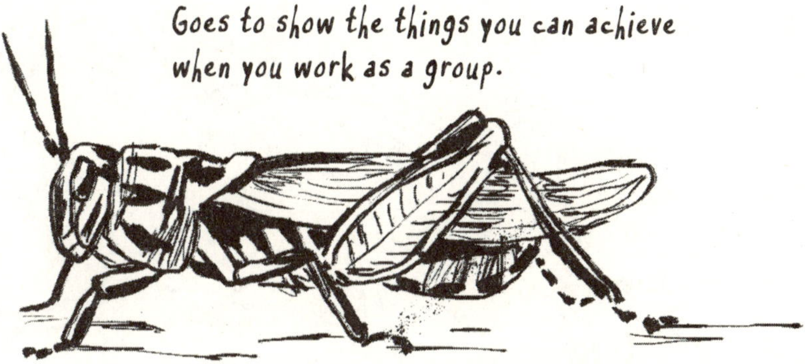

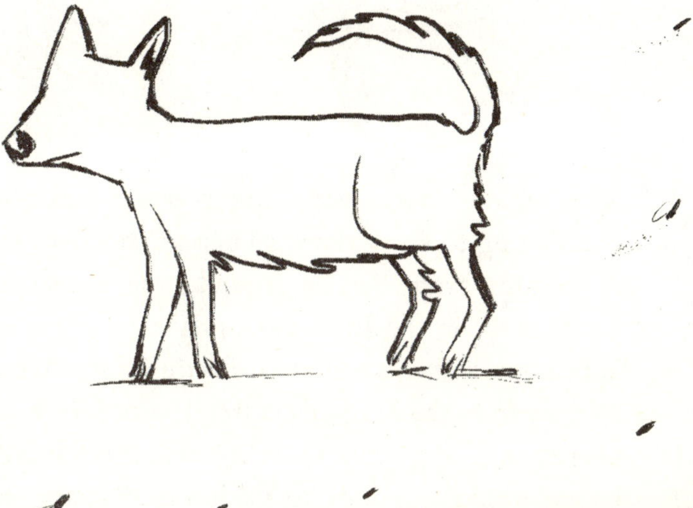

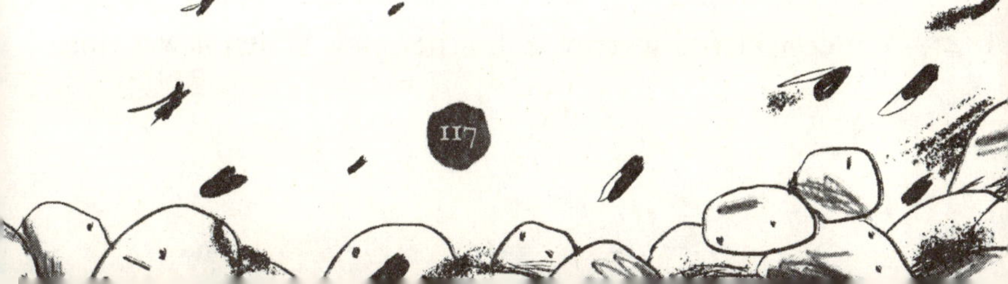

THE HOMA BIRD

the homa bird

05/11/2018

Rāebareli, UP

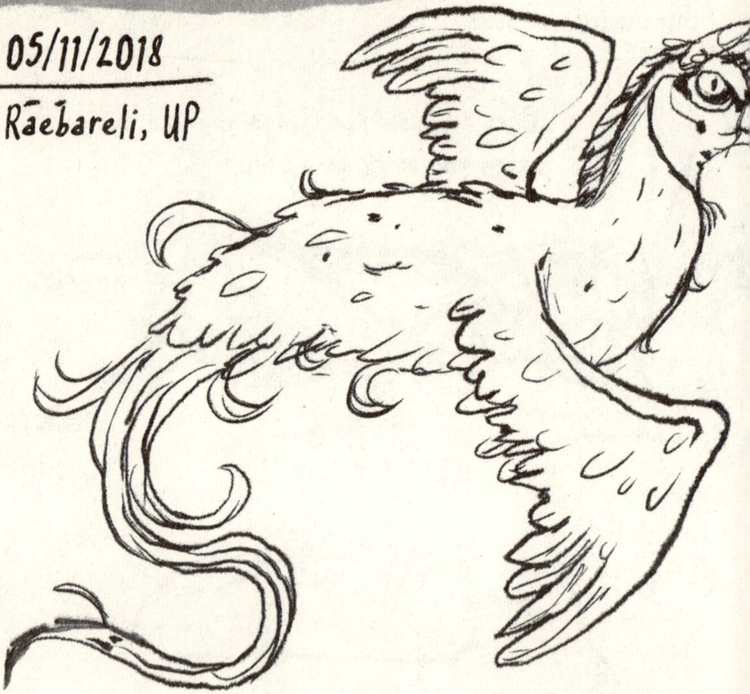

In a region where everything is out to get you, it's comforting to know there's a beast that's here to help. A creature from Persian legends, the Homa Bird is a rare sight in the Indian skies. It only makes special appearances when it comes to selecting kings. According to texts from the Mughal era, the Homa Bird would fly over crowds to predict who the next king was going to be and would only allow its shadow to fall upon the one it considered worthy to be the ruler. When it was time for his coronation, the chosen one would wear a turban with the bird's feathers.

If you're scratching your heads wondering who died and made the Homa Bird a kingmaker, the answer is probably someone who was fascinated by this bird's weird life. For starters, Homa Birds lived in the air, and I don't mean just the flying bit. They spend their entire lives in the air and they never touch the ground, not even when they lay eggs. When a Homa Bird lays an egg, it does it in the air. The egg falls towards the ground and hatches mid-air! The chick joins its mother in the air immediately after hatching.

That's not all! The best part about the Homa Birds is that they lay golden eggs and are quite generous with them. The birds often present golden eggshells to deserving people, but also have a track record of taking back their gifts if the person they help became greedy.

No, I have not been lucky enough to get one yet, but of course whenever I am in this area, I open my door every morning with my fingers crossed.

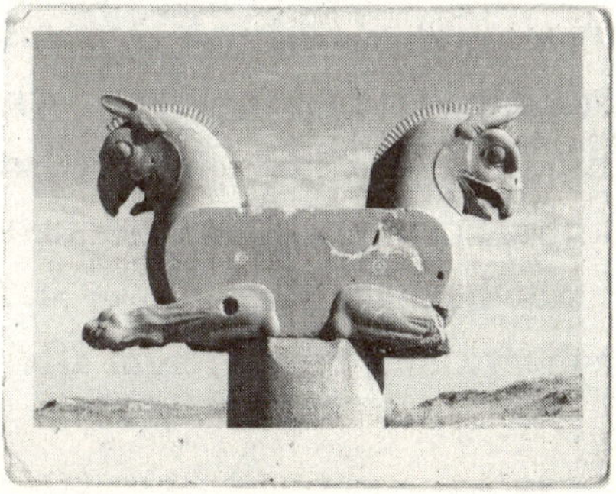

THE MONOPODS

the monopods

05/11/2018
—Aligarh, UP

What's the most defining thing about Uttar Pradesh?

If you answered anything other than yoga, then I'm afraid you're wrong. I see yoga practitioners in the parks, I see them on TV in my lodge and I see them lining the banks of the Ganga. As I watch them twist, contort and rearrange themselves into different shapes, I can't help but think about the Monopods.

Quite possibly the closest to humans of all the beasts in my journal, the Monopods – meaning 'one-legged' – are human-like creatures who have a single large foot extending from the centre of their bodies. St. Augustine, a theologian and philosopher, mentions them in his book, *The City of God*, and wonders if they can trace their ancestry to Adam or Noah. The Greek historian Ctesias, in his account of India, mentions that the Monopods are very swift. They move by hopping and can clear great distances in a single leap. They are also called Sciapods – meaning 'shadow foot' – because they often lie on their backs under the hot sun and use their large feet as umbrellas.

It tickles me how much they looked like yoga practitioners. Maybe that should answer St. Augustine's question. Maybe we aren't so different after all.

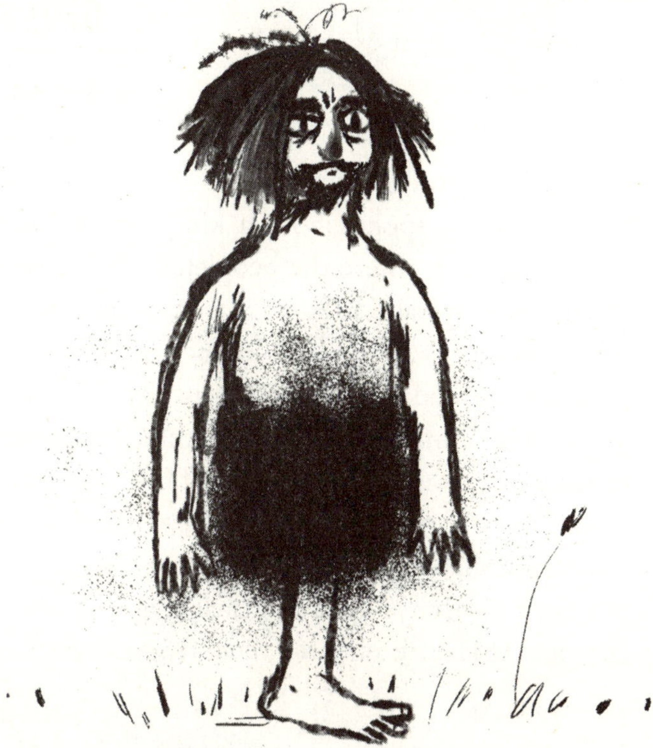

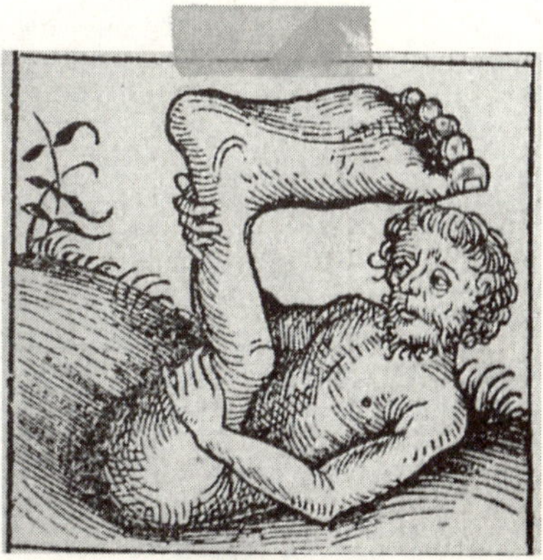

THE CALINGAE

the calingae

07/11/2018

Unknown, UP

Speaking of strange human-like creatures, Pliny the Elder also spoke about a kingdom in India called Calingae, where the people didn't live very long. Their average lifespan was just eight years. They would grow out of infancy rapidly, and would work and contribute to society at a very young age. Pliny also mentioned that the women of Calingae gave birth by the age of five, and often passed away a year or two later. These people were indistinguishable from humans otherwise. It was just their shorter heights and their tragically short lifespans that differentiated them from others.

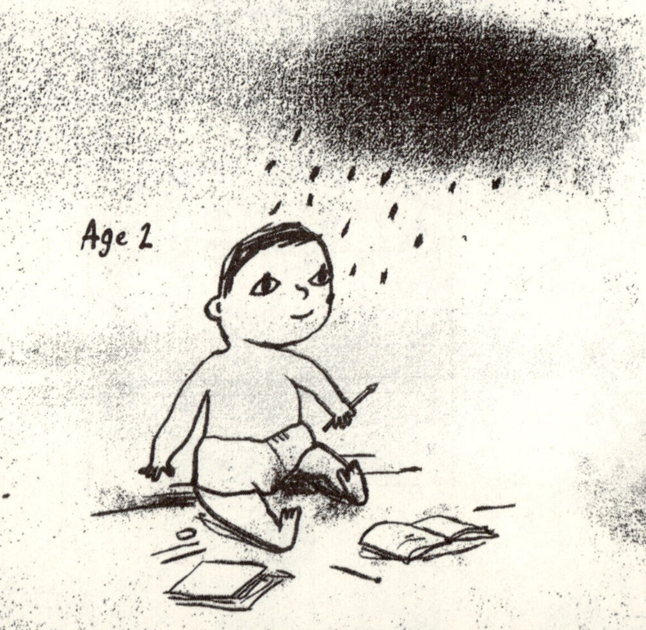

Now, what would I have done were I to live for only eight years? I'd be done studying by the time I turned toddler, would have fathered a child while in kindergarten, retired from work instead of graduating from the second grade, and I'd probably start planning my funeral the moment I celebrated my eighth birthday!

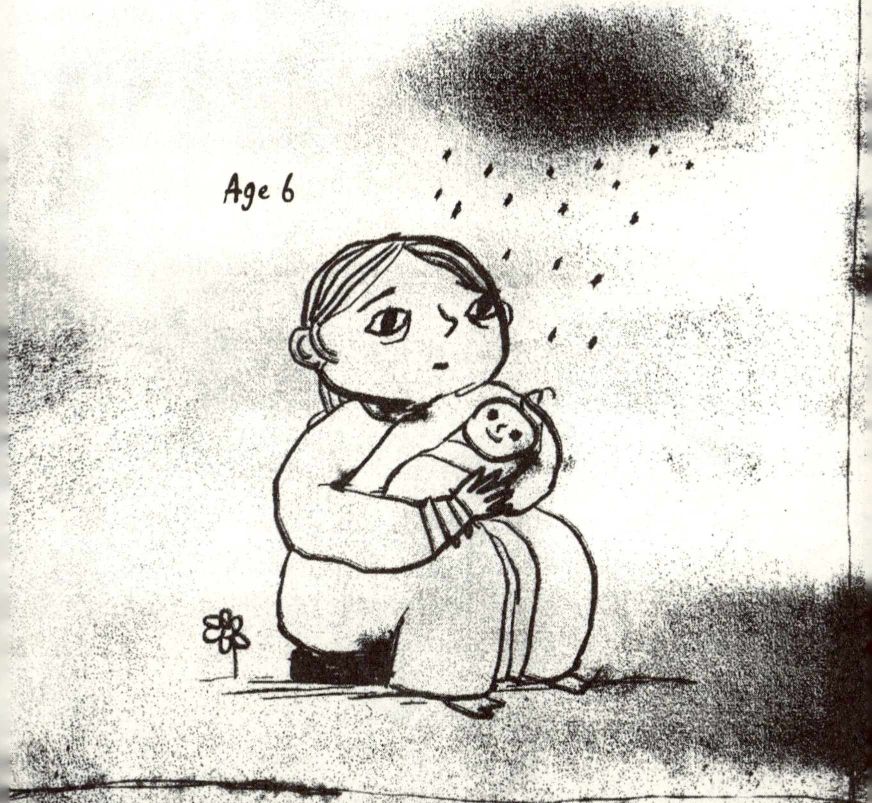

KIRTIMUKHA

kirtimukha

07/11/2018

Unknown Temple, UP

I've been temple-hopping to see the different kinds of fantastic creatures engraved on the walls, and I noticed one particular figure make an appearance in all the temples – the Kirtimukha.

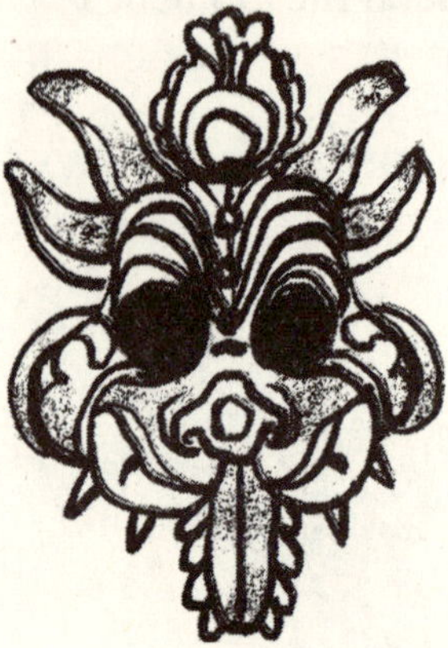

The Kirtimukha can be found on the walls and entrances of most temples. It sort of just hangs around as a kind of decoration, appearing in stone carvings as a large monstrous face with huge fangs and a wide-open mouth, looking ready to eat anything in its path. That's pretty much what it did.

According to legend, the Kirtimukha was a rakshasa follower of Shiva, who was initially sent by a powerful king to challenge the god. When the two met, Shiva overpowered the beast with ease and ordered it to appease its ravenous hunger by feasting on its own body. Kirtimukha did as Shiva commanded. Its appetite was so intense that it devoured its own tail, arms, legs and body, and stopped just short of eating its own face, but only because it was physically impossible to do it.

Shiva was so pleased with the beast that he asked for its face to be present on the doors of all his temples. And that's why the Kirtimukha's face can be found in temples across India, Nepal, Bhutan and even other parts of South-East Asia.

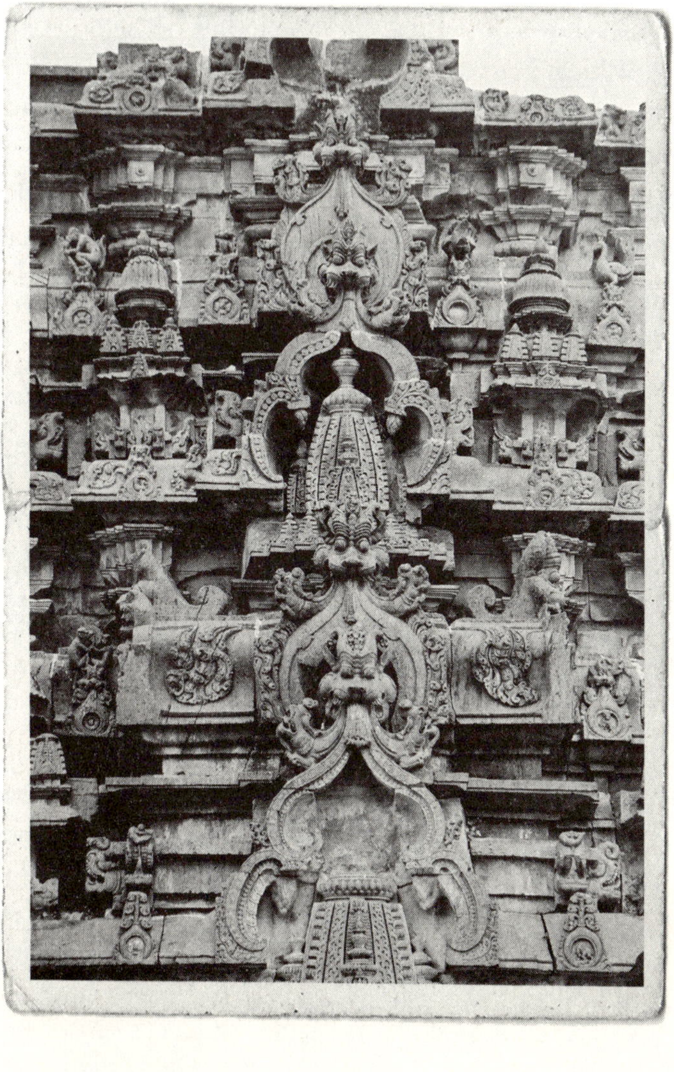

RAHU AND KETU

rahu and ketu

07/11/2018

Unknown Temple, UP

Kirtimukha and Rahu are often mistaken to be the same, especially when they are carved on the walls of temples. There is one tiny difference between the two: Rahu is always shown devouring the moon, while Kirtimukha isn't.

Which begs the question: why on earth *is* Rahu eating the moon? The short answer to that is because Rahu hates the moon and considers the moon his mortal enemy, much like how Ketu hates the sun and considers it his mortal enemy. And what exactly do they have against these luminous heavenly bodies? We'll need to travel back in time to answer that question.

A long time ago, the gods and the demons decided to churn the ocean and divide everything that came out of the ocean among themselves. The serpent king Vasuki

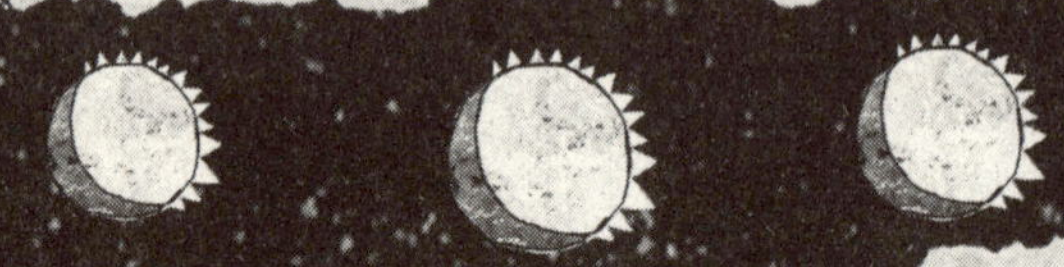

was used as the rope to churn the ocean; a mountain was used as a churning stick and Vishnu's Kurma avatar was used as the base of the churn. The first thing to come out of the ocean was a deadly poison called kalakuta; followed by Kamadhenu, the sacred cow; some unwilting flowers; Uchchaihshravas, the seven-headed horse; Dhanvantari, the first ever physician; and a whole lot of other interesting things that any god or demon would find desirable. But the thing that both the gods and the demons wanted the most was amrit, the elixir of immortality. After a lot of fighting, the gods and the demons decided to share the amrit, with the gods tasting it first, followed by the demons. In reality, the gods had no intention of sharing the elixir with the demons, and were planning on finishing it all by themselves. It just so happened that the demon Swarbhanu got wind of this, and quickly snuck between Surya and Chandra – the sun and moon gods – to have a taste. The sun and the moon soon realized that there was an imposter among them. When they deduced that it was Swarbhanu who had drunk the elixir, they told Vishnu.

A furious Vishnu used his chakra to chop off Swarbhanu's head. The demon's head became Rahu and the rest of his body became Ketu. Which is why Rahu and Ketu are involved whenever there's a solar or a lunar eclipse; the two consider the sun and the moon their worst enemies and long for revenge.

If there's one takeaway from this story, it's that telling on people is a sure-shot way of making enemies for life. And this might be an unpopular opinion, but I don't think it was very nice of the gods to keep all the amrit for themselves once they had promised to share it.

THE VAHANAS

the vahanas

11/07/2018

Coasts of Mumbai

How do the gods get around?

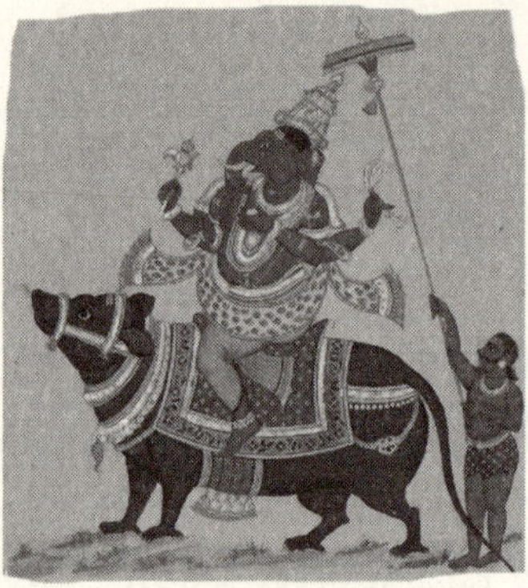

Mooshakraja: Ganesha's ride – mouse.

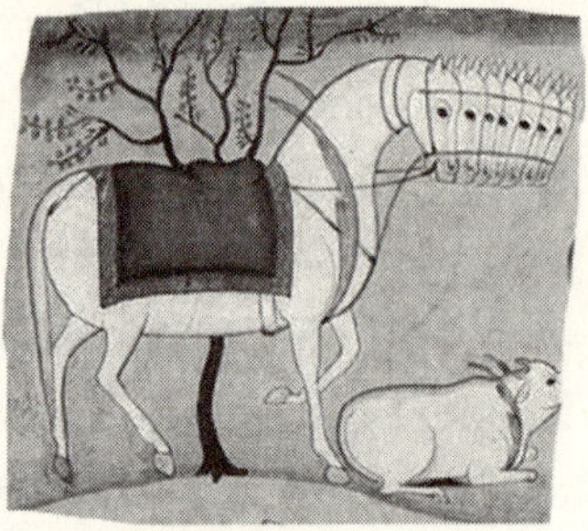

Uchchaihshravas: Indra's ride – seven-headed horse.

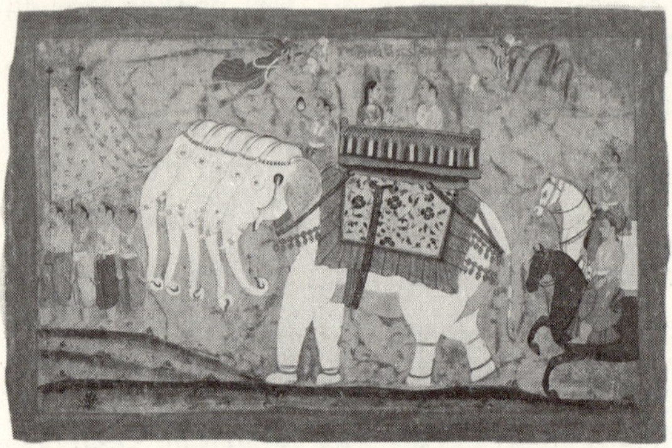

Airavata: Indra's ride – five-headed white elephant (yes, the king of heaven had more than one vehicle!).

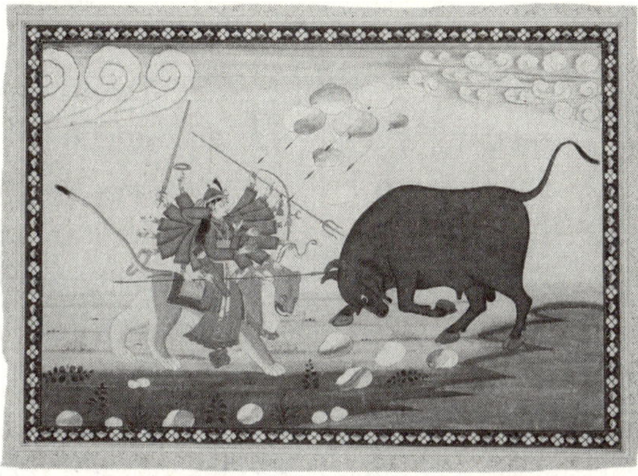

Dawon: Durga's ride – half-lion and half-tiger, according to Bengali lore.

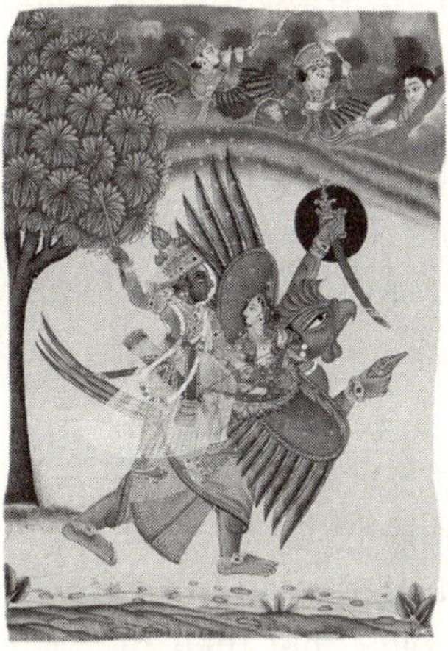

Garuda: Vishnu's ride – half-eagle, half-man.

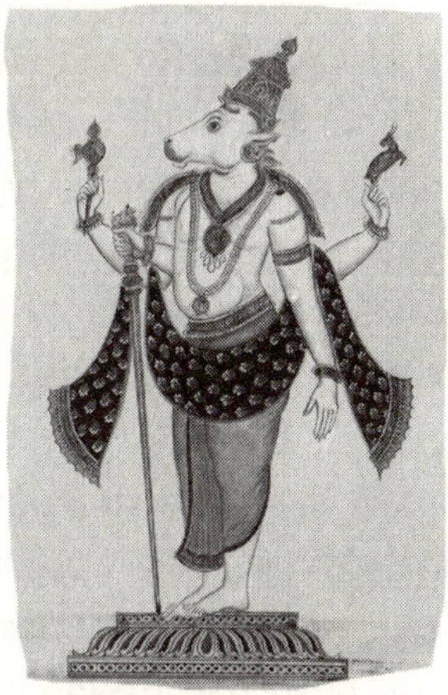

Nandi: Shiva's ride – sacred humanoid bull.

Note: Vahanas are mythical beasts that the gods use as their vehicle.

It's getting colder the further north I travel. The plains and the rivers have grown into mountains and glaciers, and I've never experienced cold weather like this before. Working the occasional odd job has got me just about enough money to buy a quality jacket and, trust me, my south Indian bones are going to need all the protection they can get.

It's really easy to get to Himachal from Uttar Pradesh. Trains to Delhi are fairly easy to come by, and there are dozens of them from Delhi to Shimla. But the way I travel often means that I book last-minute tickets, and if you know anything about that, you probably know that I'm going to have to travel in the unreserved compartment.

The first time I travelled in one was to go to my grandmother's funeral. My mother and I travelled in the muggy summer, sweating and rubbing shoulders with the rest of the people in the compartment. We remained silent throughout the way, skipping lunch because of how crowded it was.

Now, years later, my unreserved compartment journey from Delhi to Shimla was completely different. People sang songs, and seemed to know each other from earlier. A few people even had designated seats that their friends had saved for them. Peanut shells cluttered the floor, people played cards, their legs dangling from the metal benches meant for the luggage, and food was passed around for everyone to share. It's surprising how much the weather can do to lighten the mood.

I began travelling unreserved when I shuffled in and around UP, half hoping that I would run into the artist graffiting 'naalai vaa', and I think I have enough experience to write down a few rules.

1. *Try not to be too grumpy – you'll ruin the mood and attract Skondhokatas.*
2. *If the train is empty enough, you could try and sneak into the sleeper class, but there's a 600-rupee fine if you get caught. If it's completely empty, get off! You're headed somewhere no human must go.*
3. *If you're caught and pay the fine, you can stay in the sleeper class, and if you ask nicely, the ticket checker might even assign a seat for you. If the checker doesn't write you a fine or pester you for a bribe, get away, they are not who they say they are.*
4. *It's hard to get caught if you sit or stand next to the toilet. This is where people who ride short distances for free gather, and they're mostly left unchecked. If you see someone leaping off the train, there's nothing you can do to save them. You're a few decades too late.*
5. *Don't enter the AC cars – you're guaranteed to get caught if you do. If a fellow passenger offers you their seat, decline politely and walk away.*
6. *I think part of the reason I've decided to go to Himachal is because of all the Greek writers who have written about India. I've heard rumours of an entire village with people of Greek descent somewhere in Himachal, and figured it would be interesting to go exploring. I may come up empty-handed, or uncover something truly amazing. Either way, I'm excited because I'm headed into a new state without a plan, ready to take a chance.*

09/11/2018

Delhi to HP

I love winding roads! The sight of the lush green trees, the wild river flowing on one side, the sound of dry heaving coming from either the bus or the passenger behind... Okay, maybe that last bit isn't ideal, but in their defence, the bus driver did look like he wanted to go off-road and right into the River Sutlej.

As I looked out my window, I was instantly reminded of Alexander the Great and his troops. Truth be told, it's hard to say if that was the actual river he camped beside – it could have been in Punjab, for all we know – but the sight of the tents pitched along the riverbank took me back to 328 BCE.

The story goes that Alexander was waging a war against the Indian king Porus (Puru), and one day when he camped by the riverside, the men from his army saw a beast unlike anything they'd ever seen. It had come to drink water, but when it saw a crowd

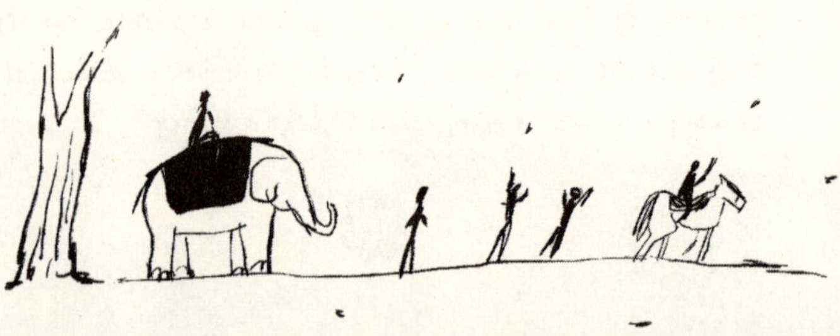

of people encroaching on its territory, it grew mad with rage. Black in colour, with three horns growing out of its forehead, the Odontotyrannos's face was horse-like and larger than anything they'd ever seen. In fact, it was so large that it could swallow an elephant in a single gulp.

According to a letter written by Alexander, the creature wasn't disturbed by fire or the arrows that his army shot at it. It charged right at them, killing 26 men and injuring 52 more. It took at least a hundred men with hunting spears to finally put an end to the beast, and it took about 200 more to drag its body out of the river (although the Armenian version says 1,300).

When the beast was finally down, Alexander's soldiers cut open its stomach only to find scorpions the size of bulls and chunks of meat that could have belonged to an elephant. Odontotyrannos means 'tooth tyrant' – named for its large jaws and menacing teeth.

If only Porus had had the Odontotyrannoses on his side!

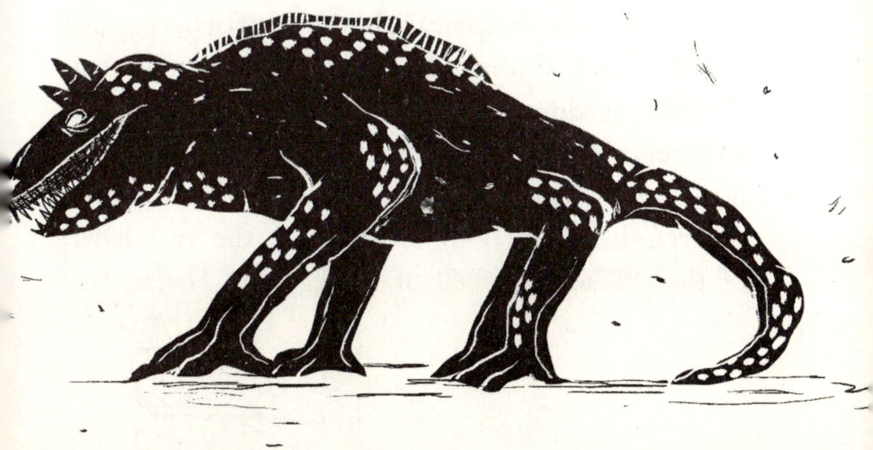

THE HAMSA BIRD

the hamsa bird

10/11/2018

En route, Jibhi, HP

I'd never seen aunties and uncles so happy to have their feet back on solid ground. Three bus breakdowns, two near-death experiences and a chorus of screams later, we'd made it to Manali. But my journey was far from over. A friend helps his uncle manage a campsite in Jibhi and he graciously offered to host me – provided I help out with chores now and then. Getting to Jibhi, however, has its own challenges. I learned from the tea seller at the bus stand that I had to either book a cab for ₹1,000, or find a bus to Banjar and then walk 8 kilometres to Jibhi.

I didn't want to get back on a bus, not after how long I'd been on one, but it really couldn't be helped – the taxi fare was too much for me. As the bus left the station, the landscape of huts and houses with asbestos roofs fell behind me and was replaced by vast stretches of icy blue mountains overlooking green forests. Now, the roads are long and winding, and the more I look out the window, the more the world starts to look like a cracked egg. The jagged mountains become the bottom half of the eggshell and the sharp whirling clouds made up the other half. I've been reading a lot about the creation of the world, and seeing the world in front of me as a broken eggshell has immediately made me think of the Hamsa Bird.

According to Hindu mythology, the two halves of the cracked eggshell of the egg the Hamsa Bird

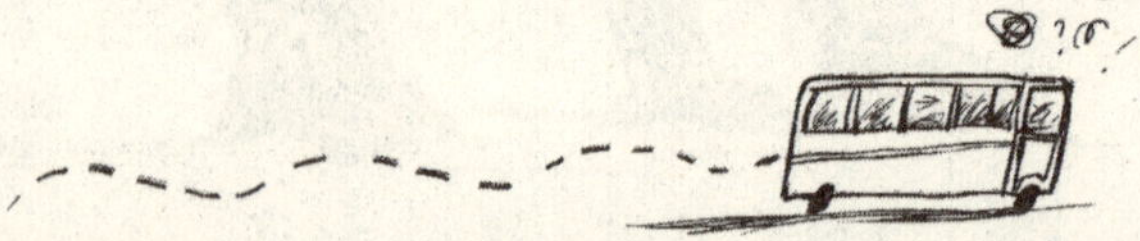

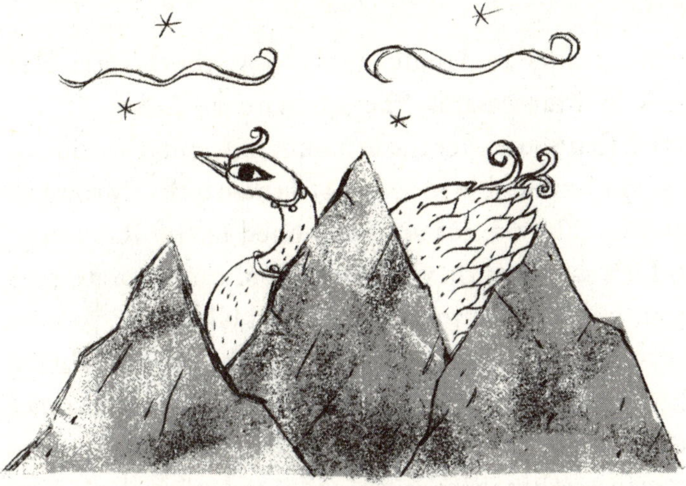

hatched became the earth and the skies. It's strangely comforting to think of the world as an egg. It makes me feel a lot safer, and I'm sure I'm not alone. According to the Greeks, Gaia (the earth goddess) laid the world egg on the waters of chaos and commanded the cosmic snake, Ophion, to encircle it and keep it warm until it hatched. In Zoroastrian legends, Ohrmazd, creator deity in Zoroastrianism, created a great egg, with the upper part forming the sky and the lower half becoming the earth. Ohrmazd then filled the lower half of the shell with water and laid a flat disc on the upper half on top of it to make the earth. The ancient Egyptians thought Ra, their sun god, emerged from the primaeval waters of a cosmic egg, and according to a Bantu myth, the upper half of an eggshell became the heavens while the lower half held Earth and Mother Nature. See, I told you I wasn't alone.

According to Hindu mythology, the Hamsa Bird lives in Manasasaras (the Mansarovar Lake). If I'm right, that's just over those mountains, and if I'm lucky, I might just be able to see one of these birds fly towards my bus. These birds are mentioned in the Ramayana, and it's said that they eat pearls and can separate milk from water. That's really cool and all, but if you ask me, their biggest contribution to the world is being the first messaging service for lovers in a long-distance relationship. In the story of Nala and Damayanti, who were in love but separated by miles and miles, the Hamsa Bird plays the role of a messenger.

I do hope that Nala and Damayanti used the bird wisely, because I can't think of anything worse than employing a poor bird to send scrolls with smiley faces and hearts drawn on tiny paper parchments.

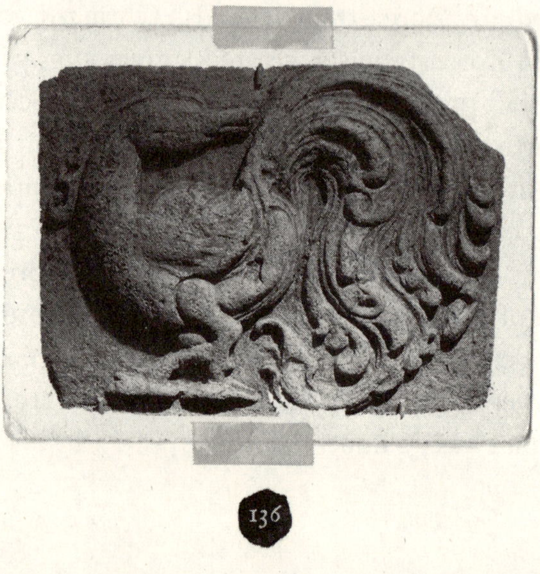

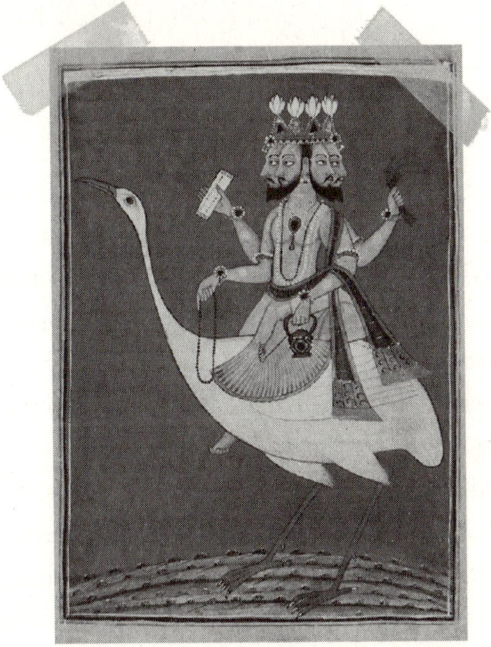

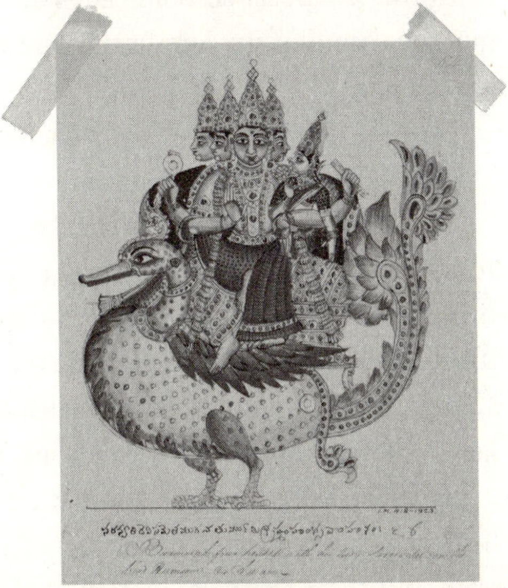

11/11/2018

Walk to Jibhi, HP

The 8-kilometre stretch to Jibhi was much longer than I thought it would be. I'd imagined a straight path along the side of a tarred road with at least a few street lights to guide me. What I got was the exact opposite. I was relieved that I had my wind-up torch with me, but I decided against using it, fearing the attention the sound of winding might attract.

As I walked down the dark curving roads, with just the light from my phone to illuminate my path, I tried my best not to think about the scary monsters and demons that could be lurking just around the corner. I needed to think of a beast so comical that, even if it surprised me, the sound of my laughter alone would be able to chase it away.

A few creatures crossed my mind, including the duckbill platypus – they always crack me up – but I finally settled on the Kumbhaṇḍa. How could any creature whose name ends with the word 'anda' scare anyone!

The Kumbhaṇḍa are a tribe of dwarf-like spirits from Buddhist mythology. These creatures have faces that resemble a friendly animal, and are usually seen sporting large stomachs that protrude up to their chests. But the most amusing part about them is that people believe that their balloon-like stomachs are not stomachs at all, but their testicles.

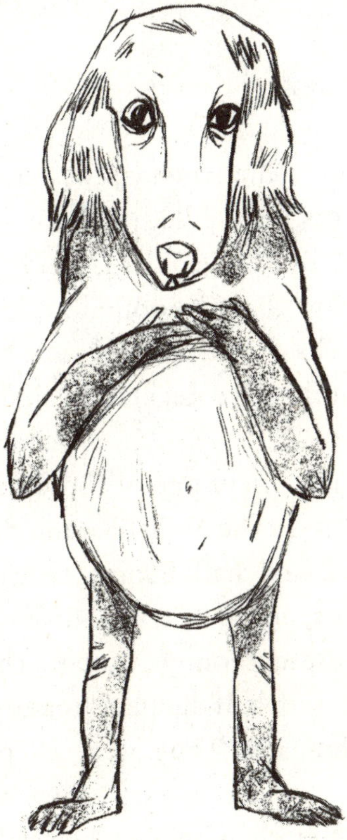

Okay, fine, I may have left out the bit about them having magical powers, and they are known to be freakishly strong and fast. And, yes, some of them are downright evil and devour humans whole. But it's also a fact that corrupt and greedy officers are reborn as Kumbhaṇḍa, and I'm never going to be bested by a pot-bellied reincarnation of a greedy bureaucrat. At least, that's what I like to believe.

KINNARAS
kinnaras

12/11/2018

Jibhi, HP

According to Vedic legends, the regions surrounding the Himalayas were filled with all sorts of tribes in around 3,000 BCE. Even the Greeks spoke about their existence. Now that I've found myself a place for the next few weeks – with a direct view of the Himalayas, I'd like to add – I've decided to find out more about these tribes.

The Kinnaras were one of those tribes that roamed the Himalayas. In the Mahabharata, they are described as half-horse and half-human creatures. They were fierce warriors, not to be trifled with.

In Buddhist mythology, though, they are described as half-bird and half-human creatures that pose no danger to humans. They were so gentle that they were known to nurse human babies when the parents went away. But their mild-mannered nature worked against them. The fact that the Kinnaras sang, danced and played instruments led to them being captured by humans and thrown into cages to perform.

I'm not entirely sure how they went extinct, but I do know one thing: being tossed into cages for human amusement isn't ideal for any species to thrive.

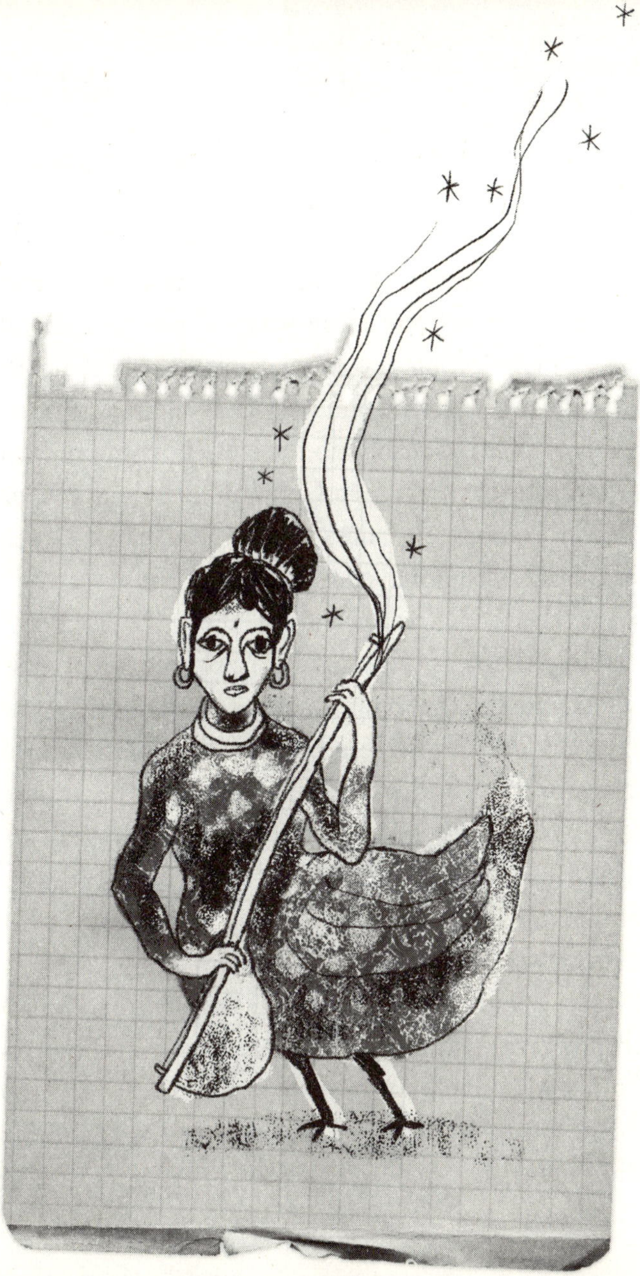

13/11/2018

A tent in Jibhi, HP

The Kinnaras aren't the only tribes that were once found an eyeshot away from where I was camping. If I were to trek along the mountainside – braving the cold, fighting off wild animals and making sure my feet stayed planted firmly on the ice – it would take me less than four days to reach Gaumukh, the place where the River Ganga originates. That's where the Greeks believed the Astomoi lived.

Pliny the Elder wrote about the tribe in detail, describing them as human-like creatures with toned muscles, and fur covering most or all of their bodies. But here's the strange thing: they don't have mouths, so they don't eat or drink! The Astomoi simply wander the mountainsides, plucking apples and flowers and sniffing their scent for sustenance. But they need to be careful about what they sniff because the faintest whiff of an unpleasant odour could kill them.

I guess I have to reconsider trekking to the place where the Ganga starts. For starters, I haven't showered in days, and I smell bad enough to make an Astomoi sick. But more importantly, it's because I'm terrible at holding in farts.

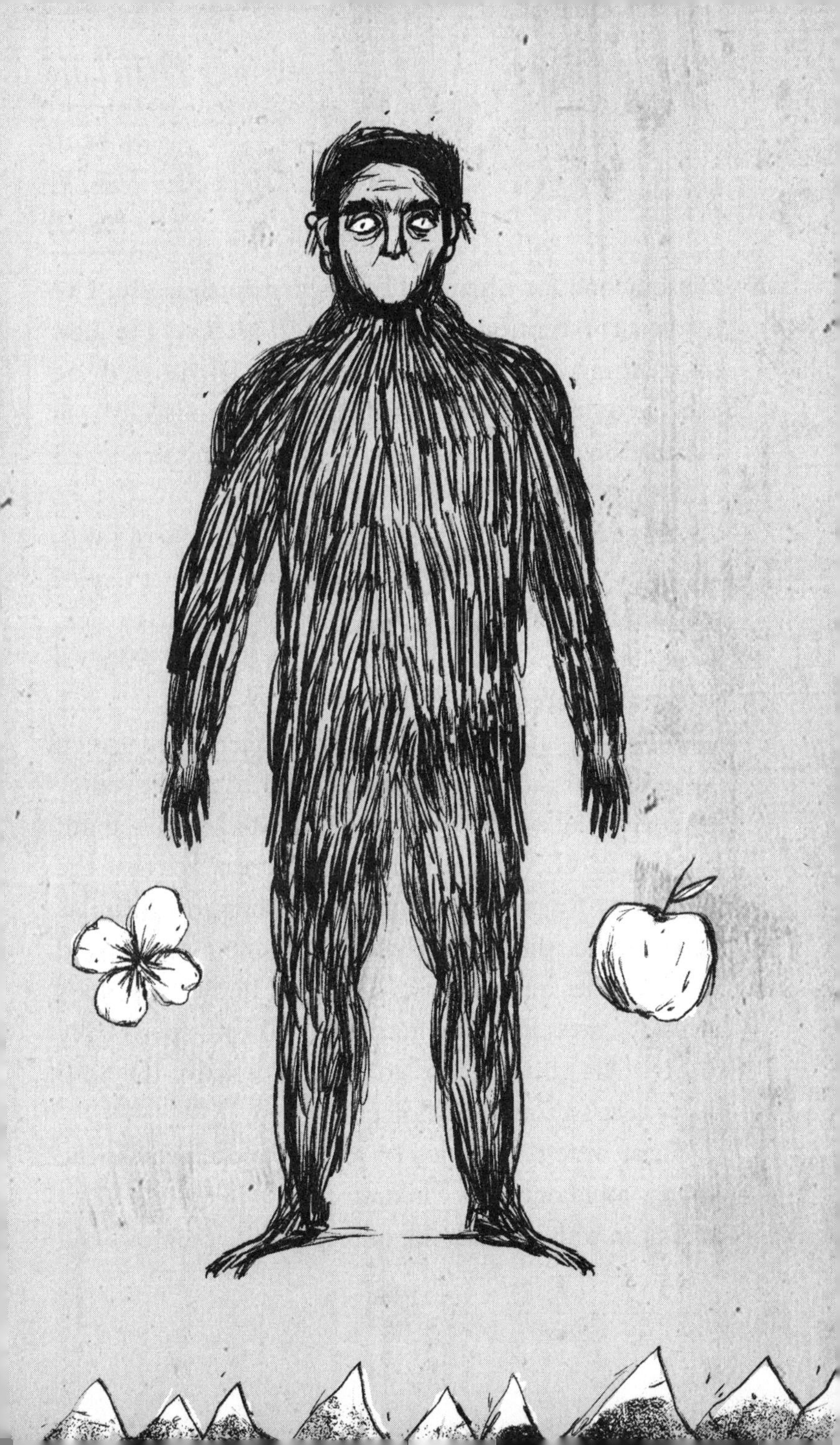

THE PANDAE

the pandae

14/11/2018

Neuli
Sainj Valley Trek, HP
(Day 1)

I'm not one for organized tours, but in this case, I've made an exception. This is partly because I'm new to trekking, but mostly because my friend told me that I could get lost in the mountains, collapse from exhaustion and crack my skull against a sharp rock if I attempted this trek alone.

Three hours and a shared taxi ride later, there I was, at Neuli village, as excited as a kid on his first day of school. (But if I'm being honest, I pretended to be sick, kicked and punched the air, and bawled my eyes out on my first day of school.)

As we began our trek, mostly walking along green pastures and paved pathways, I looked at the valley gradually falling under our feet and thought about Pandae, another tribe of humanoid creatures that the Greeks wrote about. According to them, the Pandae were a tribe who had only four fingers on each hand and four toes on each foot. Going by Pliny the Elder's account, they lived in mountain valleys, specifically those where the Indian reed grew – perhaps, the Spiti valley that's about 100 kilometres away.

There were only a total of 30,000 Pandae because the women could only have children once in their lives. They were born with a mouth full of teeth, white eyebrows and white eyelashes, and were covered in white fur. As they got older, their hair turned jet black – quite the opposite of us!

The thing that sticks out the most about the Pandae, and I mean this quite literally, are their ears. Their ears were so long that they fell all the way down to their elbows, and wide enough to touch each other when allowed to fall behind their shoulders. It is said that they would tie their ears behind their backs when they went into battle! The men and women of this tribe were mostly warriors and archers. According to the Greek historian Ctesias, they could live up to 200 years!

Hmm... Maybe we ought to have been a little more mindful while we trekked? But who am I kidding – a tribe of warriors with Dumbo-sized ears would hear us coming from miles away, regardless of how cautious we were.

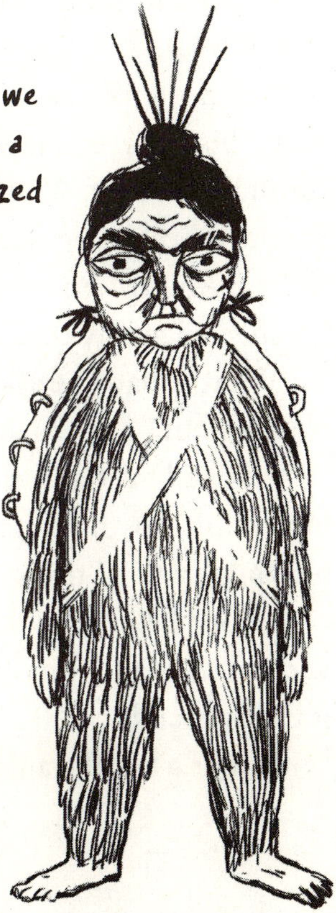

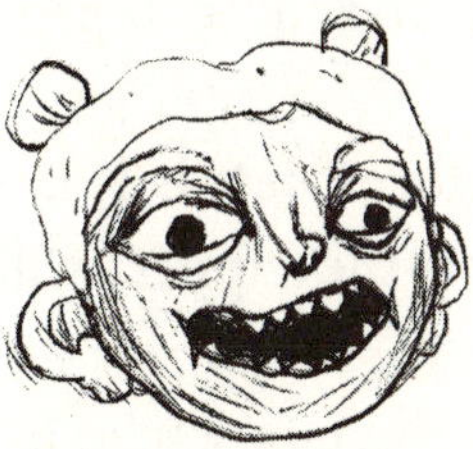

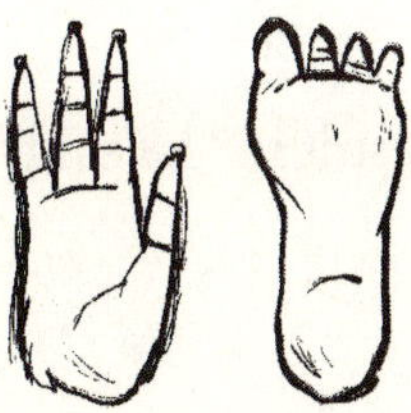

15/11/2018

Shakti

Sainj Valley Trek, HP (Day 2)

The second day of my trek started easy, but within 45 minutes, I found myself panting and gasping for air.

'Are you okay?' a voice called.

The man looked as though he were in his sixties. He had a long bushy moustache, an accent that reminded me of the American missionaries who visited us back in school and white skin that appeared more wrinkled than it was.

'From the plains, I take it?' he continued, slowing down his pace to match mine. 'You just need to get through this part. Would have helped if you'd prepared for the hike, but I guess you've got to pick things up on the go. And try not to fall – that bit is important.' He laughed so loudly that he alarmed the rest of the party.

'What's that?' he asked, pointing to a piece of paper sticking out of my backpack.

I looked at it and then at my gloves. It was almost impossible to grip, let alone close the zipper while wearing a pair of thick woollen gloves.

Before I knew it, the man with the moustache had yanked the paper out of my bag and was busy showing it to his friends.

'Looks a bit like an ape-man, doesn't it?' he said.

'It does, but it's a little too small to be –'

'Give it back!' I snapped, interrupting their conversation and snatching back my drawing.

'You're not here looking for that beast by any chance, are you?'

I froze. 'I am – but how'd you know about it?' I mumbled.

'We all are!' He laughed. 'So, what's the deal with your drawing?'

I unfurled the piece of paper and handed it back to him. 'This is a Chromandae,' I explained. 'They're a

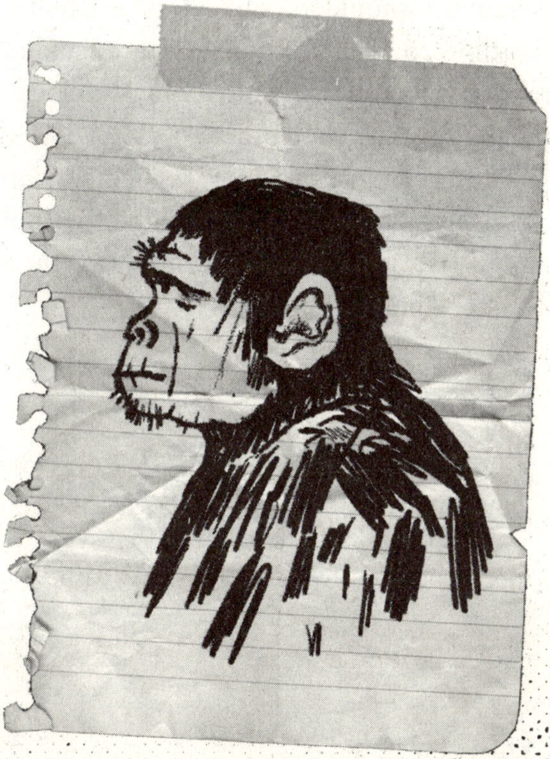

tribe of human-like apes. They're supposed to live in the valleys and caves along the Himalayas.'

The man with the moustache leaned closer to me.

'They're almost monkey-like in appearance, with bodies covered in fur,' I added. I watched his eyes widen and continued, 'They're supposed to be docile but can be dangerous, when riled, owing to their sharp dog-like teeth.'

The man with the moustache stopped dead in his tracks. 'And what about their feet?' he asked. 'How big are they?'

'Just normal feet, I guess,' I replied, and instantly watched his shoulders sink along with his interest. 'According to what I read, the Chromandae couldn't speak, and instead made terrifying shrieking noises to communicate with each other.'

'That's interesting, kid,' he replied, waving his hand dismissively, 'but we're actually here for another ape-creature!' He leaned closer to me. 'Ever heard of the "Bigfoot"?' he whispered.

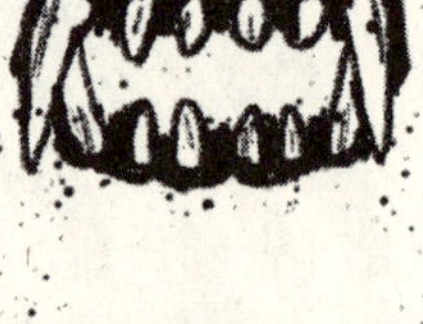

15/11/2018

Towards Parkachi
Sainj Valley Trek
(Day 2)

'You're looking for extraordinary beasts and you've never heard of the Yeti?' It's hard to convey astonishment when your face is covered with layers of clothing, but somehow my new friend Mr Robin did it quite easily.

'Oh, the Yeti,' I snorted. 'Of course, I've heard of it. Mostly in the cartoons I watched as a kid. But they're far less interesting than the Nittaewo and how we drove them to extinction.'

I don't know if it was the way I said it, but my new friends seemed quite offended.

'Bigfoot is very real!' Mr Robin whispered. 'There have been reports about them from as early as the 17th century. There's even this monk who walked all the way from India to Nepal to meditate inside a cave, back in the 1600s, and he left behind written accounts of the Yeti bringing him food to eat and water to drink.' He paused for a moment. 'Did you know that the place where he died – Pangboche, I believe it's called - was actually enshrined? Complete with its relics!'

'I... I – I only know about the fluffy ones I've seen in my cartoons,' I mumbled, regretting what I'd said the moment the words left my mouth.

'The accounts from the cartoons are only half true. If you ask me, there are two kinds of Yetis. A kind and friendly one, about 10 to 15 feet in height, that walks on two legs and lives well below the snowy part of the mountain, and a bloodthirsty Yeti who walks on all fours and kills anyone who encroaches upon its territory.

'We're here in search of the friendly ones. But if I come across a fierce one, I won't hesitate to kill it,' Mr Robin said, drilling his walking pole into the earth. 'Did you know that the government in Nepal handed out licences to hunt Yetis back in the 1950s? Look it up when you're back in the plains.

'Most people don't know what they're looking for when they're looking for a Yeti. They're supposed to be hairy ape-like figures with large feet, but the Tibetans believe them to be more bear-like than apes. Bears... apes...none of that really matters, because we'll know the moment we find one, won't we?' He winked at me. 'Judging by the tracks we found a week ago, it's only a matter of time before we do.'

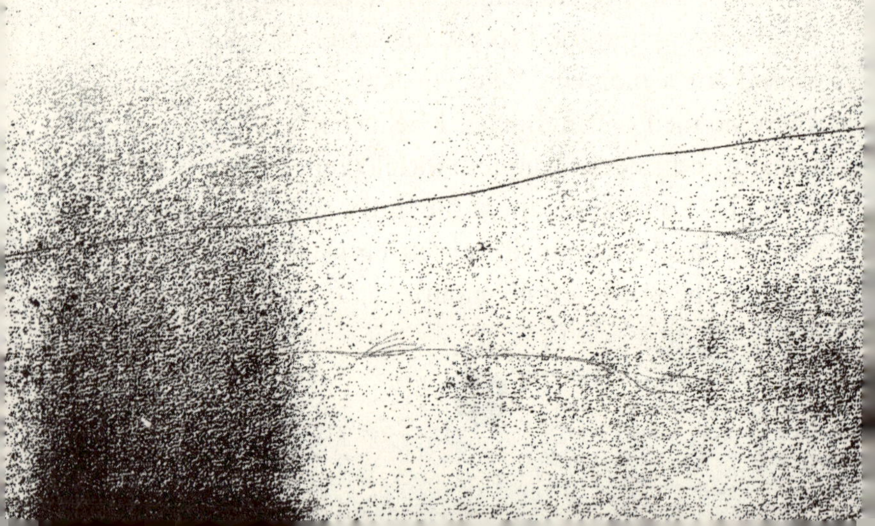

'Is the Yeti the only creature you're interested in?' I asked.

'Yetis during the summer, Sasquatches in the winter, and angels all year round,' he said, very matter-of-factly.

Mr Robin pulled ahead of me and walked on over to the front of the group. I hoped for the Yeti's sake that it never crossed paths with him. Regardless of what he told me about them, something about him suggested that he would shoot a Yeti – kind or otherwise – in the back the moment he saw one. Heck, he seemed like the kind of person who'd shoot an angel in the face as it tried to fly away.

16/11/2018

Towards Raktisar
Sainj Valley Trek
(Day 3)

On the third day, we walked through bushes, crossed streams using wooden logs that rolled over if you leaned too much one way or the other, and trudged carefully along the moss-covered rocks. But that wasn't even the worst part. I'd never seen snow before and so I thought my first time witnessing it would be life-changing. Sure enough, it was. But it took me less than five minutes to get tired of it. It made the edges of the glacier a lot more slippery. It almost gave my fingers frostbite when I tried to make a snowball, and it made me feel colder than I'd ever been.

I hate the snow. Humans aren't built to live in the snow. But at least we're far better off than the Mandoi.

According to my research, the Mandoi were a valley tribe with frail bodies and a physique unsuited to survive harsh conditions. Mandoi women only gave birth once in their life, and whenever a Mandoi child was born, they would come out of the womb looking old and wrinkly already. I know what you're thinking – most newborn babies *are* grey and wrinkly by default, but unlike human babies, the Mandoi stayed old and wrinkled their entire lives!

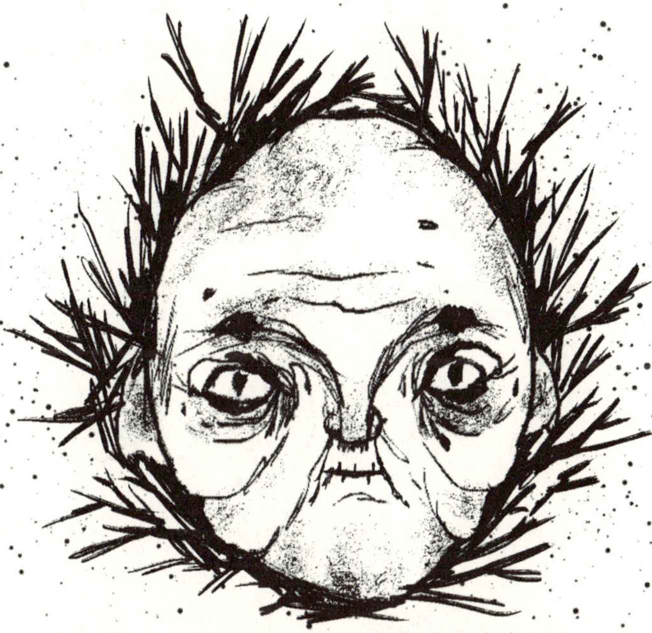

As a matter of fact, the Mandoi rarely made it past the age of forty. They ate locusts and other bugs, and were oddly swift on their feet despite their frail old bodies.

Phew, just the thought of being a Mandoi in the cold is giving me arthritis. I'm glad to be born a human. But I mustn't allow myself to get complacent, because Pliny also wrote about another tribe of human-like creatures that were far better adapted to the cold than humans could ever be – the Astomoi.

16/11/2018

Towards Raktisar
Sainj Valley Trek, HP
(Day 3)

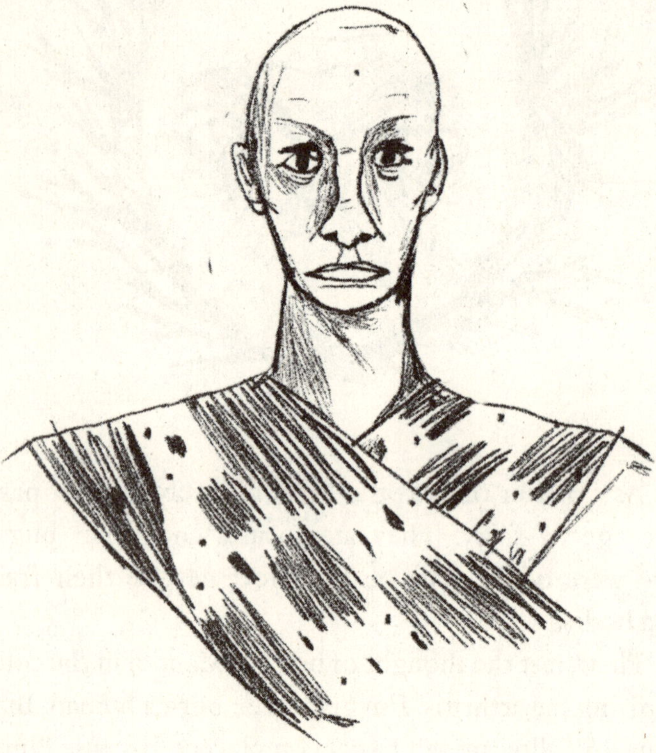

The Macrobi is a collective term for India's many long-lived tribes. Unlike the Mandoi, the Macrobi are born young and strong, and are perfectly adept at dealing with anything nature throws at them. The most fascinating among these tribes were the Cyrni, who lived by the mountains and only died when they reached 140 years.

Onesicritus, the Greek historian from the fourth century BCE, mentions a nameless race of Indians who were 8 feet tall and lived in the part of the country where there were no shadows. He thought that the Indians from this region lived for 130 years, but would stop ageing after they turned forty. He believed them to be strong and resilient, and now that I come to think about it, they do sound like Yetis (maybe after a shave and a full-body wax).

The last leg of our trek was the most strenuous. We were walking along the river, climbing over snow-dusted boulders, making sure we didn't slip, and there I was, daydreaming about something trivial. I stared at the path in front of me, and then I raised my head and glanced at the daunting glacier in front of us. I felt weary, dizzy and overwhelmed.

'We have to stop,' I gasped. 'Let's camp here! I don't think I'm going to make it if we don't camp here.'

Turns out that we were going to pitch in our tents anyway, and I would have seemed as resilient and strong as the others had I just held it in for another kilometre.

I hate how embarrassing it gets the moment after I speak my mind, put my foot down, or stand up for myself. My ears become warm, my cheeks feel red (my Tirunelveli complexion prevents them from *becoming* red), and I begin to shake on the inside.

Well, you know what? I'm happy I did that. I'm sure the others were thinking it, but I was the one to say it. No one is going to think that I cracked, right?

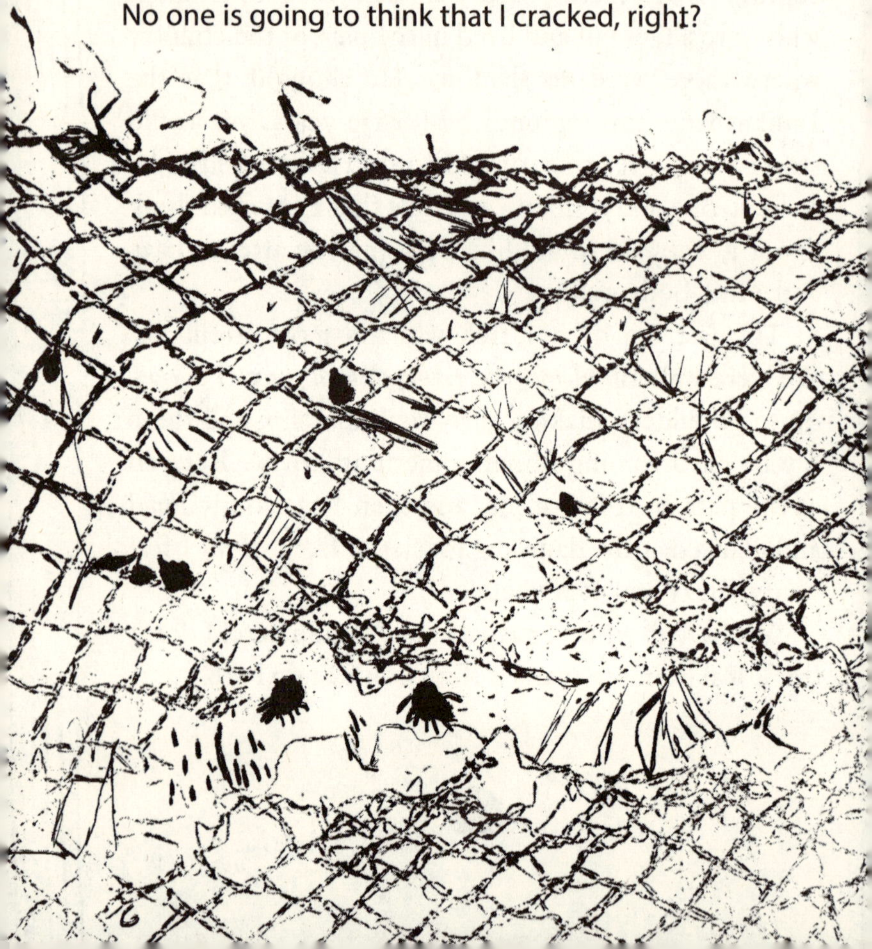

At least, I'm in my tent now, with nothing but my journal and my signal-less Nokia phone to keep me company. I don't know why, but being out here in the middle of nowhere, right under the foot of the large glacier, makes me feel like drawing something. Maybe I'll draw the tribes of the Macrobi… No, even better! I'm going to draw something bigger.

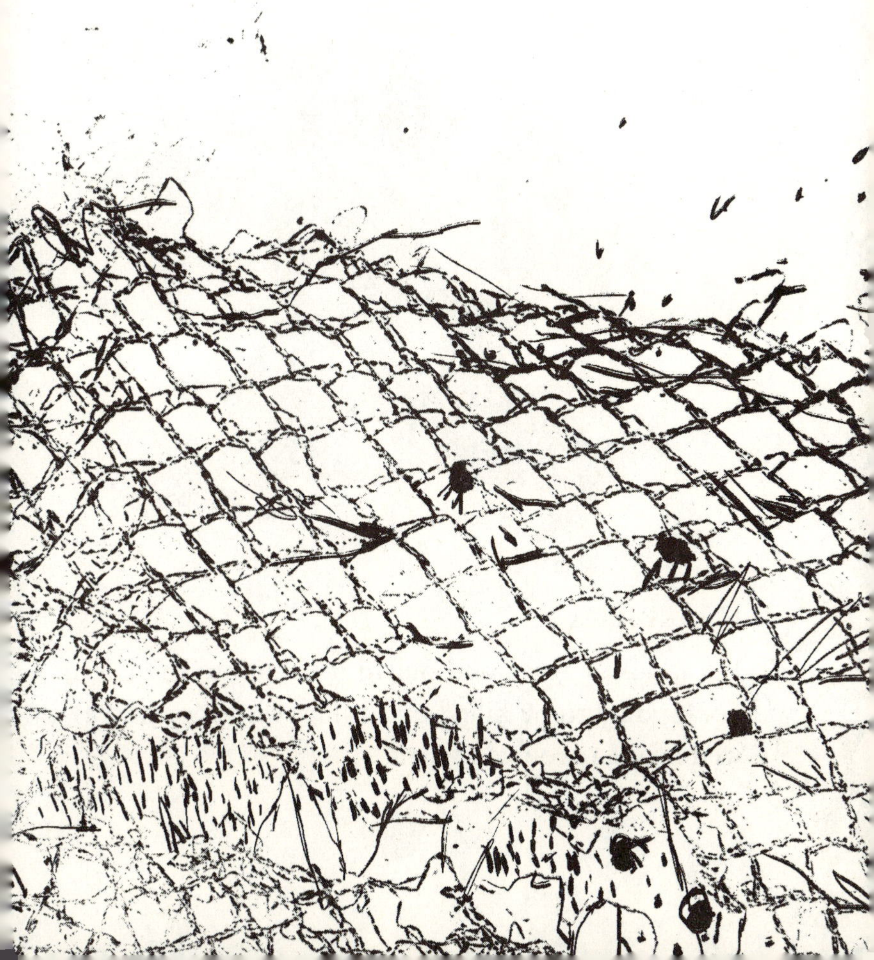

giants of india

17/11/2018

Tent by the glacier
Sainj Valley Trek, HP
(Day 4)

According to Hindu mythology, India is filled with many lovable and not-so-lovable giants. These are the ones that came to my mind.

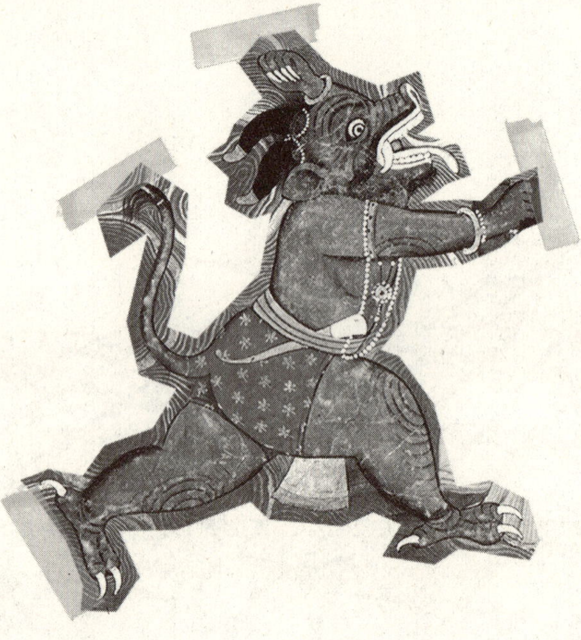

HIRANYAKSHA

He attacked Earth and pulled it deep into the cosmic ocean, only to be killed by Vishnu, who appeared as a wild boar and rescued Earth.

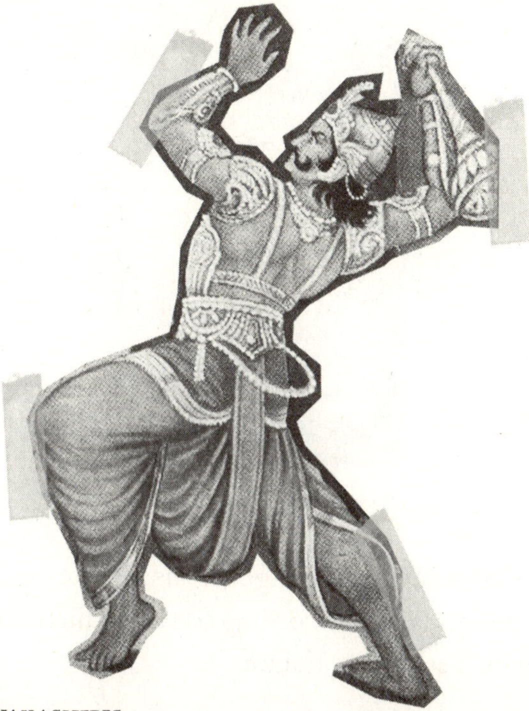

HIRANYAKASHIPU

The king of the Daityas (a race of giants), Hiranyakashipu wanted to kill Vishnu as revenge for the death of his brother Hiranyaksha. The giant performed penance and acquired a boon from Brahma. And though Hiranyakashipu wasn't granted his wish for immortality, he was granted a boon so that he couldn't be killed by any living entity, couldn't die during daytime or night, couldn't be killed on the ground or in the sky, couldn't be killed by any weapon, or by any demigod, god or demon. The loophole was Narashima, Vishnu's carefully concocted avatar that defied all of Hiranyakashipu's limitations of death.

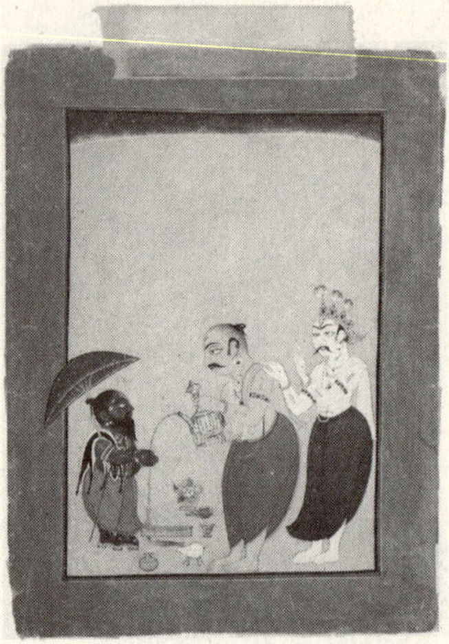

Mahabali

He was a benevolent and generous king, especially loved in Kerala. But according to some Jain texts, he was an evil, scheming demon.

Kumbhakarna

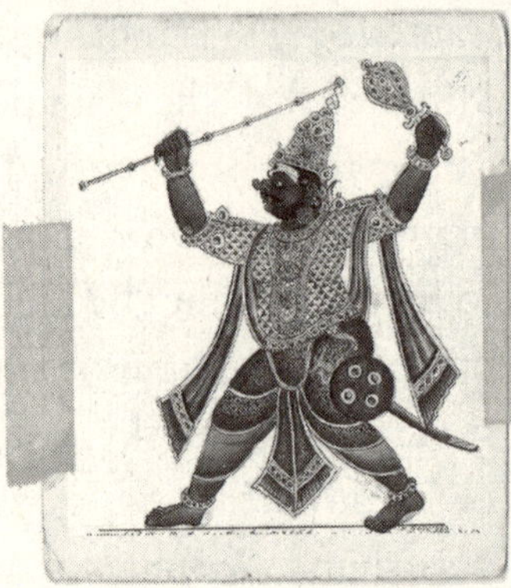

The younger brother of Ravan. He basically ate and slept a lot. He's widely regarded as a lovable, amicable giant, despite killing and eating a whole lot of his enemies.

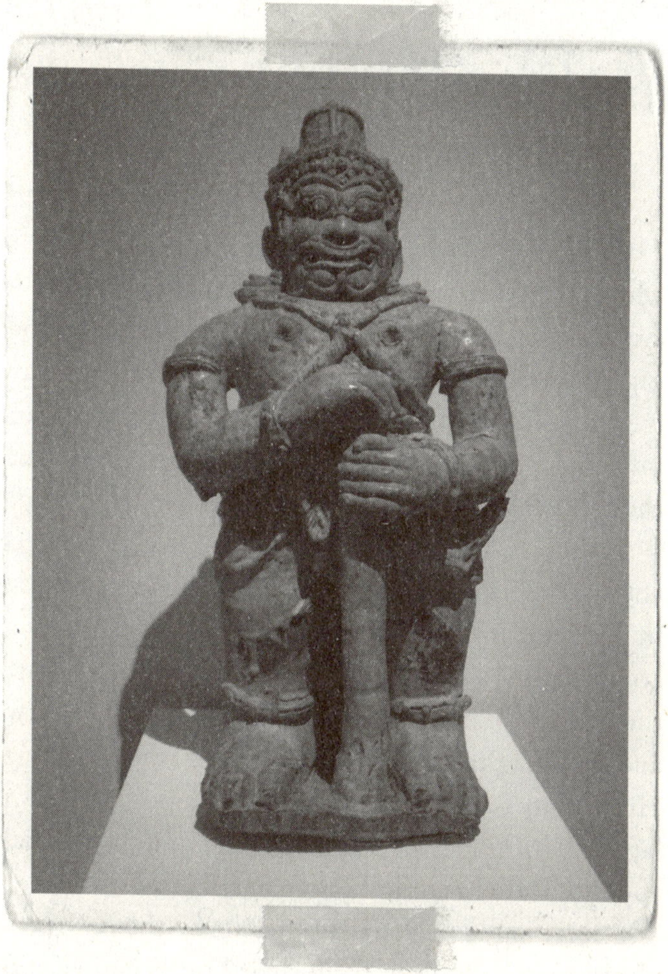

DVARAPALA

A fearsome giant warrior and a door guardian. In today's depictions, he's usually armed with a mace and can be found outside temples across India, South-East Asia and Sri Lanka.

18/11/2018

On top of the glacier
Sainj Valley Trek, HP
(Day 5)

I am on top of the world! It feels great to pen this while at the very peak of the glacier. I'm sure my legs are going to be wobblier than a bowl of instant noodles on my way down, but I don't care. Not when I have a view of the Himalayan Range in front of me. I know my mind is making this up, but being up here, I feel as though I can look down into Uttarakhand and Nepal.

I've often wondered if the creatures I look for care about borders. Do they stick to their little localities the way we humans do, or do they traverse cities, states and countries like a tiger in the Sundarbans? If it's the latter, then we might just run into the Gurumapa, a mean, wild and easily agitated carnivorous giant who lives in the Himalayan Range in Nepal. He's supposed to have a large, terrifying face, jagged fangs and an insatiable appetite for human flesh.

According to Nepalese folklore, the Gurumapa would snatch children from their homes and eat them up at leisure. The only way the villagers were able to put a stop to his rampant killing was with some good old-fashioned diplomacy. The villagers agreed to offer the beast an annual feast with all the boiled rice and buffalo meat he could eat; in return, the Gurumapa would have to live far away from their villages and stop eating their children. The giant agreed. Even today, there are people in Nepal who uphold their end of the deal and prepare a feast for him once a year.

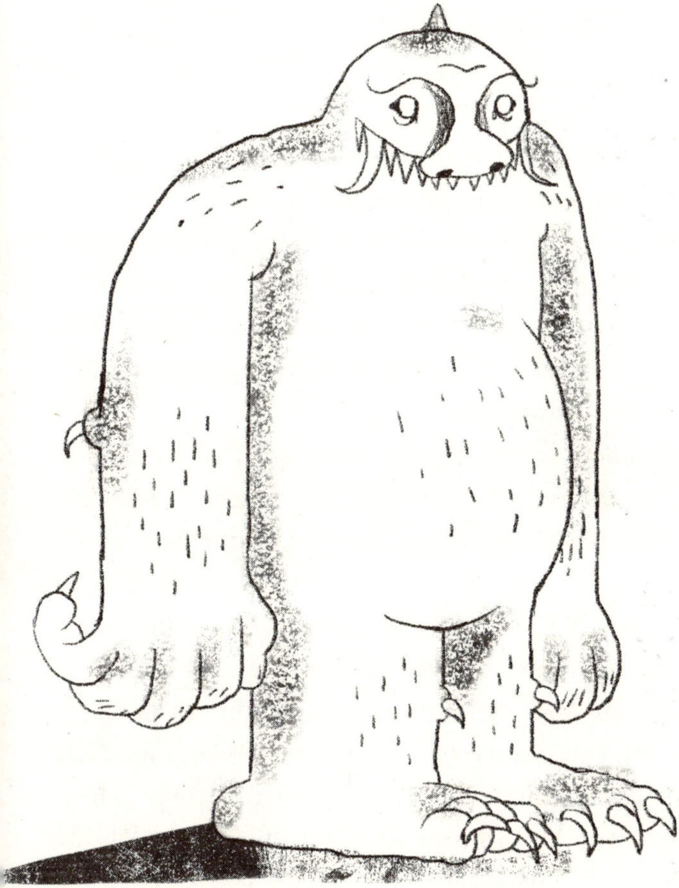

the banmanush and barmanou

19/11/2018

Down the glacier
Sainj Valley Trek, HP (Day 6)

When it was time for us to trek down the glacier and head home, I was already dreading our journey. Not because of the difficulty of the descent, but because I didn't want to leave the tranquillity of the mountains, although I suppose I'd be susceptible to attacks from the Banmanush or the Barmanou if I dared remain on the mountaintops alone.

Indigenous to the Himalayan Range, the Banmanush check all the right boxes on a Yeti hunter's list. They are furry ape-men who live below the snowline of the mountain range, only climbing to the peak to hunt and eat when food is scarce. The Banmanush is only 6 feet tall — about half the height of a Yeti – and can be incredibly vicious. They are skilled hunters, quick on their feet, and known to be very aggressive, especially when people encroach upon their territory. These creatures are also known to enter villages under the cover of night and abduct humans.

With dozens of these reported snowmen around, you'd think I would at least get a glimpse of one of

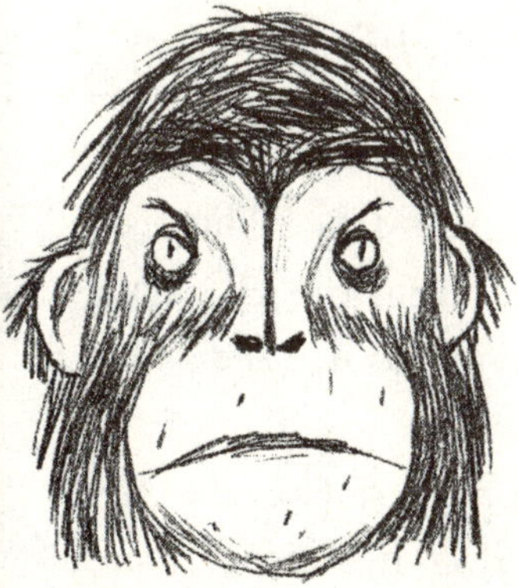

Fig 1

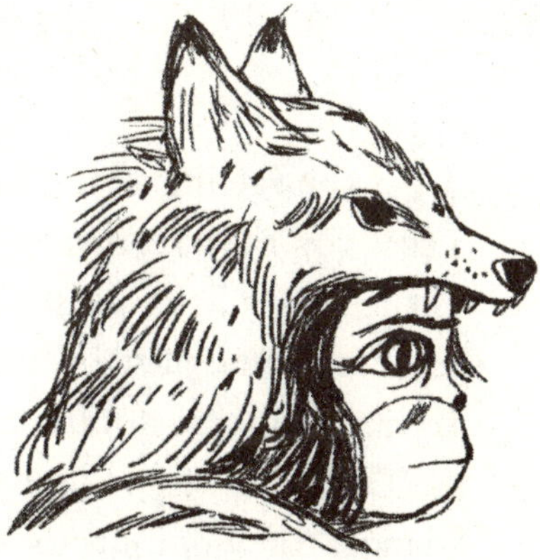

Fig 2

them. But I suppose that these creatures are spread across distances spanning hundreds of kilometres, and some of them stick to their own mountains, while others lumber awkwardly between India, Tibet, Nepal and Bhutan. Perhaps next time I'll venture towards the mountains of west Pakistan and try my luck. I heard that the Barmanou, an ape-like creature described as equal parts human and animal, live there.

Note to self: The Barmanou wear fur and animal skin that cover their head and shoulders, and are notorious for trying to hook up with humans. Plan your trip with caution.

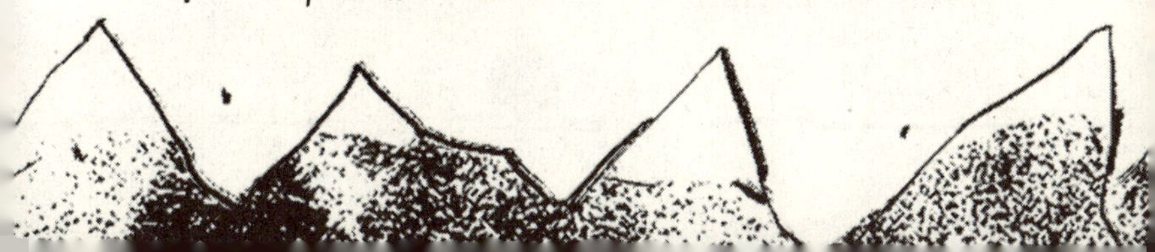

THE KYNOKEPHALOI

the kynokephaloi

19/11/2018

Down the glacier

Sainj Valley Trek, HP (Day 6)

I get the feeling that I have been dealing a lot of bad press for the creatures all along this trek. The truth is that not all the beasts that live along the Himalayas are bad. Some of them are just trying to live their lives, trying their best not to bother anyone.

Take the Kynokephaloi, for instance. At first glance, they might look like dog-headed humans, who come across as ferocious and scary, but according to Ctesias, they were actually quite civil. He said that the Kynokephaloi lived in the mountains of India, clothing themselves in the skins of wild beasts, and communicating among themselves using barks and growls. They were supposed to have teeth larger than dogs, their nails were wolf-like but manicured, and they were almost always dark in complexion and fur. Even though they understood local Indian languages, they were incapable of responding, and relied on sign language and gestures to communicate with humans as well as one another.

The Kynokephaloi didn't know how to grow plants or do any of the jobs we humans do. They survived by gathering fruits from the forest and by hunting animals, which they slow-roasted under the sun. They did, however, know how to rear animals, and the richest

Kynokephaloi was often the one who owned the highest number of sheep.

They were so well loved at one time that the kings of India sent them spears, bows and shields as gifts. And even though there were over a lakh Kynokephaloi in the fourth century BCE, they refused to live in houses, choosing the cave complexes of the region instead.

The Kynokephaloi woke up in the morning, grabbed their spears and bows, and chased after their prey. And given how they were half dogs, they were agile and as swift as the wind. Their one shortcoming was personal hygiene. It is said that the Kynokephaloi women used to bathe once a month, while the men went their entire lives without bathing. They did, however, use perfumes made from milk, so I guess that's some sort of compensation?

I like thinking about the way the Kynokephaloi lived. They wore very little clothing, slept on leaves and grass instead of beds, had tails above their hips, and were covered in silky fur. Oh my god, I think I see it now. The Kynokephaloi are golden retrievers in human form! But the Kynokephaloi lived an average of 170 to 220 years. If only golden retrievers could live that long.

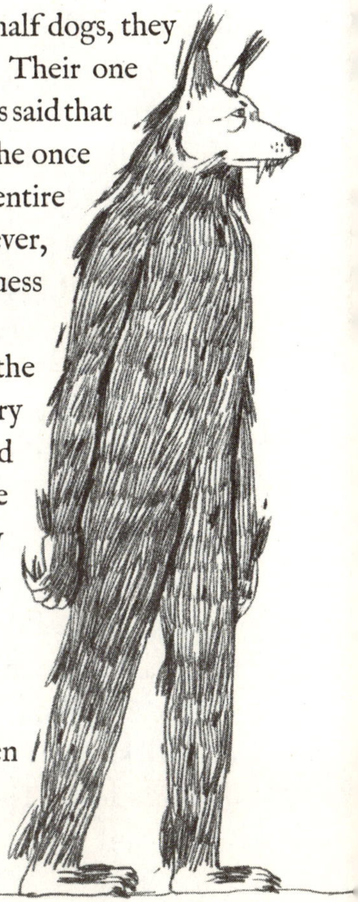

20/11/2018

Down the glacier
Sainj Valley Trek,
HP (Day 7)

We were done with the most strenuous part of our trek. I'd left the ice behind me and was ready to enter the forest. It was only a matter of time before I reached home. I just hoped that my joints would stay inside their sockets.

I must come clean – something about this trek had been bothering me. I didn't socialize as much as I ought to have, but with good reason. The others from the trek had little respect for nature. They threw their rubbish around, they walked around like they owned the place, and they stepped on tiny mushrooms and saplings, sometimes on purpose!

I wish that the Abarimon or their fiercer Brazilian cousin, the Curupira, were around to stop my companions. Almost identical to us humans in every regard, the Abarimon (and the Curupira) are different in one way – their feet are on backwards from the knee down. The Abarimon aren't violent and it's well known that they don't harm humans. The Curupira, on the other hand, would tear a human to shreds should someone pose a threat to or harm the forests and the animals that live in it.

The Abarimon can run very fast, unlike the Curupira, who tricks humans and lures them away from animals during a hunt. The Abarimon live in forests cloaked with magic, which hides their homes in the valleys from any human intruders. If a human finds their forest, the Abarimon use the animals under their command to chase the strangers out.

Only the Abarimon can communicate with and command the animals in their valley, but if a human is ever unlucky enough to still find their way to an Abarimon's house, or if they even breathe the same air as the Abarimon, they would be stuck in the valley forever! The air is supposedly filled with magic, and once someone gets used to inhaling that air, they can't go back to the air they'd breathed earlier. The Abarimon too would suffocate to death if they ever tried to leave the valley and breathed the air of the outside world!

The Abarimon do sometimes venture outside their valley, but they use magical crystals and bubbleheads to keep themselves from dying.

I was starting to feel a bit lightheaded all of a sudden, like I could hardly breathe. I hoped it was because of my exhausted lungs and tired body.

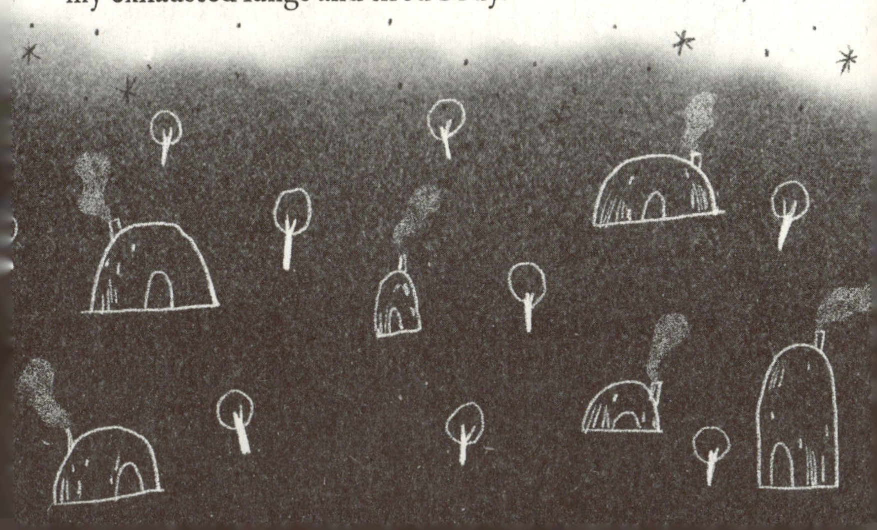

THE COW_EATING PLANT

the cow-eating plant

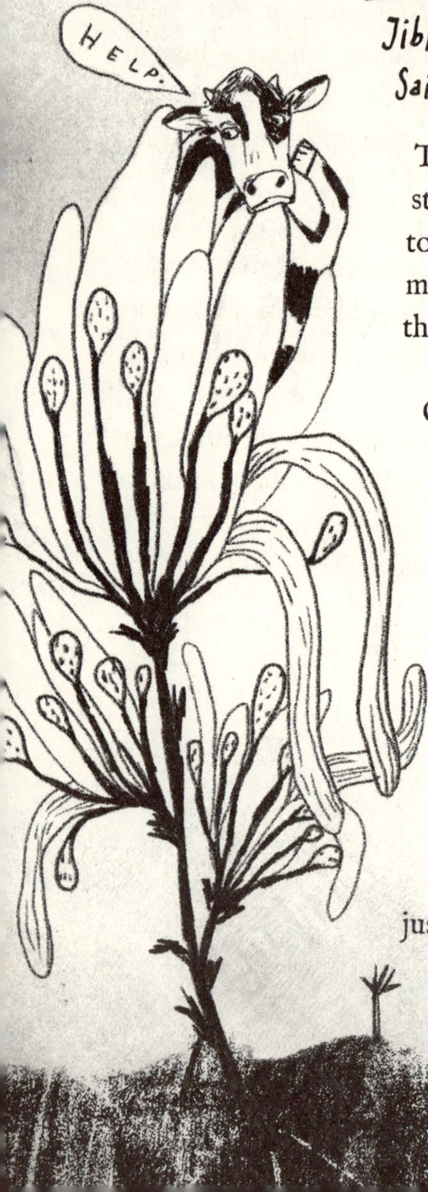

20/11/2018

Jibhi

Sainj Valley Trek, HP (Day 7)

The slopes were getting a lot steeper, despite us coming back to the plains. The trees around me seemed 10 times as tall, and the bushes...they tried to grab me!

'WE NEED TO GET OUT OF HERE!' I yelled, mustering the last ounce of energy I had in me. 'I'VE HEARD OF THESE PLANTS, THEY'RE OUT TO GET US!'

I flailed my arms and ran around, trying to warn my fellow trekkers, but they looked at me as though I was mad.

'I've heard about plants just like these in Mangaluru,' I

tried once more, this time lying down on the ground. 'People from the Uppinangady forest range saw plants just like these. They ate the cattle, and then they ate the children! These plants are carnivorous, and they're going to eat us!

'The villagers allowed their cows to graze in the forest. When they heard loud cries of pain, they rushed into the woods, only to find a plant, just like the one in front of us, gnawing on a cow's legs. But the villagers acted swiftly. They hacked away at the plant, rescuing the poor cow from it before it was too late. If we don't cut down these plants, they're going to come for us!' I groaned, still kicking and thrashing on the ground.

I woke up hours later at the campsite.

My friend tells me that I had a very public meltdown, and that it may have been caused because of the lack of oxygen at the high altitude. But I know what I saw, I know I saw the Cow-eating Plant, and I know I saved all our lives.

The downside to my heroics is that I now have a fever, and my friend tells me it's quite bad. 'House rest and a lot of fluids,' he said. And as much as I want to get up and leave, I just don't have the energy to do it. Forget cracking my skull open while on a trek, I might break every bone in my body trying to find my way down the stairs that lead to the common area.

I really hope this passes soon. I hate being sick.

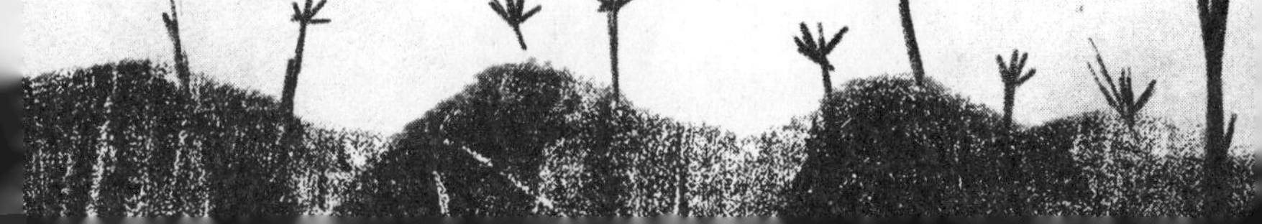

THE BHEKI

the bheki

20/11/2018

Tent in Jibhi, HP

I might be getting worse. I don't feel like eating, I don't feel like getting up, and I'm not sleeping well at all. I stay awake at night, slipping in and out of consciousness, my head filled with weird visions of a world that's impossible to comprehend.

These images come to me like dreams, and I would forget all about them if I didn't note them down here. But looking at what I've written, I'm beginning to question my sanity. My pages are filled with strange symbols and stranger drawings. No one in their right mind should be able to understand what I've penned down, and yet I can.

On the night of my alleged meltdown, my legs still sore from the seven-day trek, my body sick and my mind at unease, I had my first fever dream. The details of my dream are still a bit fuzzy, but from what I remember...

I was dressed like a king. I saw this girl seated by the well, and I was drawn to her as I had never been to anyone before. I approached her and begged her to

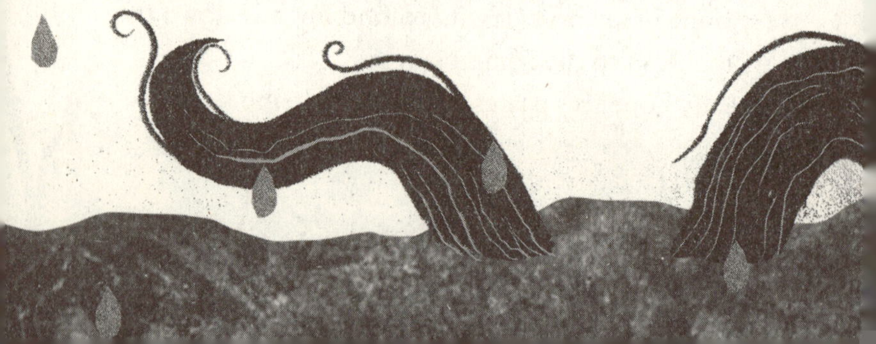

be my wife, and she agreed, but on one condition. She made me promise never to show her water – not the sea, not the river, not even a single drop of water.

I accepted hastily, and we began our lives together. We lived happily for years – we cooked together, we travelled, and we built our lives together!

I remember spending a quiet afternoon with her, when all of a sudden she asked me for a glass of water. We were sweltering and she looked tired, so I didn't think much about it. I brought her a glass of water, and as I handed it to her, I watched her slowly fade away – first the feet, then her torso, and finally her head and shoulders. She was washed out of reality, just as the sun drowns in the ocean every evening.

I woke up with a jolt, gasping for air. The woman I'd married in my dream was Bheki, the sun who fell off the earth and drowned into the ocean at the sight of water. I gave her a glass of water even though she'd warned me never to show it to her.

My eyelids felt like the opposite poles of a magnet. It was so hard to keep them from meeting.

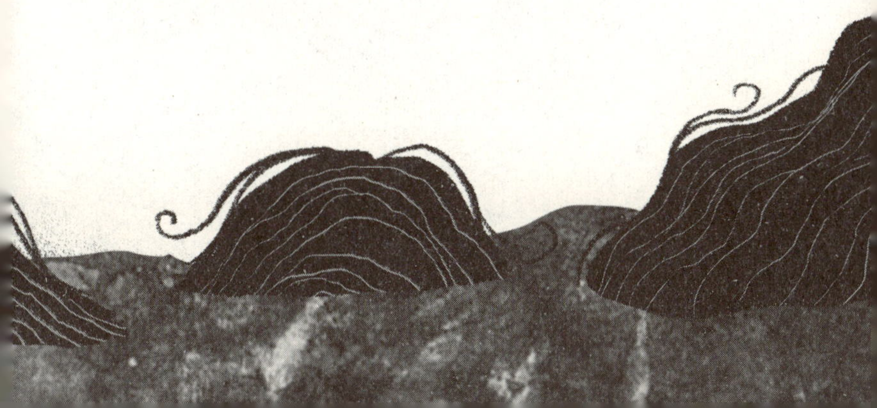

ASPIDOCHELONE

aspidochelone

21/11/2018

Tent in Jibhi, HP

I've never been a dreamer. I didn't dream much as a child, and when I did, I couldn't remember the dreams the next day. Maybe I always chose to let my dreams slip through my fingers like water, never to let them wake me up at night.

Right before my second dream, I felt my body stiffen. It was as though there was a huge weight on my chest, as though someone was sitting on me. I couldn't move, speak or call for help. And that's when I heard it: a soft humming sound, calm and pleasing to the ears. I tried following the sound, and when I turned around, I saw my body lying in the sleeping bag by the mouth of the tent – frozen, motionless, struggling to speak.

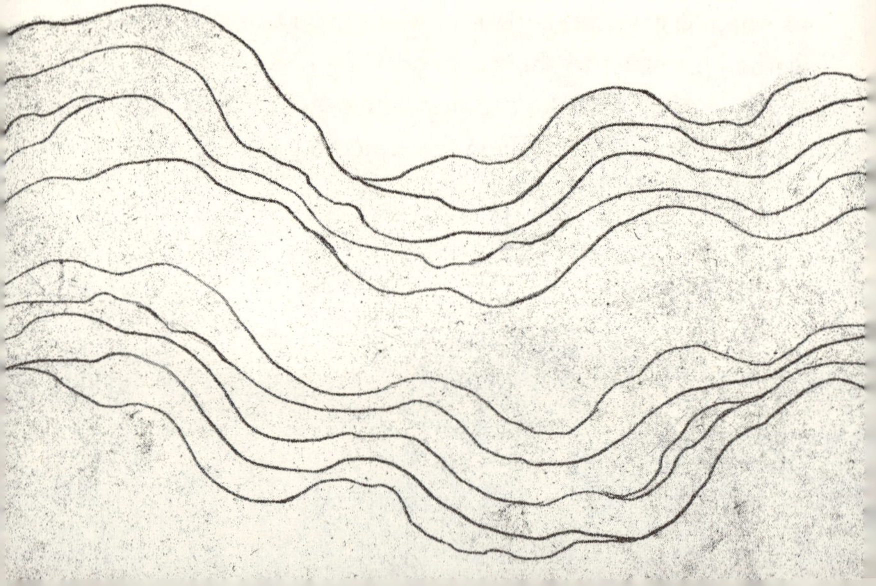

I floated out of my tent, and then upwards, towards the stars. When I looked down, I was surprised to find the land moving. The higher I drifted, the easier it was to make out what was below.

A great turtle, larger than a city, was shouldering an island on its back. I watched time speed up, and I saw the turtle swim across the oceans. Sailors would anchor their ships on the rim of its carapace, thinking it was an island. When they lit a fire to celebrate their nights, the turtle would sink back into the ocean, drowning the sailors and sending them to their watery graves.

My body convulsed, I found myself falling. Moments before I hit the ground, the giant turtle swam to me and introduced itself, 'My name is Aspidochelone – it means shielded turtle.'

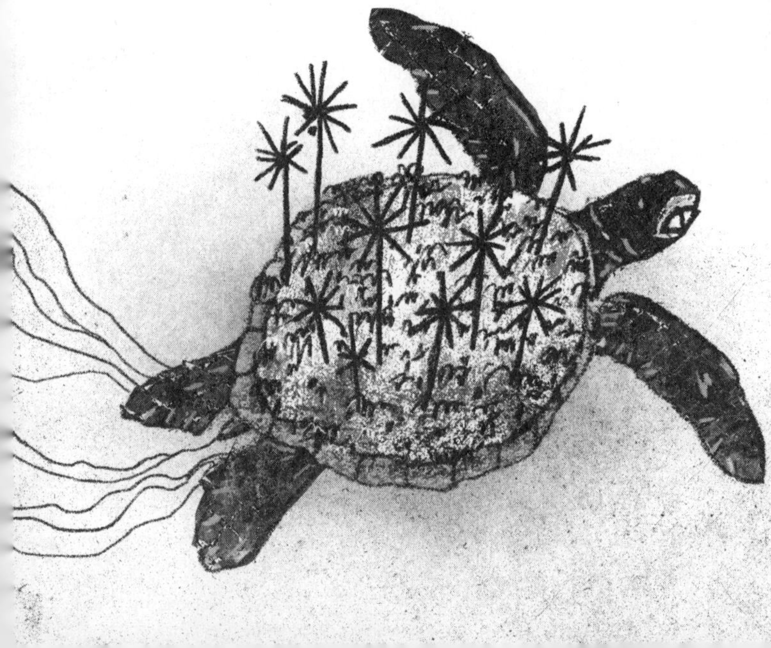

21/11/2018

Tent in Jibhi, HP

I did not wake up. Instead, I floated further into the sky. The land below me grew smaller and smaller. People looked like ants, mountains like wrinkles on a carpet, and then the earth itself was reduced to a disc.

Even though I was dreaming, I could recognize the World Turtle anywhere. I'd read about it while researching Hindu mythology, and in the pages of Terry Pratchett's *Discworld* while I relaxed. I stood in front of the colossal creature, its flippers the size of continents, its eyes as big as New Zealand and Sri Lanka. I watched the creature support the entire world on its back without breaking a sweat. I fought the urge to swim underneath the beast, curious about what the turtle stood on. But it was so big that going any closer to it would mean getting sucked in by its gravity, and spiralling to my death.

I stayed a respectful distance from the turtle and thought about all the life it supported – the world it was burdened to carry, as well as the elephants that stood on its back.

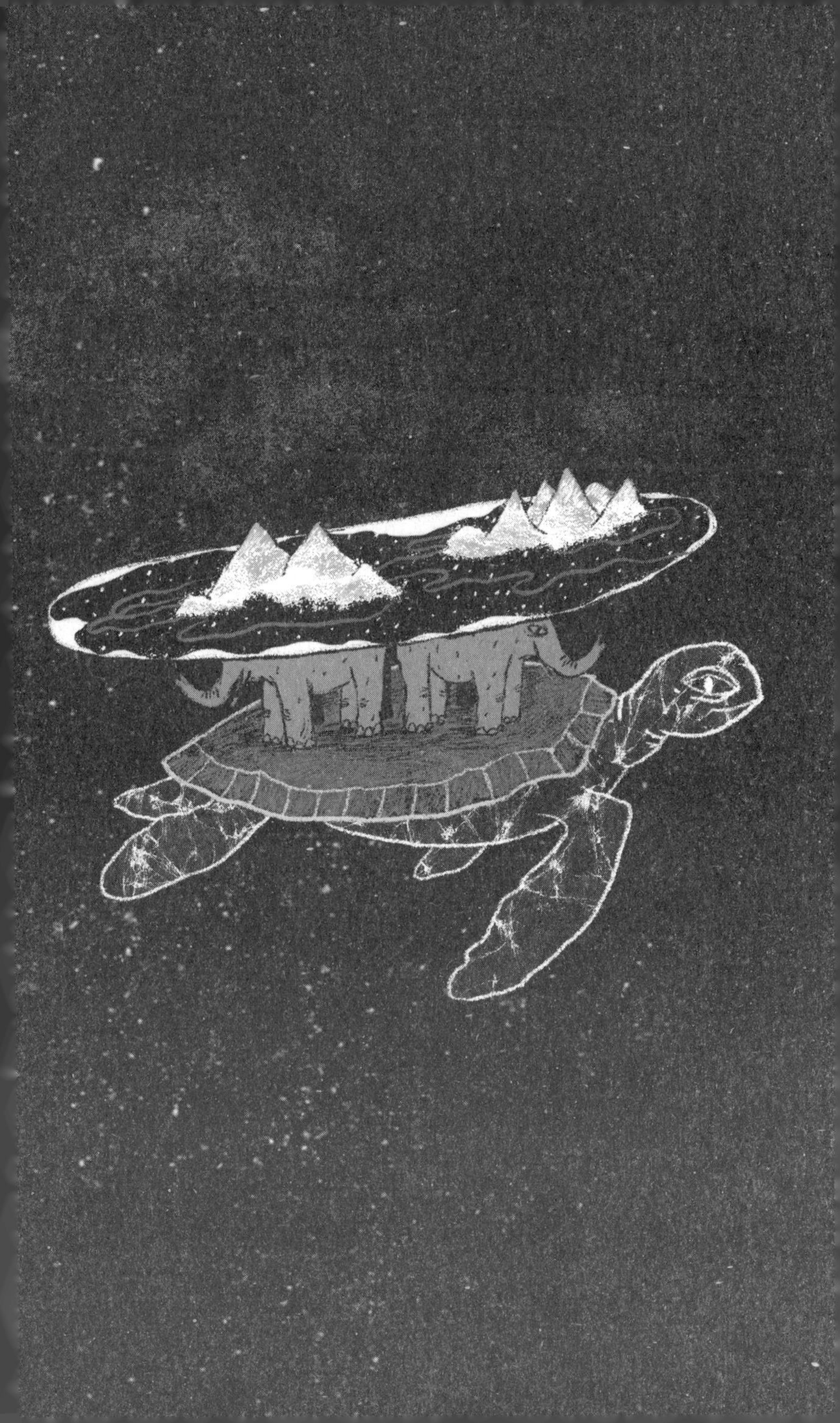

WORLD ELEPHANTS
world elephants

21/11/2018

Tent in Jibhi, HP

The elephants on the turtle's back barely moved. They remained calm and focused, the weight of the world distributed among their shoulders evenly. I tried imagining what would happen if the elephants lost interest. What if they shrugged off their responsibilities and chose freedom instead?

I can imagine one elephant going its own way, but not all 16 of them, not all at the same time. I know this is just a stupid dream, and I know my pride is misplaced, but I can't help but grin like an idiot knowing that our ancestors dreamed up a nearly foolproof interpretation of the cosmos. Unlike the Greeks, our ancestors didn't place the earth on an easily distracted and perpetually bored Titan named Atlas. They placed it on 16 elephants.

I do, however, sympathize with Atlas. He must have been lonely, having to carry the world all on his own. The elephants on the other hand are paired in twos – husbands and wives, the lot of them.

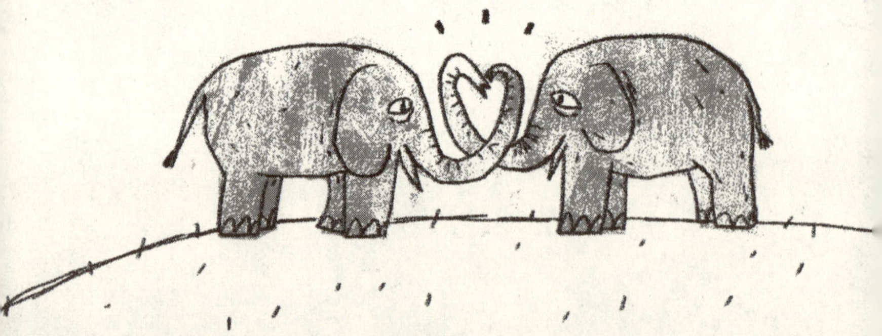

ABHRAMU ♥ AIRAVATA

PUNDARIKA ♥ KAPILA

VAMANA ♥ PINGALA

KUMUNDA ♥ ANUPAMA

ANJANA ♥ ANJANA

SARVA-BHAUMA ♥ TAMRAKARNA

SUPRATIKA ♥ ANJANAVATI

PUSHPA-DANTA ♥ SUBHADANTI

22/11/2018
Tent in Jibhi

Next, I floated beyond the moon, beyond Jupiter, beyond our galaxy, and even then, all I could see was a fraction of the beast's head. I had never heard or read about such a creature before, but I knew its name the moment I saw its body twist and curl in the cosmic waters. It was almost as though it conveyed its name to me telepathically.

'I am the Antaboga, and I am all-knowing.'

I glanced into its eyes and at once understood how everything came to be. In the beginning, there was nothing but the Antaboga. The celestial beast swam the emptiness of space, meditating worlds into existence. And when it swam towards our corner of the galaxy, it willed the World Turtle into being. Antaboga shed a tear once its creation came to life, and its tear transformed into an egg. And when the egg cracked open, Dewi Sri, the rice and fertility goddess of Java and Bali, emerged and populated the world with life.

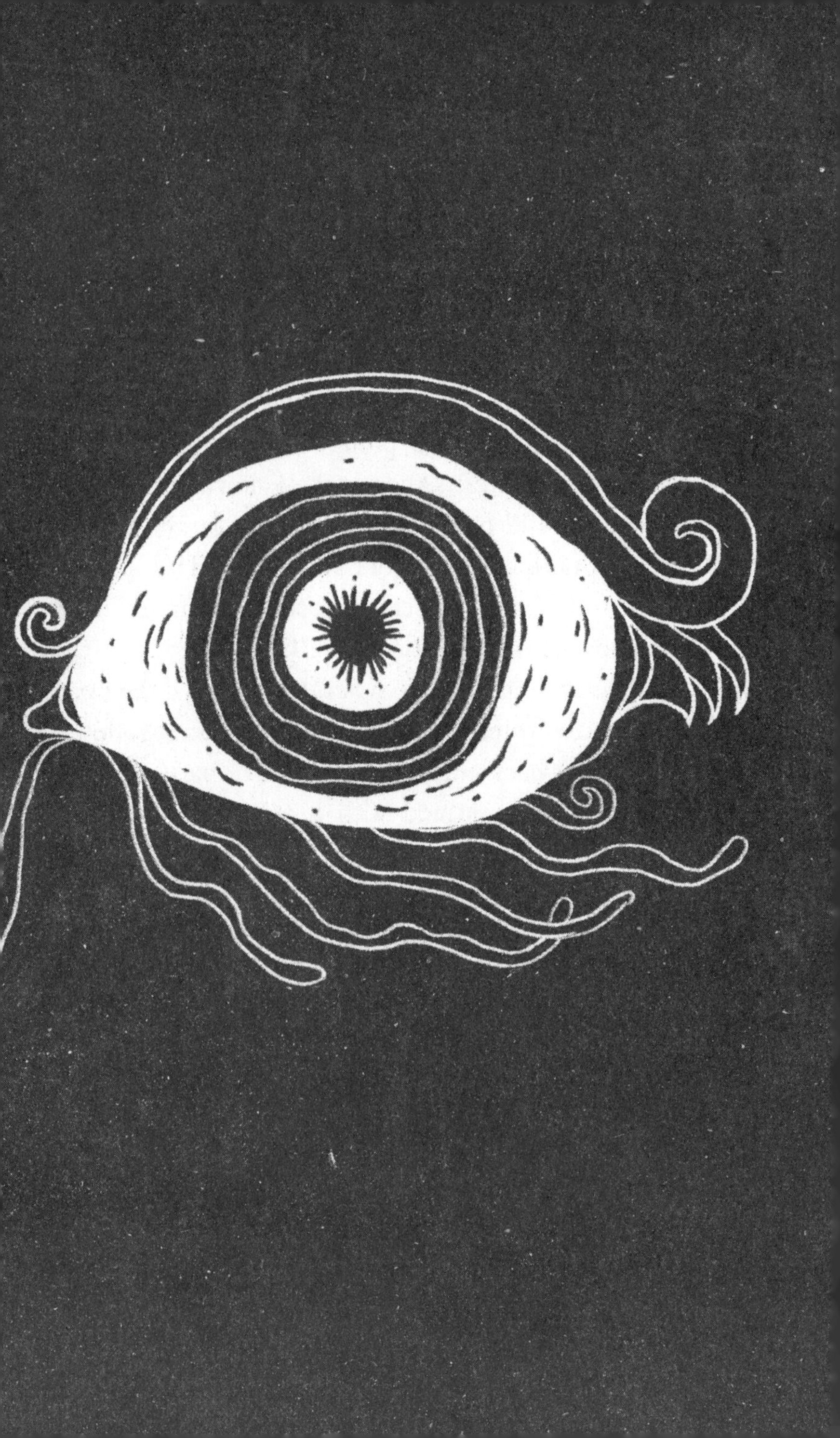

THE VARAHA

the varaha

22/11/2018

Tent in Jibhi, HP

Everything around me began to rumble; the primaeval waters began to shake. The world transformed into a ball, and within seconds I saw it plunge deep into the primordial waters. Then, out of nowhere, I watched a wild boar appear, growing larger and larger until it was bigger than the world itself. The boar dove into the cosmic ocean, swimming deep under. It used its tusks to lift Earth back to the surface. Earth shook violently each time the boar moved it around, and just when the boar was about to bring it back up, a giant blocked its path.

Hiranyaksha, armed with a gada, fought the boar, blocking it from returning above the water. But the boar struck back, and fought fiercely before finally maiming the giant demon with its tusks.

I watched the boar swim back to the surface and snapped back to reality as bhajans for Vishnu blared from the speakers of the neighbouring tent of the temple on top of the far hill.

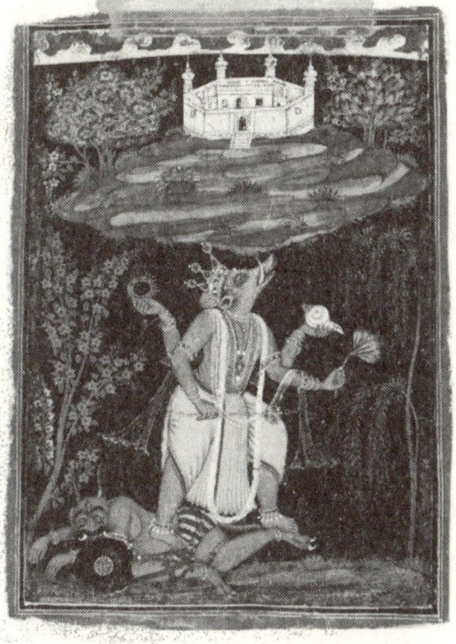

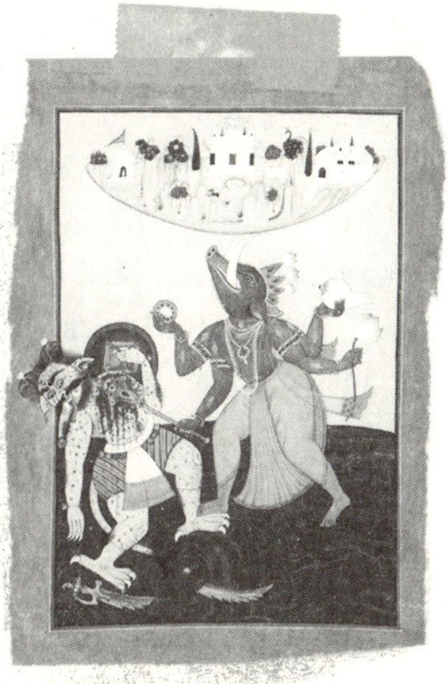

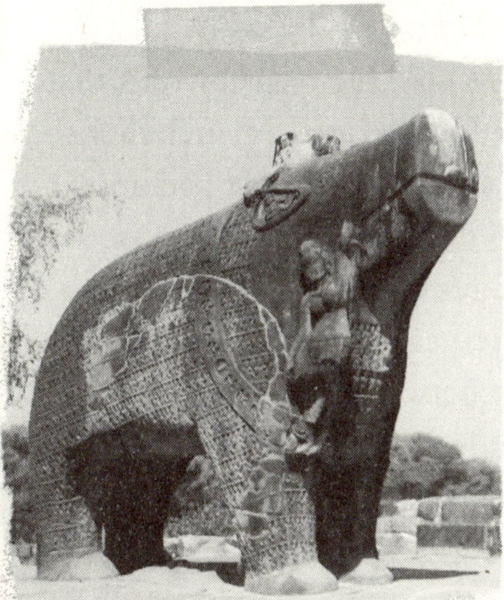

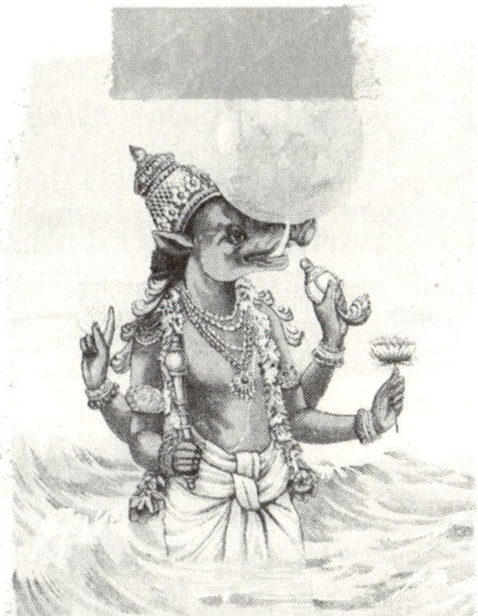

22/11/2018

Tent in Jibhi, HP

I tried my best to stay awake. The sun was out, the birds were chirping, yet I couldn't lift my heavy eyelids.

As I drifted back to sleep, I began dreaming once again. This time, it was about a beast bigger than anything I'd ever conceived – even bigger than the Akupara. I sat among the gods as they pulled the monstrosity out of their imaginations – what use could such a gigantic creature have?

This is what the gods whispered in my ears:

The beast was built to support Earth. Because when Earth was created, it rocked and wobbled like a boat in a storm. And so God created a large ruby rock to support it, and on the rock, we punctured 7,000 holes, from which 7,000 seas emerged.

Yet, there was nothing to hold the red ruby rock that Earth was placed on, and so God created a giant bull with 7,000 horns to hold up the rock. The beast had 40,000 eyes, 40,000 noses, 40,000 ears, 40,000 mouths, 40,000 tongues, 40,000 legs...you get the picture. The creature was so big that it took 500 years to travel between its two legs, and the distance between its horns was much wider than between the ends of the earth.

The beast only breathed twice a day. And since half of its nose was under the water, its breathing caused the waves to swell and crash onto our shores. There were earthquakes when it shifted, storms when its hairs

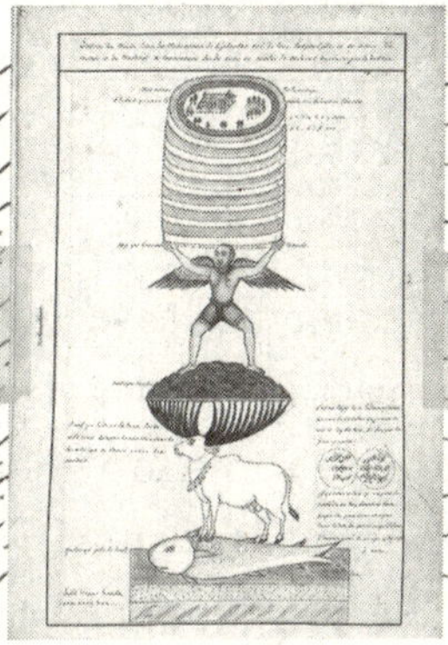

moved. The giant bull remained very still, even though it stood on the back of a great fish. The fish was so large that all the seas of the world were about the size of a mustard seed in comparison with it.

I tried to get a glimpse of what was under the fish, but all I found was more water. I saw earth, storms, sand, darkness, sickness, and things that were unimaginable to the human mind.

When I woke up, I realized there was no way my mind could come up with this. I'm not nearly creative enough to think up a new animal, let alone a bull with 40,000 eyes. I got off my sleeping bag and rushed to the common area, desperate to find something, anything, about the beast I'd dreamed about.

I was shocked to learn that it was real. It was called a Kuyutha (or Behemoth, or Leviathan, depending on the translation) and was described in near-perfect detail by the Islamic cosmologist Zakariya al-Qazwini.

PICHAL PERI

pichal peri

23/11/2018

– En route to Shimla, HP

I've never been happier to leave my room and head back out into the world. It's such a strange feeling to be sequestered inside one's room in a strange land. Try and picture yourself in a town far away from home, unable to head back, unable to go out to buy your groceries, unable to even leave the confines of your home to get some fresh air. I'm wasting my breath here.

I do think that I jumped the gun because the moment I felt better, I stuffed my backpack with all my belongings and left. I simply had to get out of there. You will never understand what it's like to be quarantined, to be locked in, left alone with your thoughts and subconscious. So there I was, walking down dirt roads late at night, with nothing but the torchlight on my phone to keep me company.

I didn't have any network, my phone was close to dying, and I wasn't even sure if the buses left town that late at night. But at least I was close to the bus stop, and I guess sitting under the lone bulb on a quiet night was some consolation.

Just as I was reaching into my backpack for my notebook – I really felt like getting some work done – I thought I heard something.

HA

HA HA HA HA HA HA HA HA HA HA HA HA HA

'Who's there?' I whispered, backing away from the abnormal sound. This time, it was muffled laughter, unexpected yet innocuous.

'I'm sorry, you startled me,' I said.

I watched her emerge from the darkness, and was surprised to find a young woman, no older than me, walking towards me.

'I can sit there,' I said, shifting my backpack one bench to the right. To my surprise, she ambled over and sat next to me.

'I'm Thomas,' I said, introducing myself. But she looked at me as though I were speaking a different language. 'I'm sorry, my Hindi is not good,' I explained.

The girl gestured for my pen and notebook. I'm usually overprotective about my things – except for when I leave them lying around carelessly – but something about the way she looked at me told me that I could trust her. I passed along my book, and she scribbled something down in a language I could not read.

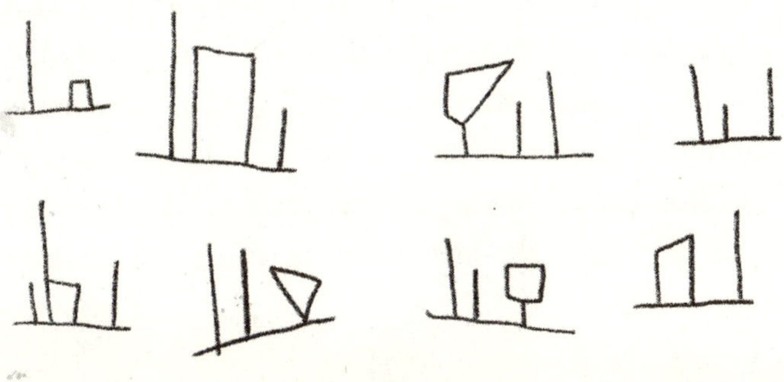

'Is that your name?' I asked, but she didn't respond. 'I'm from the south!' I said, drawing a rough map of India with a tiny drawing of me on Tamil Nadu.

She grabbed the book from me and drew a picture of the mountains just north of where we were.

'Oh, I was just there!' I exclaimed.

She nodded enthusiastically and closed her eyes, gesturing that she knew.

'Were you part of the trek?' I asked, using my fingers to pretend-climb the steep armrest on the side of the bench. 'I'm sorry about the way it ended. I didn't mean to inconvenience everyone.'

The girl shook her head and looked straight into my eyes.

'You're not from the trek?'

She shook her head again.

'Were you working in one of the shops along the way?' I asked, drawing a rough picture of a tea shop.

Once again, she shook her head. She snatched my notebook out of my hand and began sketching away.

'Wow, you draw very well!' I said, leaning closer to her. She had drawn the most difficult part of our descent, the part where we crossed gushing streams and clambered over boulders.

'I thought you were going to draw a picture of where we met,' I said, closing the book when she handed it back to me.

The girl rolled her eyes. She inched closer to me, and then she yawned, feigning tiredness.

'You can sleep on my bag if you want,' I shoved my backpack towards her. 'I don't think there's a bus coming this way anyway,' I added.

When I passed along the bag, she tossed it aside and grabbed my arm to lean against. She plucked the book from my hand and drew a quick picture of my arm. She pinched her index finger and thumb together, and gestured that my hand was better than the backpack.

'Thanks...' I replied, still remarkably clueless about what was going on.

I kept my eyes fixed on my notebook as she drew a couple of eyes, a pair of oddly shaped legs, a head that looked remarkably similar to mine. I shifted myself, giving her enough room to lean against me comfortably, and watched as she began crossing out the eyes and twisting the part of the page where the legs were.

'Stop that! I have something written on the other side,' I said. The girl continued to draw on my notebook, this time scribbling on the picture of my head. Just as I was about to look at it, my eyes were blinded by a powerful beam of light.

'Is this guy troubling you?' I heard someone yell, after a loud honk.

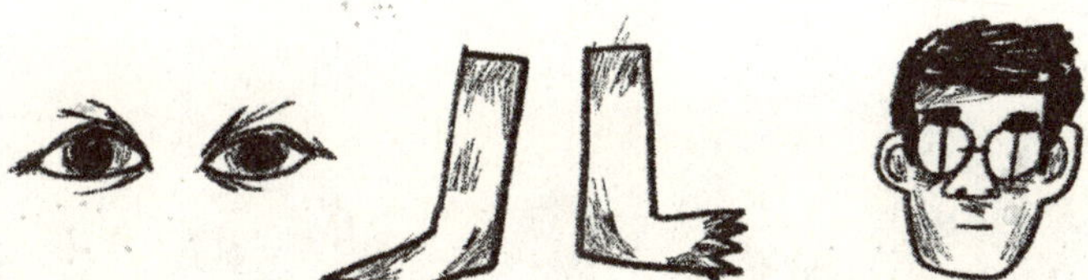

The girl got off the bench, skipped towards the bus, and turned to smile at me before she got on. As I stood up to follow her, the conductor scolded me.

'But I need to leave too,' I explained.

'Take the next one,' he snapped as the bus drove away.

My stomach burned and my throat was filled with bile. What gave him the right to not allow me inside the bus? Who did he think he was? I threw my head against my backpack and rested, and was woken up early in the morning by a conductor.

'Going to town?' he asked.

I nodded and lumbered into the empty bus.

The conductor looked at me from head to toe. 'Don't sleep out in the open like that again, and don't leave your house in the middle of the night. You have no idea about the kind of creatures that walk this part of the woods,' he warned. 'My colleague had to rescue some fool from a Pichal Peri just last night.'

I was too groggy to pay attention to the conductor, so I ignored him and shuffled to the back of the bus. I pulled out my notebook and flipped through it under the morning light. And that's when I saw it.

I flipped over to the previous page, and almost threw my book out the window when I saw the image that she'd drawn.

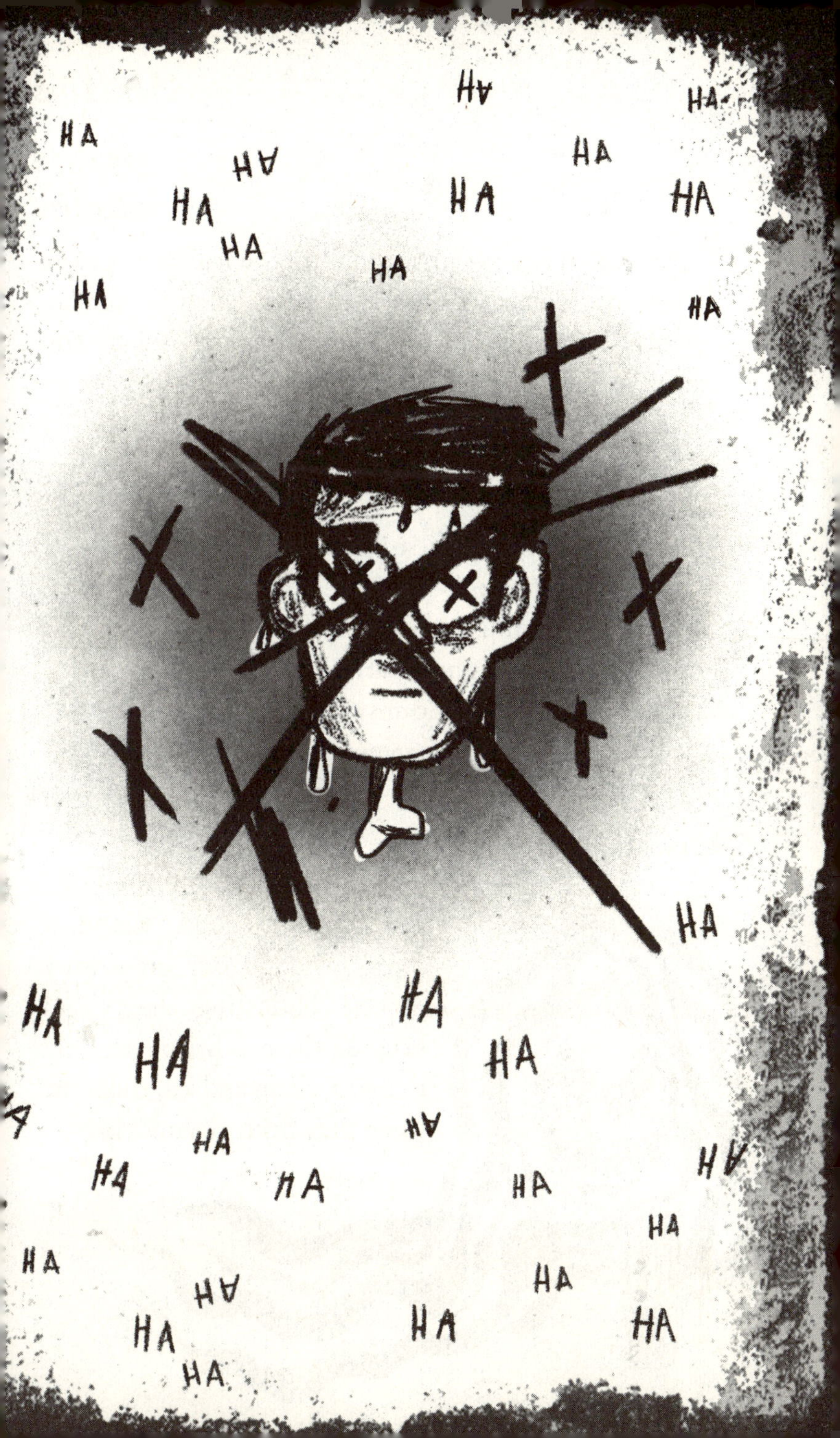
HA
HA
HA
HA
HA
HA
HA
HA
HA
HA
HA
HA
HA
HA
HA
HA
HA
HA
HA
HA
HA
HA
HA
HA
HA
HA
HA
HA
HA
HA
HA

FEET ON BACKWARDS

feet on backwards

24/11/2018

Location Unknown

There are other creatures like the Pichal Peri spread across the country, almost all of them with similar stories. They are ready to wreak violence on men for the injustices suffered in a past life.

You've got creatures like:

The KINDURIS, who are Sri Lankan ghosts of pregnant women who knock on doors in the dead of night, sparing women and children who answer the door, but killing the men.

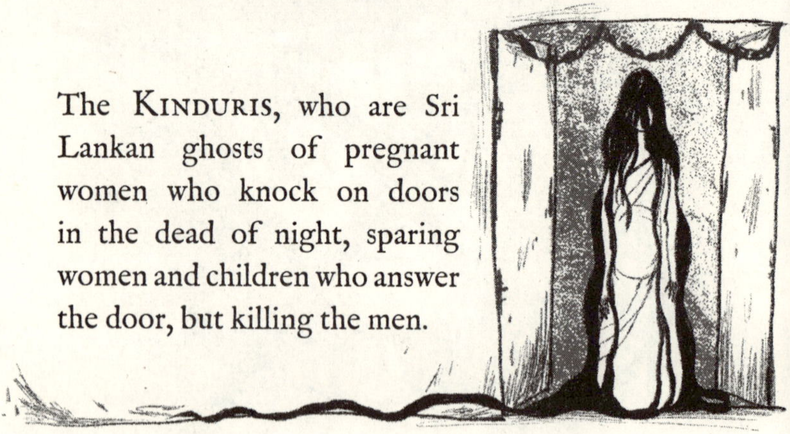

The RANTAS are Kashmiri spirits who go out on stormy nights, abducting men and keeping them as prisoners, only to marry them and kill them off when they become annoying.

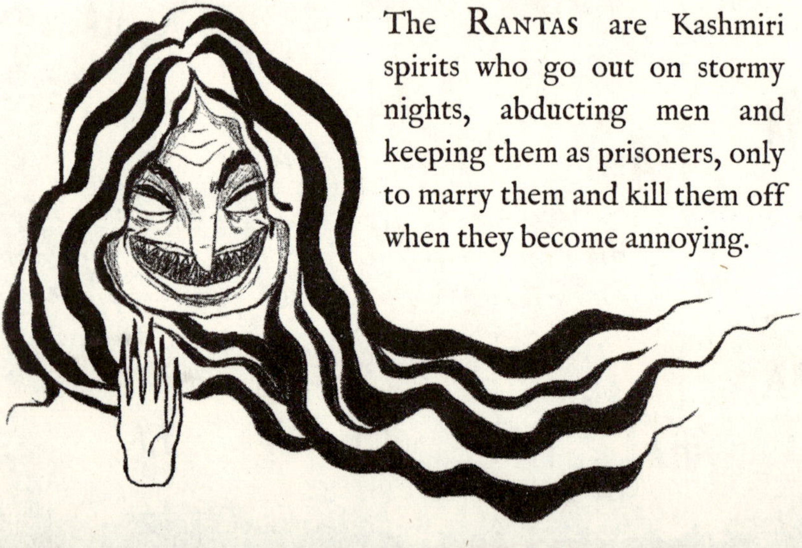

The CHUDAILS are creatures with the ability to shape-shift and take the form of any woman. They carry lanterns and charm men they meet on the roads, only to kill them.

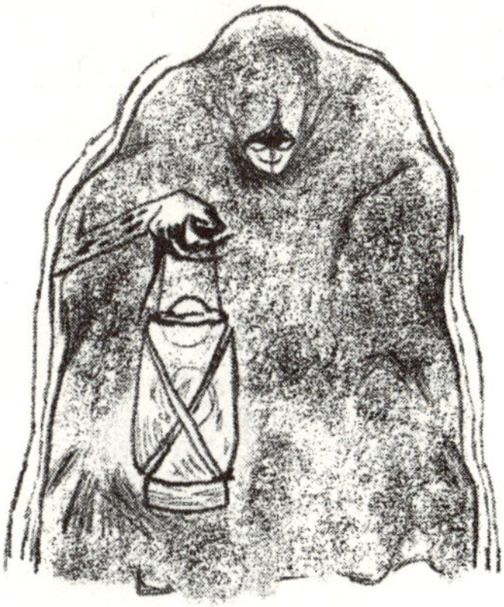

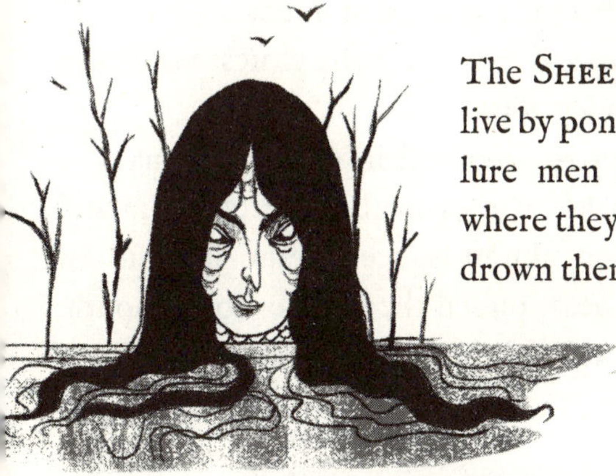

The SHEEKOL BURI, who live by ponds and lakes, and lure men into the water, where they use their hair to drown them.

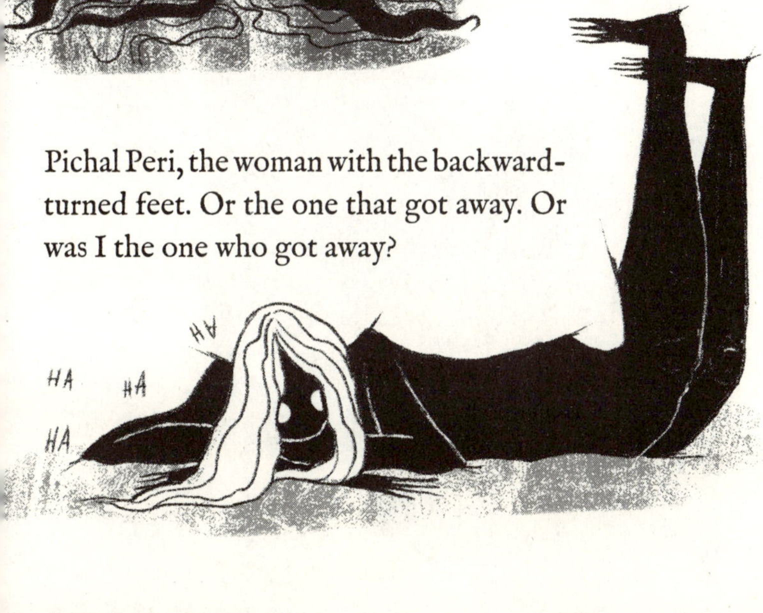

Pichal Peri, the woman with the backward-turned feet. Or the one that got away. Or was I the one who got away?

THE KABANDHA

the kabandha

24/11/2018

Shimla, HP

Kabandha is as big as the mountains that surround me. His arms stretch on for kilometres, his skin is darker than coal and his body is covered in prickly hair. Deprived of a face, Kabandha has one yellowish eye and a mouth that cuts across its body. With a broad chest and a neck that looks like freshly tenderized meat, Kabandha is the closest an Indian beast gets to a Cyclops.

The demon is described in the Ramayana as a horrendous beast who managed to catch Ram and Lakshman, and almost squeezed the life out of them. As the beast pulled them closer to its mouth, the brothers realized that its weakness was its arms.

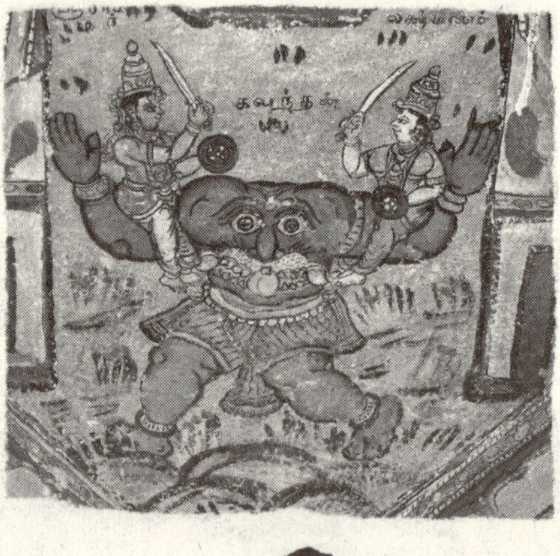

Without wasting a moment, they brothers drew their swords and cut off the demon's arms.

However, it's not just Indian mythology that mentions Kabandha. About a thousand years later, around 700 BCE, the ancient Greeks mentioned a similar creature – the Anthropophagi. Herodotus, the Greek historian and geographer, wrote that they were savage cannibals who lived nomadic lives and spoke in a strange tongue. According to Isigonus of Nicaea, they drank out of human skulls and wore a tapestry of human scalps (with the hair!) around their neck.

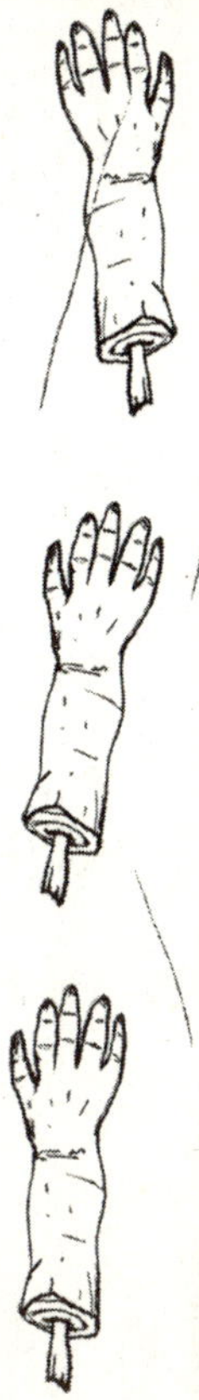

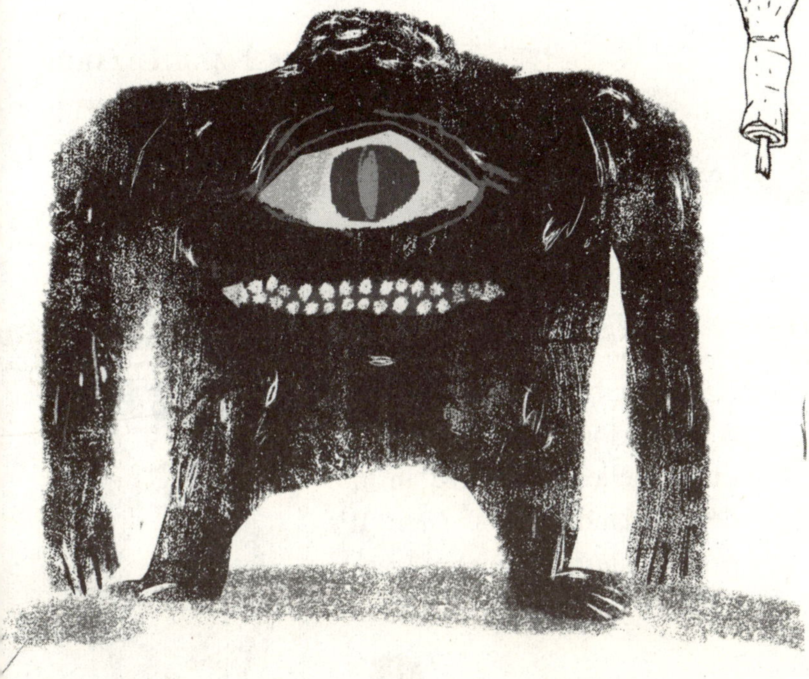

BEASTS OF THE ANDAMANS

beasts of the andamans

??/??/????

??????????????

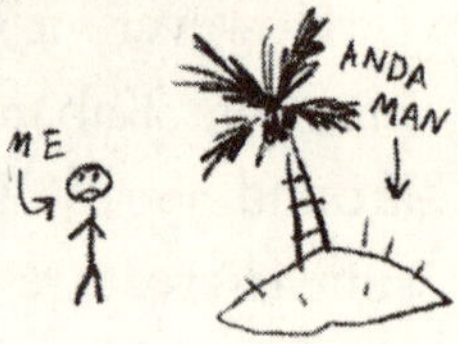

I've never been to the Andamans, and I don't think I'll be able to visit any time soon, but I do look forward to the day I can explore the less inhabited islands. In the forests of these tiny isles are tiny beasts, lurking in the bushes, waiting to be discovered.

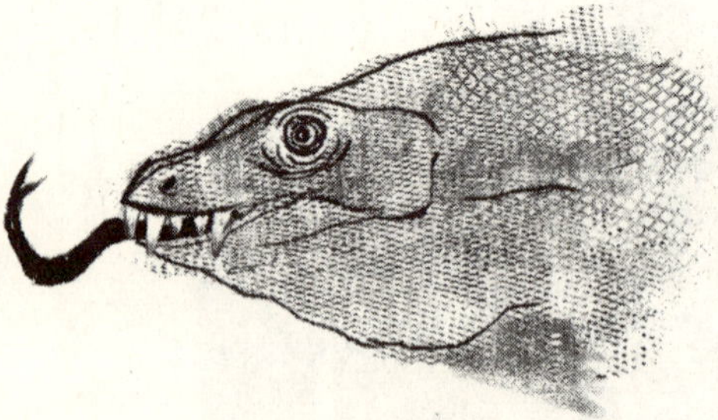

The Kara Lizard: A giant lizard with extremely sharp teeth that are larger than a crocodile's.

Andaman Wooden Owl: A mysterious owl-like creature that's believed to live in the dense island forests. *Note*: It's probably just a regular old owl.

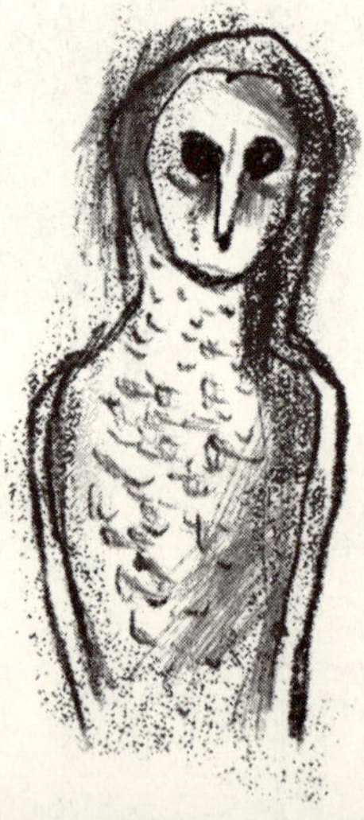

The Jirmu: A reptile so large that when elephants were first introduced in the Andaman Islands by the British, the locals mistook the elephants for the Jirmu. Though we aren't sure what they look like, I surmise from my research that they look like dinosaurs from *Jurassic Park*. Or, perhaps, the Jirmu were Platybelodons, the predecessors of the elephant.

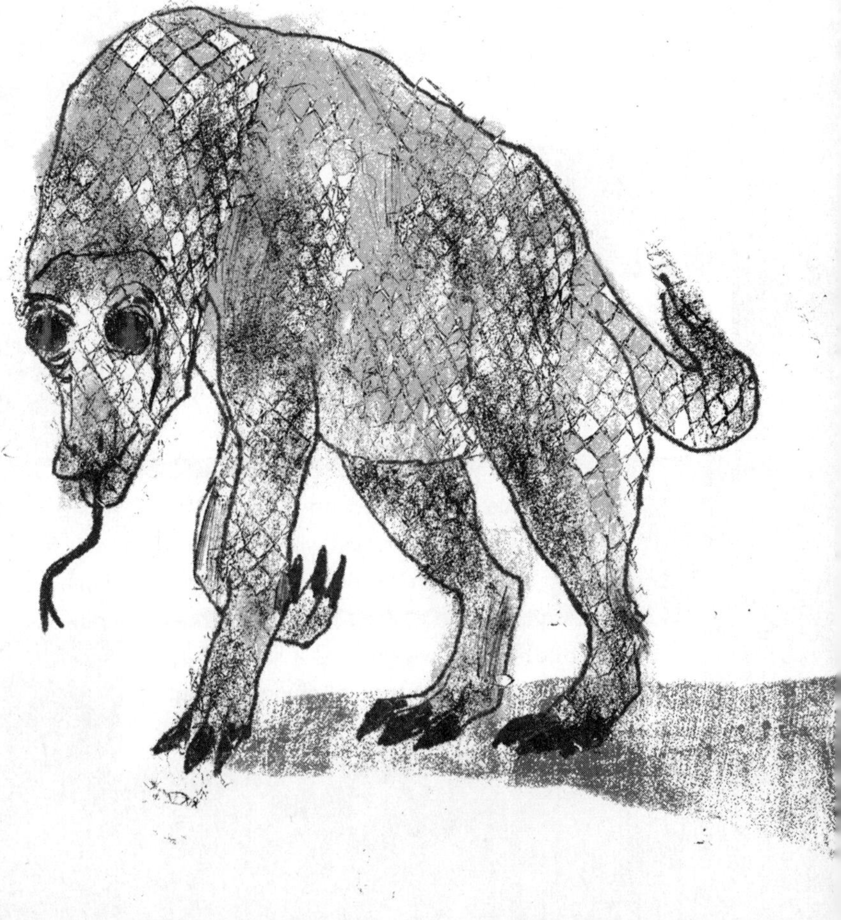

You won't believe what just happened! I was on a train making my way across Uttarakhand when, out of the blue, I received a string of text messages.

+91 9978985744: Dear Iravathur, I'm writing on behalf of my employer, who chooses to remain anonymous for the time being. We have heard about your journey to catalogue mythical beasts, and I think your expertise could be of use to us.

Me: Hi, it's nice to hear from you, but could you tell me how you got my number?

+91 9978985744: Not important. The assignment is time-sensitive, and we would like to discuss the same with you at the earliest. When can you get to Kolkata?

Me: Not for another week. I'm travelling at the moment, and will reach Prayagraj in a few days. Can we discuss this over the phone?

+91 9978985744: Have emailed a link to your plane tickets. Your flight leaves tomorrow night. More instructions will follow, Mr Iravathur.

I couldn't help but pace up and down the length of the train when I first received the text messages. What on earth is happening? How did they get my phone number? How did they know my last name? Almost no one knows my last name! Most importantly, what did he mean by a link to my plane tickets?

It took me a while to calm down and think about this rationally. I thought it could be a phishing scam or maybe they were luring me to an unidentified location to harvest my organs. But then again, who pays for a last-minute flight ticket?

I thought about the text messages and even called the airlines to check if my tickets are genuine. They are! But it would be reckless to accept a ticket from a stranger. The last time a rich person gave me something for free was when V. Chettiar fed everyone in the village on the death anniversary of his late wife. He looked far too happy for someone whose wife had died only a year ago, and the food we ate that day just didn't sit well.

Something about the free tickets feels very wrong. Call it an instinct or a gut reaction, because my stomach feels exactly the same as it did on the day V. Chettiar fed our entire village. Rich people freak the heck out of me.

THE MAN_EATING GOONCH

the man-eating goonch

30/11/2018

Banks of the River Sharda, UP

I decided not to take up the mysterious stranger's offer after all. Instead, I travelled to check out the ghats along the River Sharda. I've been dying to go there ever since I stumbled across a documentary on river monsters. People criticize me for spending more time flipping

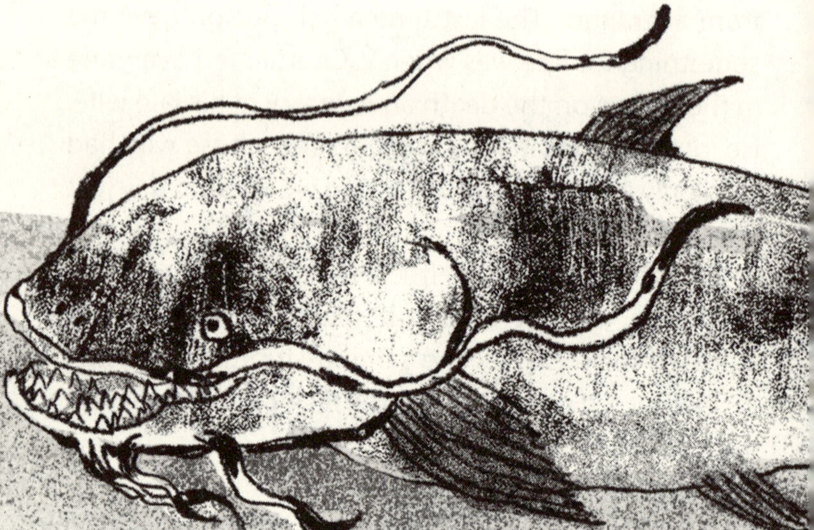

through channels than actually watching something, but if it weren't for my pernickety channel surfing, I'd have never found out about the Goonch. But I didn't stay on the channel long enough to find out exactly what a Goonch is. So the criticism stands, I guess.

The villagers who lived near the Dharma Ghat were very enthusiastic to talk to me about the Goonch. Almost everyone had their own version of a Goonch story – close encounters with the monster, stories of lost livestock and anecdotes of a loved one who'd almost been taken away by the monster. Oddly enough, I couldn't find a single person who didn't believe in the beast.

'So...what exactly is a Goonch?' I asked.

'It's a very big catfish, the biggest in the world!' a middle-aged woman replied.

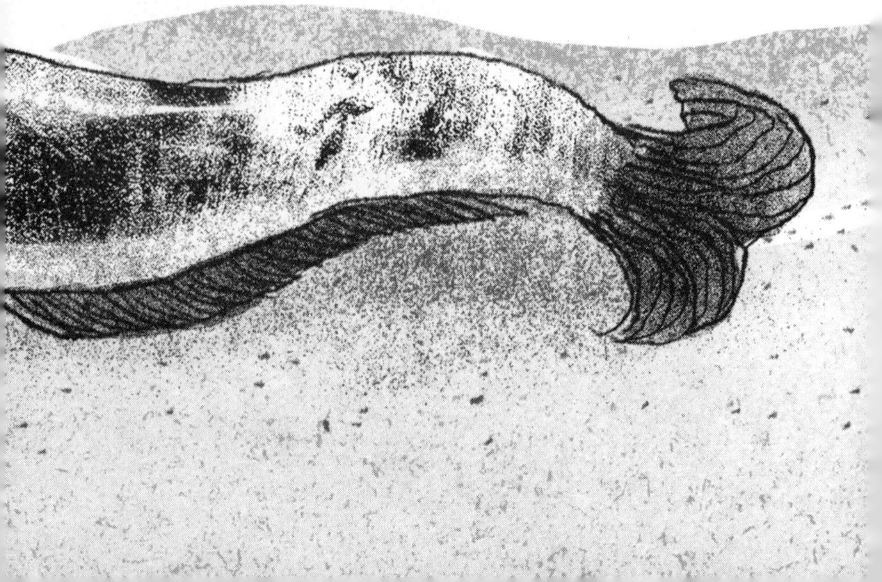

'A big catfish?' I almost chuckled at the thought of an entire village being afraid of a catfish.

'It's not what you think,' the lady replied. 'I was by the river when it attacked for the very first time. Around 20 years ago, when I was swimming in the ghat with Baluvanth, it came out of nowhere. It happened in seconds, leaving nothing but a small whirlpool of blood in the water.'

'A catfish ate a person?' I asked, still a bit doubtful. 'Are you sure it wasn't a mythical beast? Perhaps it was something ancient in the water, maybe a Makara that had swum upstream.'

'It was a catfish, and I saw it with my own eyes,' the lady snapped. 'It swam back to the same spot three days later and made away with a child. The entire village searched for it, and we looked for months, but it was gone.' Her voice became softer; she began to sound more sombre. 'We've been offering our cattle as a sacrifice ever since. It has certainly helped reduce the number of attacks, but they have a taste for our flesh now, and they're not going to stop any time soon.'

'What do you mean, "a taste for our flesh"?'

'Catfish aren't known to harm humans. The ones in the River Kali are the only exception because they've been snacking on the burnt corpses that float down the rivers. They're growing bigger every year.' She looked me dead in the eye. 'We only caught Goonches as long as

3 feet until a few years ago. But then, last year, we caught one that was over six and a half feet long. It weighed 73 kilograms. Big enough to gobble up a child!' The woman inched closer to me. 'And you know what? There are Goonches much bigger than the one we caught in the river, ones strong enough to drag a water buffalo into the water. We have no idea how big they can get, and we know that they've been multiplying. All we can do is pray for fewer corpses in the rivers.'

'What are the odds of more corpses floating down the river?'

'There are only so many burnt corpses that float down the river each year. It's not like there's ever going to be a plague or a natural disaster or something. I can't think of a possibility where there will be tens and thousands of deaths, with bodies cremated in a hurry. The villagers can rest assured that something like that will never happen.'

I pulled out my mobile and found a couple of unread messages. One from Cherian – I wondered what she wanted – and the other from the same unknown number as before.

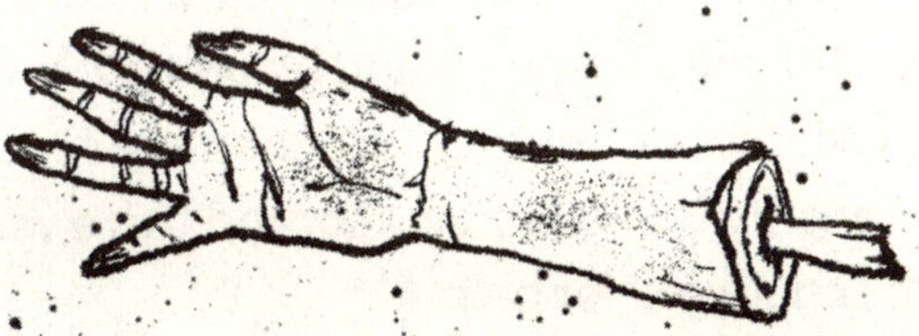

+91 9978985744: Where are you?

Me: Along the River Kali.

+91 9978985744: Your flight leaves in 16 hours.

Me: I don't think I'll be able to make it, sorry.

+91 9978985744: Will text back in 5.

+ 91 9978985744: Arranged a cab to drive you to Kanpur. My employer is eager to meet you.

Me: Are you really arranging a cab?

I didn't have a chance to send the last message. The driver from a white Innova all but accosted me. He opened the door to the car and helped put my luggage away. I felt scared, nervous, and thoroughly confused. I was probably being kidnapped, and there was no one whom I could call for help.

I tried making a run for it when I reached the airport.

Okay, not really, but I did politely stand near the entrance, ready to flee the moment my driver left. My flight was to leave in two hours, and my backpack was already on my shoulder. I took a step towards the exit. But then, all at once, I heard my name.

'Good evening, Mr Iravathur. I'm Ali and I'm your concierge for the evening. May I help you with your bag?'

'I didn't know domestic flights had concierges.'

'They don't, but we make exceptions for our more esteemed clients, like your employer.'

Mr Ali grabbed my bag and began marching toward the gates. We bypassed the luggage check-in with our personal security officer. Before I knew it, I was boarding my flight.

'Hold on,' I said as I stepped towards my plane. 'My employer. You know him, right? Who is he?'

Ali didn't respond. 'It was a pleasure serving you this evening,' he replied, smiling at me.

On the plane, I was treated like royalty. I sat in the first row, I was served a warm meal, and the cabin manager made sure I was well taken care of. With nothing to do but wait to meet my 'employer', I decided to get a bit of sleep.

DOG_HEADED PEOPLE

dog-headed people

30/11/2018

Location Unknown

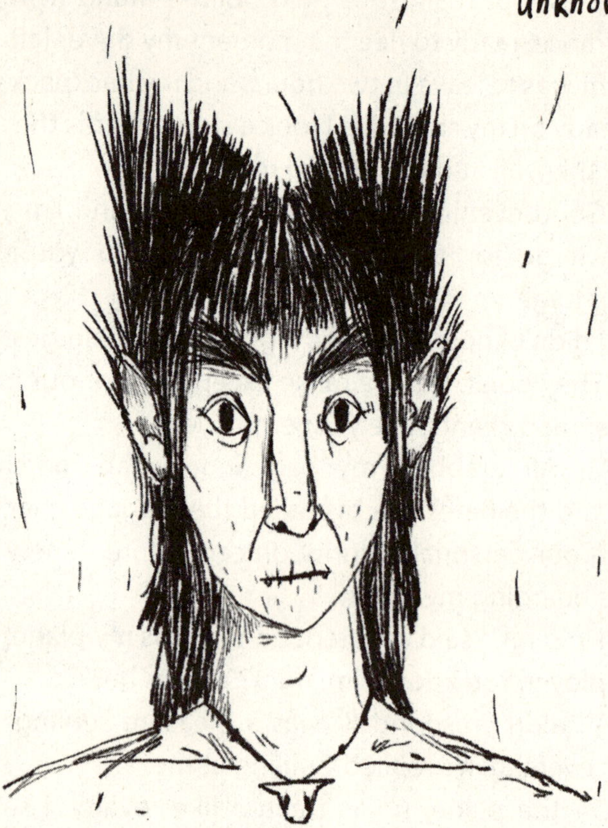

While on the hills in Uttarakhand, I learned about the Cynocephali. Humans with the heads of wolves, who were sometimes thought to be giants. The Cynocephali were kind and gentle and fought alongside the humans during wars. The Dog-headed People however, were a different story. They were thought to be shape-shifters and could transform into their wolf-like state at will. If this sounds just like a European werewolf, don't get ahead of yourselves, because unlike werewolves from the west, the dog-headed Indian counterparts could transform at will, but they did come with one catch – they always retained wolf-like features when they transformed back to their human selves. This could be a long snout-like nose, eyes that glowed in the dark, or pointy ears that resembled a dog's.

There are different accounts of the Dog-headed People from different parts of the country. According to Sir John Mandeville, a medieval English traveller, the Dog-headed People whom he met in the Nicobar Islands worshipped an ox, and wore ox-shaped ornaments around their necks and heads. Sir John mentioned that the Dog-headed People were great warriors, and would kill and eat anyone they defeated in battle. He also spoke at length about the king of the Dog-headed People, describing him as someone who was rich beyond measure – he wore 300 pearls around his neck, and a ruby about the size of five fingers that was presented to him the moment he became the king. There are also contradictory accounts by Marco Polo, who called the Dog-headed People nothing more than beasts, who had neither laws nor manners, nor a king.

01/12/2018

Flight to Kolkata

It's a bit strange to find the first row of the plane empty on an otherwise crowded flight. Did my mysterious abductor book the entire line for me?

I fell asleep across the three empty seats and was woken up a couple of times, once when my meal was served and the second time by a couple of frazzled whispers coming from behind me. I closed my eyes and tried to pay closer attention to them.

'What on earth did we just see!' a man said.

'Whatever it was, I haven't seen anything like it before. Maybe as a one-off case, but the entire village?' his co-passenger replied, his voice sounding much older than the first.

'I came here thinking it was all just a hoax, but there might be something to this.'

'Don't be silly! Do you actually believe in the Muhnochwa?' the elderly voice scoffed.

'How else do you explain all those faces? They were scratched so badly! Why would anyone do that to themselves?'

'Religion, mass hysteria, an abuser we don't know of...' the elderly voice replied. 'It could be anything, but I certainly know it isn't some creature of the night, ambushing villagers.' He chuckled. 'That's just plain absurd.'

'What makes you so sure?'

'For starters, the villagers all had different descriptions of the creature. A few called it a dark, shapeless ominous spirit, while most described it as a giant spider.'

'You can't discount the fact that their accounts of the attack sounded so similar,' the younger voice protested. 'The way they were attacked in the darkness, their claims of the beast scratching their faces repeatedly, leaving them for dead.' He paused. 'I don't know, but there's something here that we're missing.'

'So, what are you saying? A giant spider did this?'

'No, I'm saying that the creature is real, people saw it and were so terrified that they didn't sleep for days.

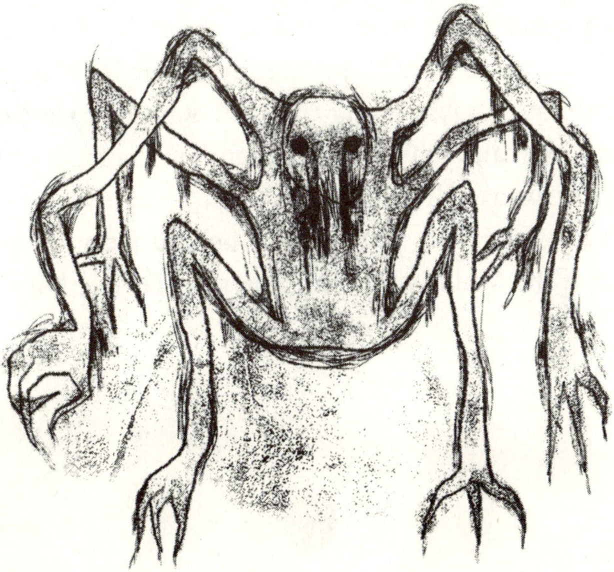

The lack of sleep slowly drove them to the brink of insanity, and they began scratching their own faces!'

My curiosity had gotten the better of me. I sat upright and turned my head around ever so slightly to hear them better. I don't know if my sudden movement startled them, or if they realized that I was eavesdropping on their conversation, because the two stopped talking almost immediately.

'We'll talk about this later,' the older voice muttered. 'We're men of science, and we can't be caught entertaining boogeyman conspiracies out in the open.'

I scolded myself for turning around. I hoped that they'd continue with their conversation. But all was not lost because the creature that they spoke about wasn't hard to find. I learned later that the spider demon was called Muhnochwa, and that it terrorized the villagers near Kanpur and Prayagraj. There were reputed newspapers that carried articles about it, describing the monster in detail, speculating about its existence, and almost always ending the same way: that the beast didn't exist and that the scars found on the faces of the survivors were self-inflicted.

But what if the young voice behind me was right? What if the Muhnochwa had a part to play in all of this?

01/12/2018

Flight to Kolkata

ROC BIRD
roc bird

As I fastened my seatbelt, waiting for my plane to land, I couldn't help but wonder if I was actually being abducted.

I stared out of my window, at the distance between the plane and the ground, and I suddenly knew how it must have felt to be a victim of the Roc Bird, to be picked up by its sharp talons and flown so high up in the air, to be scared and helpless, waiting to be set back on the ground.

Roc Birds did eventually set their prey on the ground, but not the way you're thinking. According to

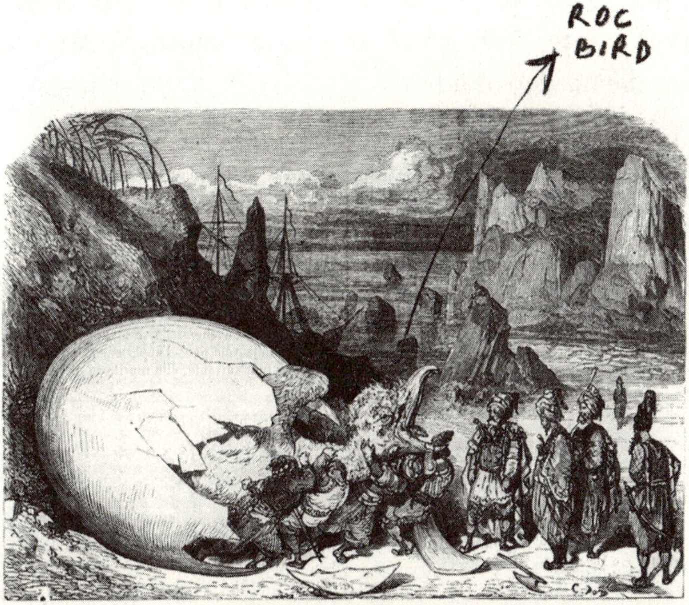

Les marchands cassèrent l'œuf. (Page 147, col. 1.)

the traveller and writer Marco Polo, these birds looked like enormous eagles, so big that a man would have to walk 12 paces to cover the length of one of its feathers. Marco Polo claimed that Roc Birds swooped down on their prey – gazelles, lions and even elephants! – at exceptionally high speed and carried the prey into the air using their large talons. The birds would then drop the poor animals to the ground, causing the prey to splatter into large meaty chunks, which the birds then fed on at leisure.

I looked out of my window once more, and my stomach sank at the thought of dropping out of the sky. I heard the landing announcement from the captain and began to calm down a bit. Unlike the Roc's prey, what good am I to my captor splattered on the hard ground?

Note: Roc Birds are often considered to be Persian or Iranian, but according to Rudolf Wittkower, an art historian, the Roc may have come from the story of the Garuda saving an elephant by carrying it to safety while it was battling a crocodile.

Another note: Dwayne the Roc Johnson is a good name for a Roc Bird.

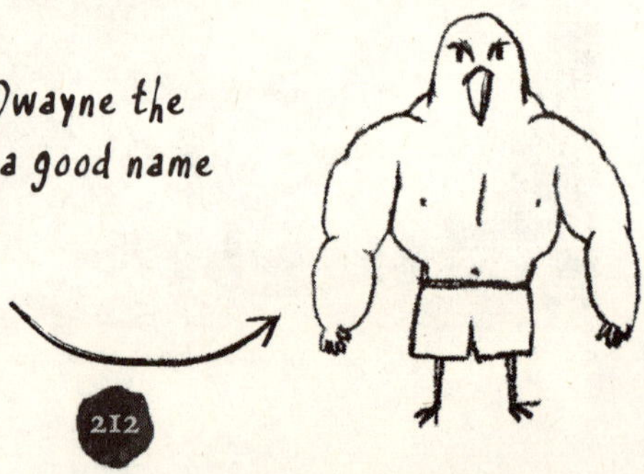

01/12/2018

Kolkata Airport, WB

THE SCIRITAE

the sciritae

Why is Kolkata so humid! I was drenched in sweat just from the short walk between my plane and the airport. I'm usually excited about travelling to a new city, so much so that I end up neglecting my work. This time, however, I'm making an exception. I intend to sit in the uncomfortable airport chairs and make this entry. I'm going to draw a member of the Sciritae tribe. And maybe if I sit here long enough, my mysterious employer will forget about me.

At first glance, it looks like the Sciritae have very little in common with humans. They don't have noses, or rather have snake-like slits in place of noses (much like a certain He Who Must Not Be Named). They're

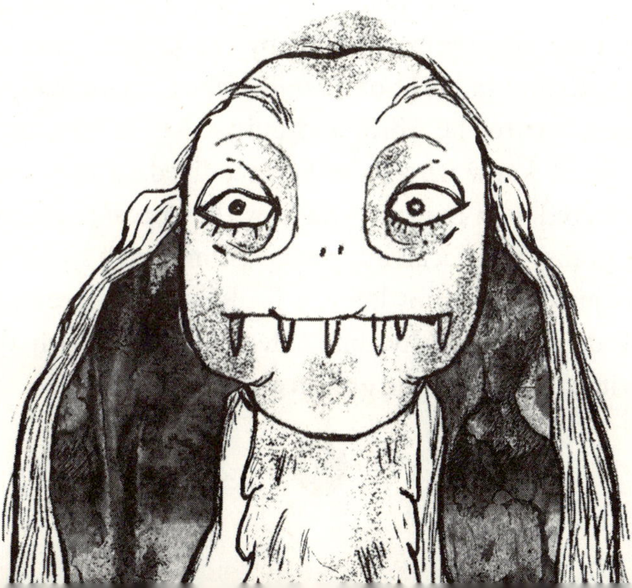

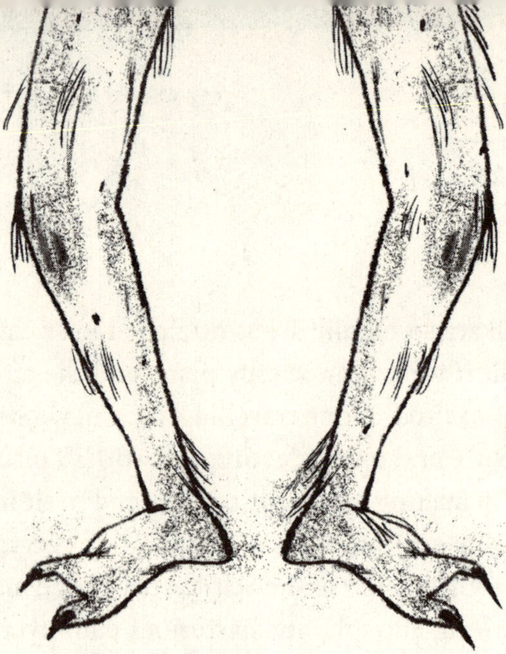

tall and lanky, and their legs bear a serious resemblance to the hind legs of a reptile. But Dark Lord nose aside, the Sciritae were not unlike humans. They were a tribe of wandering nomads, they lived in communities and they took care of their young.

We don't know much about the Sciritae, except that they were written about by the Greek historian Megasthenes in his book *Indica* – which incidentally is largely lost to the world and only exists in fragments. We don't know where the Sciritae lived, if they ever interacted with humans, and how they became extinct. But going by a recurring pattern, I'm pretty sure they were just killed off by humans for looking different.

I don't know why, but I feel a kinship with the Sciritae. I feel I'd have gotten along with them.

The person who picked me from the airport turned out to be the one who'd sent me the text messages.

'I know this must all be very strange for you,' he began, 'but my employer has been dabbling with the occult for quite some time now. When he heard about you, he insisted on hiring you for a small assignment.'

'Heard about me?' I asked, genuinely surprised.

'That's right, you were recommended by a Dr Cherian during our search for a mouse-sized elephant known as Ye Thin. She was all praise for the way you research and catalogue the paranormal, and my employer insisted that we fly you out here at once.'

If only I'd read the text messages Cherian had sent me, it would have spared me the anxiety. But I routinely let my inbox fill up with the hope of answering everything together one day.

'Can I ask you why your employer is so taken with the occult?'

'Yes, you *may* ask me,' he replied.

01/12/2018

Kolkātā, en route to my employer

'It all began years ago, when my employer was eight. He was vacationing in the Sundarbans and decided to go for a stroll. He was only a child and despite his advanced navigational skills, found himself lost by the water.

'He was scared at first, but when the water began to glow, he became curious. He walked closer and closer to the swamp, thinking what he saw was bioluminescence. But he soon realized that the light was a green spherical orb, and it was floating in the air, just a few inches above the water. He was elated and he began running towards the light, not realizing that he'd entered the marsh and was sinking into the quicksand by the water.

'My employer swears that he was engulfed by the water at least twice, and that he would have drowned had it not been for a slightly older boy pulling him out. Here's the interesting bit: my employer claims that the boy was decked in golden jewels, carried a bow and spoke the purest form of Bengali. When my master returned to Kolkata, he wanted to thank the person who saved him. When he began researching the strange phenomenon of the floating light in the Sundarbans, he learned about the legend of the drowned boy.

'This is how the story goes. Legend has it that King Shrutanjaya was hunting with his son Alyanjaya. During their hunt, they found a tigress with her cub. Not wanting to let the opportunity slip, Alyanjaya sprang to action, and cornered the cub and its mother. He took aim and shot the tigress through the heart. But even at the brink of death, the tigress didn't give up. She carried her cub and tossed it into the forest, buying it enough time to get away. The cub roamed the forest, hungry and alone. When it became very thirsty, it returned to the marsh. But the poor cub drowned in the quicksand.

'A few months passed, and Alyanjaya and his father went to hunt for tigers once again. Hoping to find more tigers in the same spot where they killed the last one, Alyanjaya and his father arrived at the marsh. Once there, the young prince found a floating green orb of light above the water. He was so thrilled and captivated by the sight that he rushed towards it, stepping into the marsh and losing his life.

'My employer is convinced about the occult because he says he would never forget the name of the boy who saved him. "Alyanjaya, but you can call me Aleya," he'd said with a smile.'

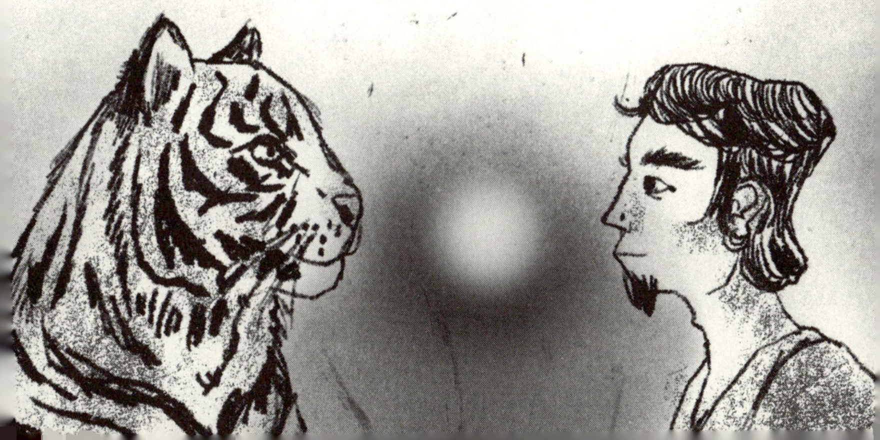

ELDRITCH LIGHTS

eldritch lights

01/12/2018

Kolkata, en route to my employer

That wasn't the first time I'd heard of floating lights by the marshes. That wasn't even the first time I was hearing about ghostly lights in Bengal. The versions I'd heard were a little different, of course – I was told they were the souls of fishermen who were lost at sea, and that they spent their afterlife floating over the water, distracting the living fishermen and putting them in seriously life-threatening situations. I've heard versions that suggest that the floating orbs were good and kept the fishermen safe. Heck, I've even heard versions about these lights causing people to lose their minds and never recover.

These eerie lights have made appearances in other parts of the world as well. In Nordic countries, they're

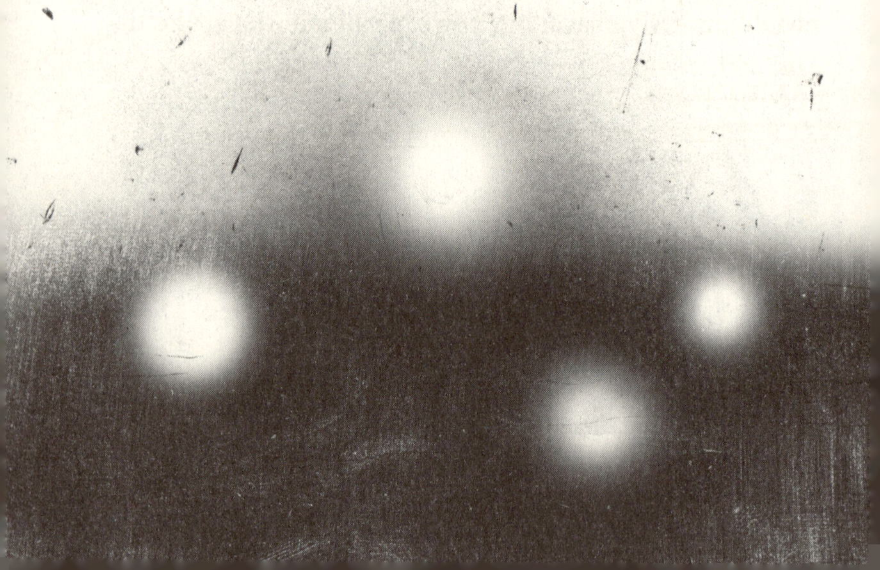

believed to mark the locations of buried treasure. In Christian lore, they're believed to be the spirits of the unbaptized, travelling to the water, desperate to be baptized – which is sad when you think about how the lights never touch the water. The Welsh believe they're fairies. The Australians think the lights play tricks on people by hiding and revealing themselves by turn. In mid-western America, they're believed to be the spirits of railroad workers killed on duty on account of terrible accidents. And the Argentinians consider these lights evil and always keep away from them.

It sort of makes sense for these lights to be all over the world. After all, they are capable of literally moving at the speed of light. What's interesting is the meaning that different cultures have assigned to these floating orbs.

I feel a lot better about meeting this mysterious employer now. I bet he's frail and wizened, living in an old colonial bungalow. And I bet he has a big moustache inspired by the paintings of equally old men that adorn his walls.

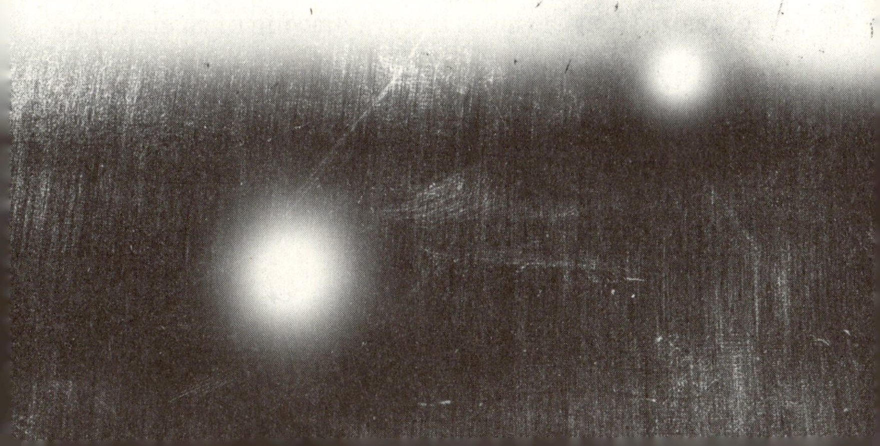

YE THIN

ye thin

01/12/2018

Kolkata, at my mysterious new employer's abode

The house was exactly how I'd imagined it – old and crumbling, with marble pillars, winding wooden stairs and floors that creaked under the slightest weight. Paintings adorned the walls, plants grew wild inside and outside the house, and there was even a knight's suit of armour near the fireplace. I was ushered along a dimly lit corridor, over the restored staircase and finally into my employer's room.

Drawings of strange beasts were plastered on the walls; scripts with unidentifiable letters lay crumpled on the floor. All the objects in the room looked like they were wrestling for space, like a badly curated museum of oddities or a disorganized killer's basement.

'You mentioned Cherian before,' I said. 'May I ask you what you were looking for?'

Mr 9978985744 – I didn't really get a chance to ask his name – walked across the room and pulled out a piece of paper from the mess. It was a drawing of an elephant.

'This is what we were looking for,' he said, passing the paper over to me.

'You were looking for an elephant?' I asked.

'Flip the page over, Mr Iravathur.'

I flipped over to the next page and was surprised to find a drawing of an elephant as small as a mouse, grazing on daisies in a garden.

'This is a lot smaller than the Kalanna,' I replied. 'So, did you manage to find one?'

Mr 9978985744 looked at me as though I'd said something incredibly stupid.

'Of course not!' He chuckled. 'They may only be as big as a small rat, but they're probably more dangerous than the largest, maddest wild elephant. They sometimes cross the borders from Myanmar and they almost always go unnoticed, given how small they are. If you had the misfortune of spotting one, you could drop dead in an instant. My master wasn't looking for them; he was looking for their footprints.'

'Looking for their *footprints*?'

'That's right. There are rumours that if Ye Thin pricked your footprint presumably with its tusks, or even your reflection in the water while around the watering hole, you would die instantly. My master wanted to snuff out their footprints and check if the reverse was true.

'Needless to say, we weren't successful. But you can go ahead and ask the master all about it. I think I hear him coming,' Mr 9978985744 said, before leaving the room.

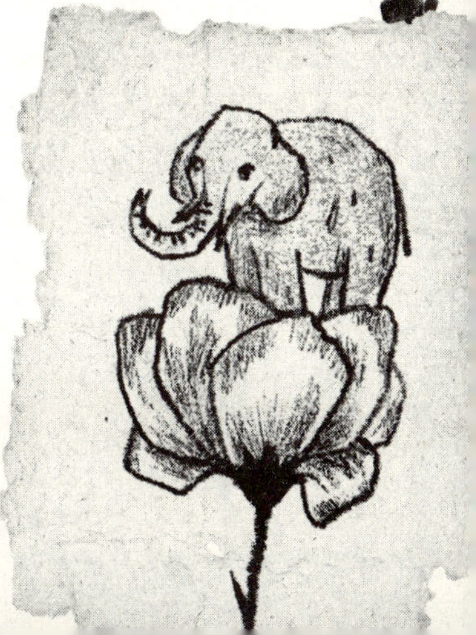

My mystifying new employer's shadow, cast by the candlelight, sailed frighteningly across the corridor. I stood up in my chair, expecting to find a monster of a man, but instead the person who entered the room was hardly 4 feet tall.

'Hi, what's your name?' I asked, getting down on one knee. 'Do you know if your father is coming? I'm waiting for him.' I almost ruffled the boy's hair.

'Mr Iravathur, I am the one who summoned you,' the boy replied. He looked not a day older than 11 but had somehow managed to sound eighty.

'You're the one who paid for my tickets?' I asked incredulously.

'That's right.'

'And that story about your seeing the floating orbs, that happened three years ago?'

'Four,' the boy corrected.

I was taken aback. I didn't know whether to laugh or slap my forehead. 'There's no way I'm working for a little boy,' I said, almost scoffing.

The young 'employer' didn't reply; he simply walked over to his desk and pushed a button under the table. Within the blink of the eye, Mr 9978985744 popped his head around the corner before entering the room.

'Could you show Mr Iravathur the drawings we collected from the children across the country?'

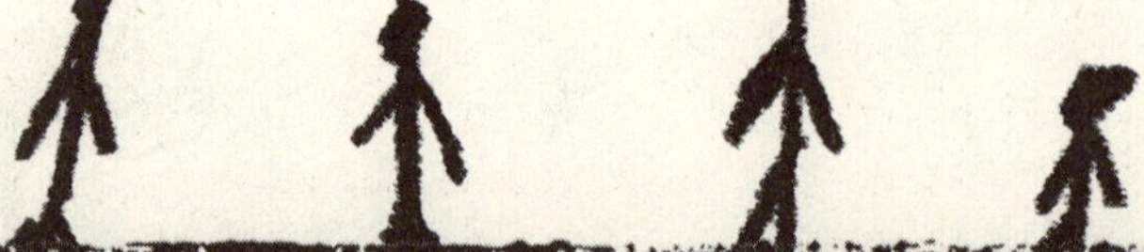

Mr 9978985744 marched over to the largest cabinet in the room. A few creaks and clicks later, he brought out a large binder, stuffed with drawings. He walked over to me, placed the binder on the table and left.

'What is this?' I asked.

'See for yourself,' the boy replied, opening the folder.

At first, I didn't think much of the drawings. They were of oddly shaped men, with slender frames and sharp teeth, dressed in clothing from across the country.

'You see this? This is a drawing I made of the Poochandi when I was six,' the boy said calmly. 'And this is one from Kerala, titled Kokkachi. It was made less than a month ago.'

I flipped through the pages, and in the corners of each page, I found dates accompanied by states and the names of cities. At the very top, were the names of the creatures they'd drawn.

04/12/2018

Location Unknown

They didn't look remarkable at first glance, but the more I looked at them, the more I began to notice the smaller details. The drawings weren't of different people; they were of the same person dressed in different clothes, appearing in different states across India, and documented over a period of 100 years.

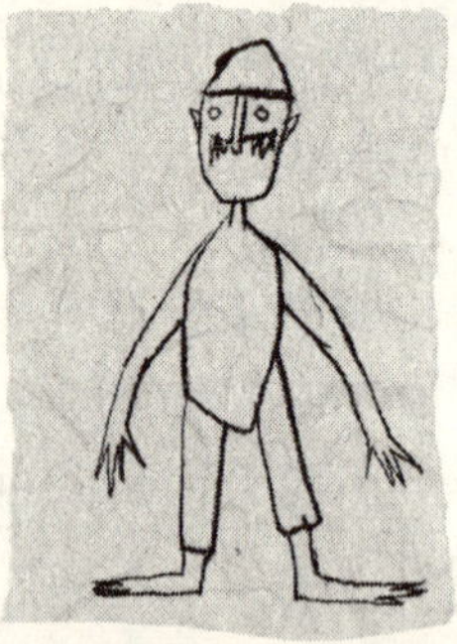

Urdu - Shaitan/Shaytaan

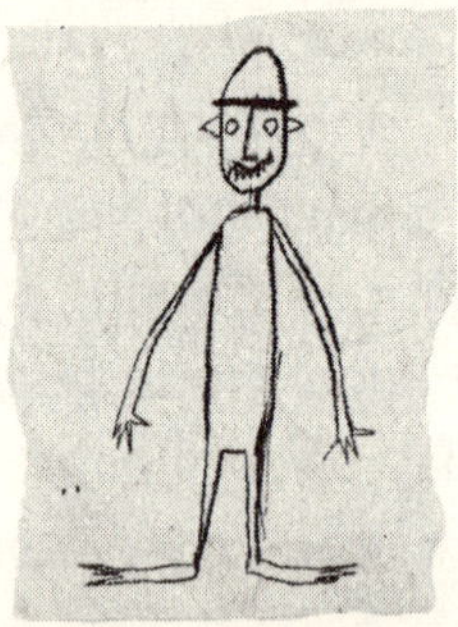

Bihar - Bhakolwa

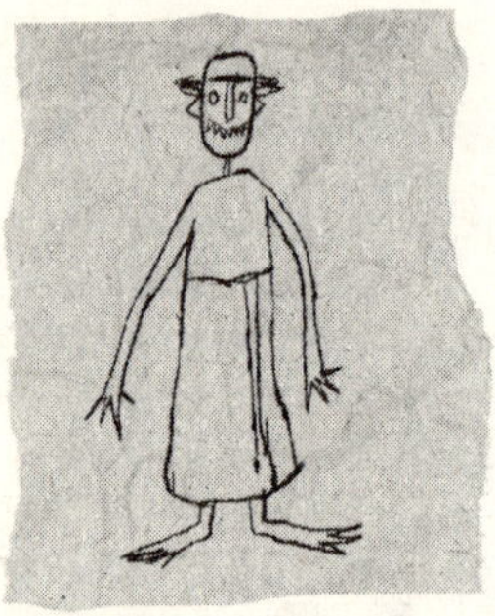

Karnataka - Goggayya

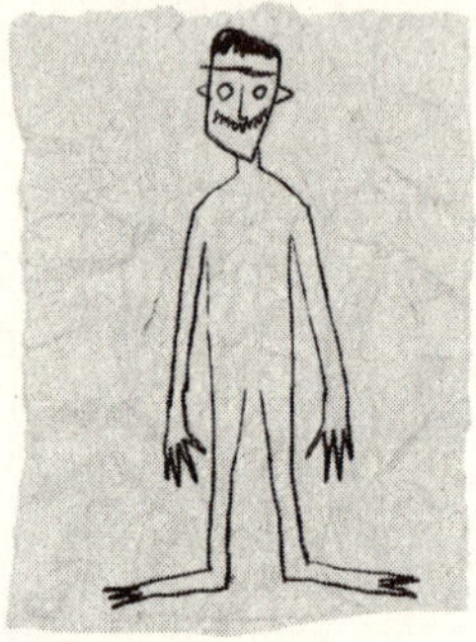

Tamil Nadu - Poochandi

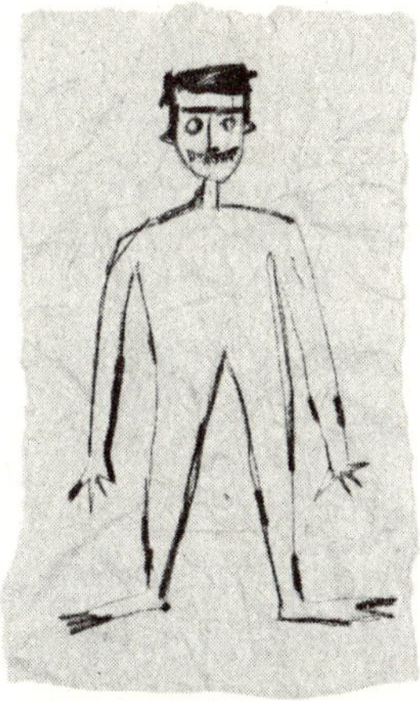

Kerala - Kokkachi

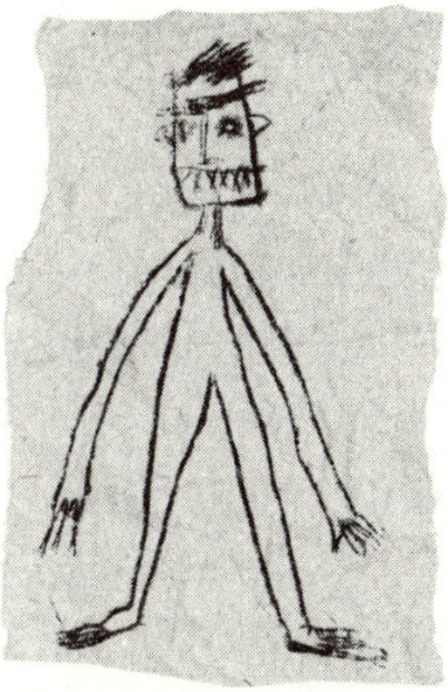

Konkani - Gongo

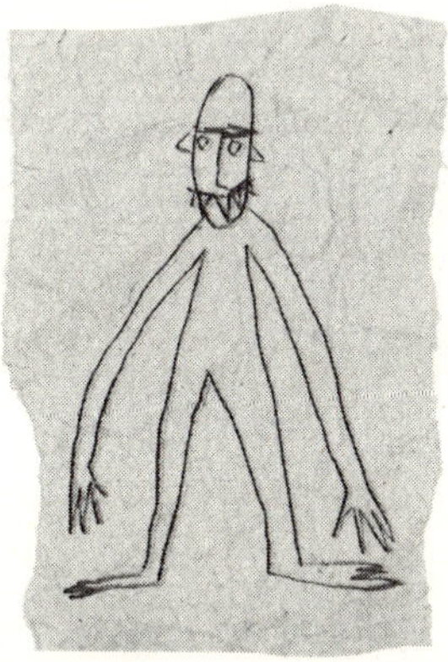

Marathi - Bagul Bua

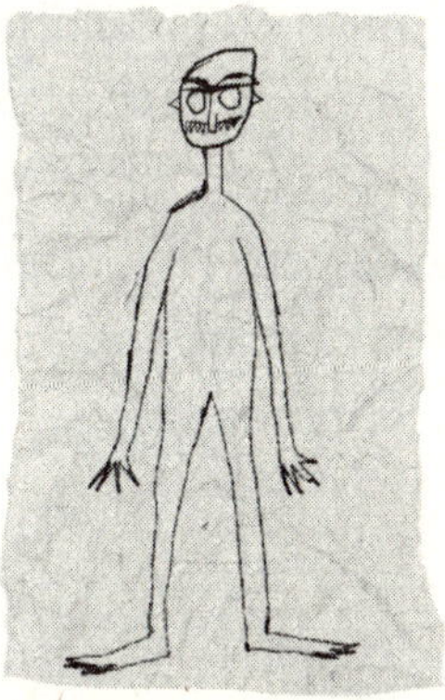

Odisha - Baaya

I stared at the creature's eyes, studied its posture and examined its clothes. The kids, they'd all drawn the same thing. They'd all drawn the Boogeyman.

'How on earth did you find these?' I asked, my heart almost leaping out of my mouth.

'That isn't important,' the boy replied. 'What is crucial is the work I want you to do for me.'

'You want me to hunt down the Boogeymen?' I asked.

'The Boogeyman is old news. I'm looking for someone to work on something completely different.'

I stared at the boy blankly.

'Witches,' he said, walking closer to me. 'I've been hearing stories about witches from different parts of the country. I would go and check them out myself, but I'm busy with other work. Which brings me to why I want to hire you.' He paused. 'I want you to be my eyes, to visit Chhattisgarh, Bihar and the villages of West Bengal, and find out all there is to know about these witches.'

'I don't think I have the time to look for witches,' I replied.

'You'll be compensated for your work, of course,' he continued, as if he hadn't heard me. 'I'll be more than happy to share my research with you.'

I thought about this for some time.

'It's not going to be cheap,' I said, thinking up the biggest fee I could conjure. 'It will cost you ₹60,000!'

'Is that a lot?' the boy asked.

'Per week,' I added hastily.

'Done!' the boy replied and shook my hand. 'All your transport and boarding has been taken care of. You leave tomorrow morning.'

And just like that, he waved me out of the room.

THE KAFTARS

the kaftars

06/12/2018

Rural West Bengal, en route

I know very little about witches. The only accounts of witchcraft that I've heard of were from back home, where neighbours performed pujas because a kannu – an evil eye – was cast on them. I've always considered witches and witchcraft superstition. But I did come across the name Kaftar many times, mostly because they walked the slim line between witches and beasts.

According to urban lore, the Kaftars were female yogis who were capable of great evil. They were considered to be shape-shifters who took on the forms of hyenas – 'Kaftar' means hyena in Persian, by the way – and stalked and killed their victims by draining their blood and eating their hearts. The Kaftars were said to possess strong magical powers, and there are even accounts of Kaftars being accused of witchcraft in ancient India.

Ibn Battuta, a 14th-century Moroccan traveller, talked about the trial of a Kaftar who, after being found guilty of killing a boy and eating his heart, was brought to him for judgement. The traveller had no idea how to deal with such a case, and simply stood back and watched the people handle their own trial. The Kaftar was brought in front of a council and it was decided that four jars filled with water would be tied to the accused before tossing her into the river. If she sank

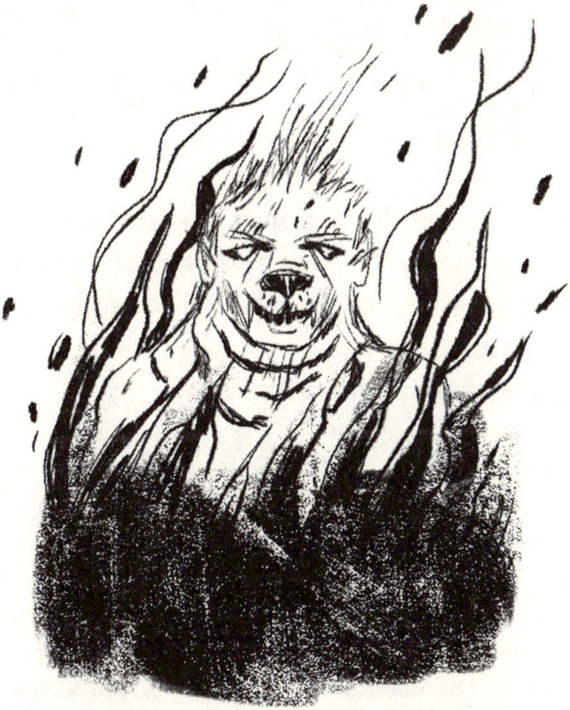

and drowned, oops! – she was innocent (but dead), and if she floated, she was guilty of being a witch and would be put to death. A lose-lose situation, if you ask me.

Turns out that the woman floated and was fished out of the water and later burned. Ibn Battuta went on to add, with scorn and disgust, that burning the witch would keep the villagers safe from the Kaftars for another year.

Truth be told, I feel a lot like Ibn Battuta, uncertain about witches and a bit conflicted by what to do. Something about this feels wrong, and I'm starting to feel a bit sick.

THE DAYAN

the dayan

06/12/2018

Rural West Bengal

My employer was kind enough to share his findings on witches across India. There wasn't much to go on, but it did give me an idea about what I was supposed to be dealing with.

This is what his report had to say:

Though technically not beasts, the Dayans have supernatural powers that allow them to transform into beastly figures. Dayans, or Indian witches, come into existence whenever a woman or a girl child dies because she's ill-treated or neglected. The spirits of the deceased are reincarnated as vengeful spirits and they spend the rest of their existence haunting their family, or hunting down the male family members responsible for their deaths.

However, like a vampire, a Dayan needs human blood to continue living. So they lure men into the forests and feed on their bodies until their victim is completely drained of his life force. Dayans are often described as old women with long black nails, long plaited hair and feet facing backwards. They're known to dabble in black magic, and just being looked at by a Dayan's evil eye is enough to bring ruin and misfortune to an entire household.

One of the ways to stop a Dayan, as well as identify one, is by paying attention to her hair. A

Dayan's source of power comes from her long braided hair; she can move it around like a prehensile tail or use it like an extra limb. The hair can be stretched, hardened, and used to strangle people.

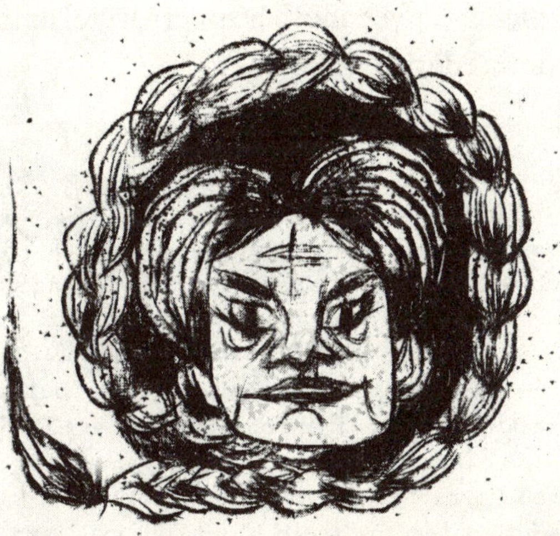

Note: There are different kinds of witches and beasts in the forest to be wary of, and almost all of them need human blood to survive. So be extra careful.

Pretty impressive notes for a child, especially the spelling. I'm sure my employer had no trouble passing the occasional dictation test at school. Maybe I'm just being paranoid, but something doesn't feel right... Call it intuition, but hunting down witches...something sure feels off.

THE CHUREL

the churel

06/12/2018

Rural West Bengal

Right after his notes about the Dayans were a few paragraphs about yet another supernatural entity that's often confused with witches.

Churels are extremely ugly creatures, much worse than my classmate Subupriya who called me spoiled and delusional. Their tongues are darker than tar, the ends of their mouths look like they're always stained with blood, almost as though their lips have been freshly cut out, and their breasts sag all the way down to their knees. They have claws instead of nails, large protruding bellies, and noses that are flat and squished like an ageing pug.

However, Churels can shape-shift, and often take on the form of beautiful women to lure their prey, slaughter them and then feed on their blood. 'Churel' and 'Dayan' are often used interchangeably, but the two couldn't be more different.

Churels are actually weaker beings, usually women who die tragic or sudden deaths and aren't given a proper cremation. They spend most of their time in the graveyards, cemeteries and abandoned battlefields. Churels are also known to attack men, and suck their blood and life force out of them, leaving a young man old and withered when they're done. The biggest difference between the two creatures is that a Churel can be fought off with ease.

The document went on about how to prevent the creation of a Churel: the suspected Churel corpse had to be placed face down on the pyre. There was also something about how the corpses of women who died under mysterious circumstances and the earth where they lay needed to be cleaned, and mustard seeds sown. Sowing mustard seeds meant mustard plants shed more seeds, so when the spirit of a Churel resurfaced to haunt her family, it would be distracted by the mustard seeds and would spend the entire night picking them up, only to sow them back in the ground and return back to the afterlife by the time the sun rose.

It was only after I read the brat's notes that I realized what an eye-opener this document had been. It had made no sense whatsoever – not the bit about the mustard seeds; that part made a lot of sense to me – and the entire document sounded like it was written by a pubescent child. Everything – from my employer's hatred of Subupriya to the description of a Churel, even the instructions about the proper disposal of female corpses – sounded like it had been made up by a silly little boy who was afraid of cooties. In reality, however, these rules and superstitions were all made up hundreds of years ago by respected elders from villages.

I set down the document and began to laugh. It felt like I had been sent on a wild goose chase. I glanced at the time on my mobile, and then I looked out my window – we were now well within the boundaries of rural Bengal. I was just in time for my appointment with the witch-hunter.

Ojhas are sent by the gods to help lowly mortals like you and me fight witchcraft. They can tell if someone is cursed or under the influence of witchcraft, they can spot a Dayan hiding in plain sight, and they are the only ones who could get rid of witches.

Not just that, Ojhas apparently have the power to cure cancer, to perform elaborate religious rituals and to communicate with the gods at will. The man standing in front of me is an Ojha, and I strongly believe he and his kind are the scourge of the earth.

'Dayans cause pain and suffering…they are the source of all sadness and disease.' Every word that left the Ojha's mouth was laced with hatred. 'But with my help, you can put an end to the suffering.' He grinned, waving his arm over the crowd that had gathered. 'Do you have old women in the village? People who live on the outskirts, far away from the village?'

The Ojha waited for the muttering to die down, and when it did, he moved to the centre of the crowd. 'The women who live outside your town…they're the reason your water tastes bitter, the reason your sons fall sick, and the reason daughters don't have children.

'Remember, there are ways to spot them. The Dayan will reveal herself if we write down the names of the old women living on the outskirts of the village, stick their names to small sacks of rice and toss them in front of an anthill. The name on the sack that's the emptiest after a day is the witch's.'

'Are you sure that's how you find a witch?' I asked.

'Yes – to be doubly sure, we must write their names on different branches of a tree, and the one that sags the most reveals the witch,' he added.

The more I listened to the Ojha, the more I hated him. He was an absolute charlatan, preying on a village's fears and naiveté, using the supernatural for his own personal gain. What's more, there were serious consequences for the people he suspected of being witches. I've heard stories of women accused of witchcraft because they'd refused someone's hand in marriage, or because their families wanted to claim their property. The victims were dragged through the streets and beaten within an inch of their lives. Some of them have even died – around 200 women a year.

This Ojha may not be mythical or a beast, but he certainly is the vilest creature I've ever encountered.

Annoyed and disgusted, I picked up my phone and called my employer. 'Witches aren't real!' I explained, and I'm glad he was understanding. I told him that I was more than happy to return the money he'd given me, but he insisted that I had earned it. Then he suggested that I run a small errand for him.

08/12/2018

Birbhum District,
Rural West Bengal

I decided to ditch the car and find my own way back to Kolkata. Big mistake.

Not only did I get lost along the way, but I also found out, when I finally got to the railway station, that my train had been delayed by eight hours. I ended up spending the night at the station, and if you've ever spent the night at a railway station, or a bus stop, you know that they attract some of the most colourful characters.

I honestly thought I wasn't going to make it through the night. I was all alone in a village I'd never heard of. All kinds of shady people were around – gamblers using the platform lights for their card game, a sprightly vegetable seller who was clearly selling something other than vegetables, and people who just glared at me as though they were looking to start a fight.

I kept my head down and didn't make eye contact with any of them. When I felt it was safe, I got off the bench and marched towards the exit. Bigger mistake. Because the road outside the railway station was darker than black. The air was crisp, the night was quiet, and the farther I walked from the station, the better I heard the sounds from the trees.

I continued to walk, hearing hooting and scratching, the flapping of wings and the rustling leaves. When I looked towards the treetops I saw a pair of glowing eyes, blood-red, like a pair of rubies. They glared at me. I began to walk faster. Then, all at once, I felt the gentle fluttering of wings almost touching the nape of my neck. Something was terribly wrong. I felt the hairs on the back of my neck stand on end, and I couldn't really explain it, but I knew I had to get out of there at that very moment.

I turned around and began sprinting towards the station, while all around me the hooting became louder. More bloodshot eyes glared down from the treetops. Had I accidently annoyed the owls? Had I disturbed their hunt? No, it was something much worse. I ran faster than my legs could carry me, harder than my lungs allowed me to. I jumped over the low wall between me and the railway station, and then I dove to the ground.

I could feel the feathers again, gliding and swooping down. Call it intuition or just an evolutionary response to danger, but I was certain that whatever was chasing me was aiming for my neck.

Walking further into the forest would have been the biggest mistake I could have made. Because the thing that was chasing me wasn't an owl or even a bird. It was the Penchapechi; though it looked, sounded and acted like an owl, it wasn't. The beast would have sucked the life force out of me, like a vampire does, had I walked further into the forest. The station made me uneasy, but at least it wasn't trying to kill me. You won't believe how happy I was to be back on my bench.

the skondhokata

09/12/2018

Dubrājpur village railway station

I woke up to the sound of my train finally arriving. I'd successfully ignored everyone in the railway station. As I got on the train and found my seat, I thought, perhaps, I'd imagined the stares and the hostility. Maybe they were just there minding their own business and my overactive imagination blew things out of proportion.

I reached into my bag to fetch a new pen and accidentally shone my phone's torch on the person opposite me.

My co-passenger was somehow awake at 4 a.m.

'An awful lot of people at the railway station for such a small town, right?' I asked.

'What are you talking about? The station's empty,' he replied.

'Um...look out of the window – there's a vegetable seller and people playing cards,' I corrected him.

'A vegetable seller, at this time?' My co-passenger stuck his head outside the window to look, causing the people on the platform to drop what they were doing and amble awkwardly towards the train.

'Look! They're walking towards you!' I said.

'Very funny,' my co-passenger scoffed, rolling his eyes and cursing me under his breath.

I looked out the window, and that's when I truly saw them. The gamblers, the vegetable seller, the goons...they had no business being there in the middle of the night. I glanced at their feet, their chests, their shoulders. Then I made eye contact with them. At least, I tried to.

'Help,' one of them wheezed, 'help find my head.'

His voice grew louder. I glanced at his face, and I almost threw up. He was missing everything above his upper jaw. Blood spurted out of his neck and clumps of hair wet with pus sat directly over his upper jaw, like an unconvincing toupee. I let my eyes wander and saw others – their heads sliced off their bodies, some of their necks coagulated with blood, others with old jagged wounds. One even had the oesophagus wrapped around the neck like a meaty scarf.

I began to panic. I didn't know what to do, so I climbed up to my berth and curled myself into a ball as the headless figures stuck their hands through the window.

'We lost our heads here...help us find them.' The voice sounded laboured and close to incomprehensible. I closed my eyes and clenched my fists, I curled up my body, trying to make myself as small as I could. A minute later, I felt a cold breeze on my feet.

The train had left just in the nick of time.

BYANGOMA_BYANGOMI

byangoma_byangomi

10/12/2018

Kolkata, en route

My co-passenger woke me up, and offered me an orange and a banana. 'Are you okay? It looked like you were having a bad dream. You've been sleeping the entire trip. I thought you could use some food.'

'Sorry, I hope I wasn't making too much noise,' I replied, before climbing down from my berth. 'How far is Kolkata from here?'

'Ten or fifteen minutes. The train's just stopping here until it gets the green signal.'

I grabbed my toothbrush and toothpaste, and shuffled awkwardly past the co-passengers in my cabin, and then the others in my coach, feeling a little embarrassed and self-conscious. Had I shouted out during my night-time terror? I honestly didn't want to find out. I inched closer to the open door and brushed my teeth, standing almost on the footboard of the train.

I glanced at a nest with a couple of birds and felt a little calmer. The birds were small, a mix of beige and

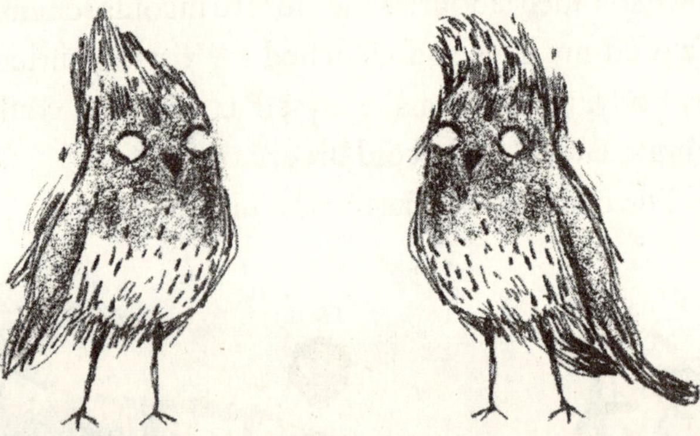

black, with a crown of feathers that stood upright like a mohawk. I watched the two birds feed their young, and then I saw them fly closer to the train. They gathered the crumbs and the peanuts spilled by the footboard, mere inches from me, and gave me a better view of their faces. I noticed a thin white film covering their eyes, and then I heard them sing. Only, it was different from the thousands of other times I'd listened to a bird sing. The song from the two birds translated into visions. Before I knew it, I was seeing my future self in a strange new land, among rice fields, looking for yet another beast.

All of a sudden, I snapped back to reality. When I took a closer look at the birds, I realized that they could be the Byangoma-Byangomi. Mythical birds no bigger than a hoopoe bird, the Byangoma-Byangomi are born blind, but they can gain eyesight when human blood is sprinkled on their eyes. It's not like they need their eyes; according to folk tales from Bengal, the birds have the power to tell the future. It stands to reason that creatures who can see the future don't need eyes because they see and know everything in advance anyway. So I guess that means they'd know how to dodge a stone from a catapult or a bullet from a gun.

I looked at the birds in their nest and felt a little uneasy. I'd been travelling for close to a year now, and for the first time since I'd set out, I felt like I was missing home.

THE PHEICHHAM

the pheichham

11/12/2018

Aizawl Airport, MZ

Staying true to my end of the bargain, I recounted my experience at the railway station, and how I'd stayed the night there as instructed. Something tells me he already knew about the headless monstrosities because, as a parting gift, my almost-teenaged employer gave me a cheque for ₹1,20,000, as well as a promise to pay for my flight ticket to a destination of my choosing. Naturally, I chose the North-East – the Aizawl Airport in Mizoram, to be specific.

You see, somewhere in Mizoram, hopping along the countryside, are one-footed creatures called Pheichhams. Sound familiar? Well, I thought so too, but the Pheichham are nothing like the human-esque Monopods that I tried to track down earlier. As a matter of fact, they couldn't be more different. While the foot of a Monopod is just used to hop around and shield themselves from the sun, the Pheichham's foot is said to possess magical powers. Anyone who manages to catch one will be granted three wishes, sort of like catching a genie.

Catching a Pheichham brings wealth and fortune, but there's just one little catch – the Pheichham doesn't like to be caught. Despite having just one foot, it is extremely swift, like a wild hare on steroids. Seeing as how they are tiny little goblins with dangerously sharp teeth, one really must be careful in approaching them.

Which is why I was dressed like a hockey goalkeeper. Okay, that wasn't the wisest way to start spending the money that I'd just made, but think about it. Catching the Pheichham would mean being granted three wishes. That's catching one mythical beast as well as wishing for all the others to appear in front of me. I'd have my cake and eat it too.

Well, as my quest to track them down is still afoot, you've probably guessed that my attempts to catch a Pheichham weren't successful.

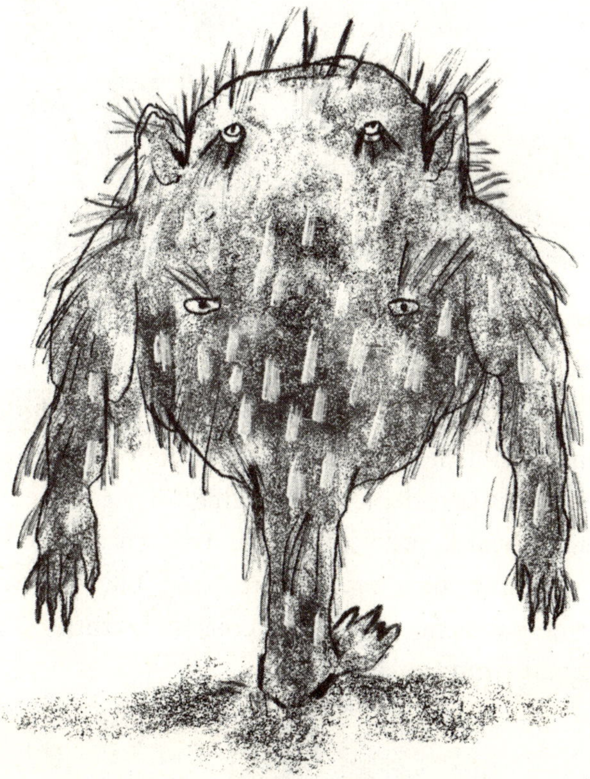

SATYR

satyr

12/12/2018

MC

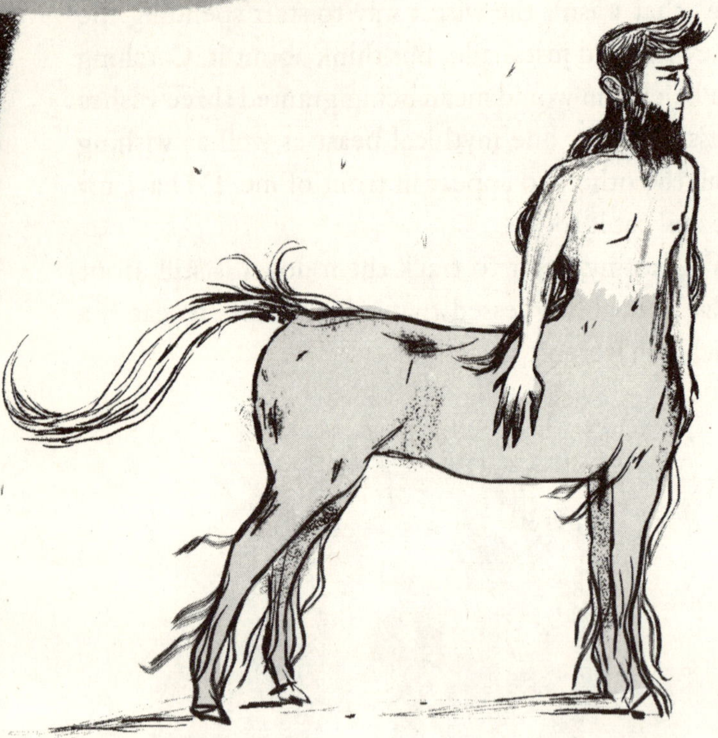

A Satyr is a mythical beast with the torso and head of a human, and the legs and body of a horse or a goat. Satyrs are usually depicted as having barbaric faces with unkempt beards and wild hair, and are known for their love of music, dancing and drinking. They are often described as being rowdy, raucous and, truth be told, pretty far from Indian.

Still, just because they weren't from the Indian subcontinent doesn't mean that they weren't here. It just so happens that there's an entire epic poem, the *Dionysiaca* – written by Nonnus, a Greek poet of the fifth century BCE – that talks about Dionysus and his army of Satyrs fighting an epic war against the kings of northern India.

There's a lot that goes on in the poem. There are detailed accounts of the Satyrs and Indians fighting many battles that lasted several days, and accounts of where the Satyrs lived and partied during their siege. Satyrs didn't sleep in the forests. They didn't build huts like the humans. Instead, they marched into the caves of lions and bears, and used their sharp claws to oust the wild animals out and to sculpt beds for themselves to sleep in.

So it comes as no surprise that the Satyrs fought so many battles. Why wouldn't they, when they had claws that could literally cut into stones and boulders? I think it's very likely that a few Satyrs stayed back in India after the war. And what better place for them to stay than in the caves of Meghalaya!

Note: There are also accounts of Satyr-like tribes in the Mahabharata. Referred to as Kinnaras, these half-man, half-horse tribes lived in the Himalayas.

It's a lot harder for me to travel in the North-East. For instance, I wanted to visit the Laitlum Canyon the other day, and I couldn't find public transport to get me there. I tried my best to use the shared SUVs but ended up shelling out for a personal cab. Here's the thing about travelling in comfort – once you get used to it, it's really hard going back to roughing it.

I was going to the Laitlum Canyon because I had heard rumours of moving rocks, tree spirits, and a cable car that transports you to a completely different world when used on a misty day. The rumour turned out to be a mere child's tale. What's worse, there was absolutely no point visiting a canyon on a misty day – I couldn't see anything!

However, the trip did give me a chance to gather my thoughts. I decided to head to Cherrapunji (Sohra) next, partly because I've always wanted to visit the second wettest place on earth (the wettest place, Mawsynram, may be too wet for my liking), but also because I was curious to learn about the Thlen.

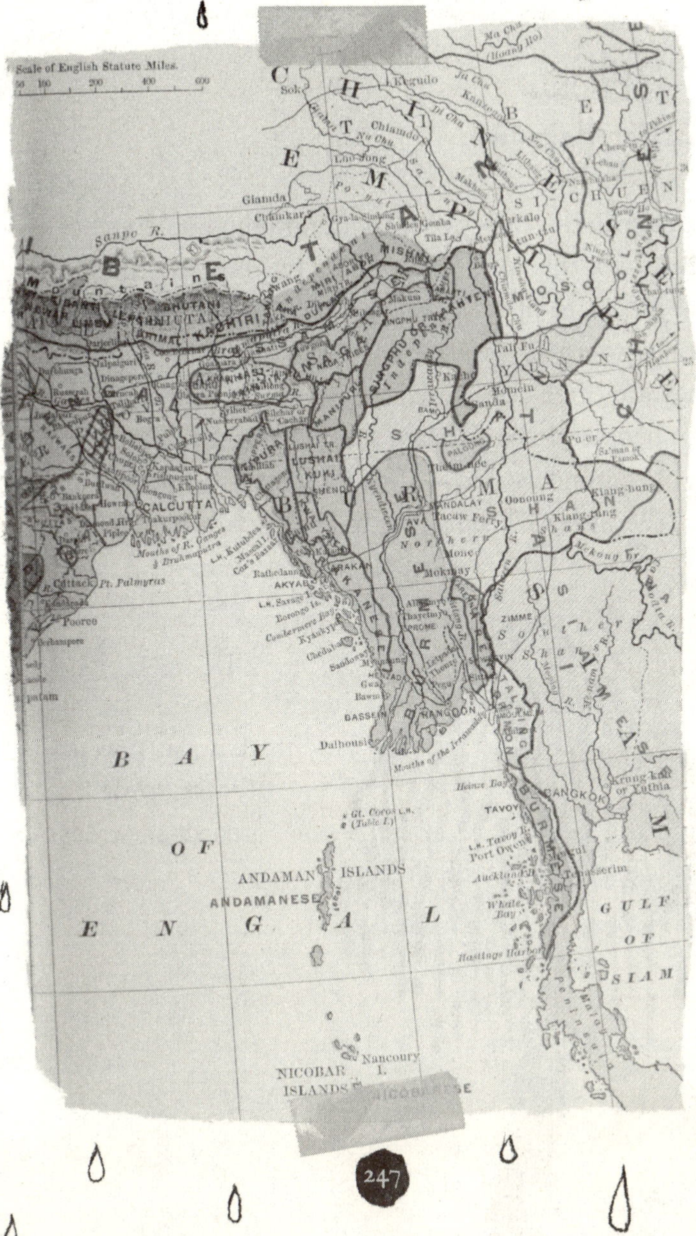

Scale of English Statute Miles.
50 100 200 400 600
CALCUTTA
Mouths of R. Ganges & Brahmaputra
Cuttack
Pt. Palmyras
Pooree
AKYAB
ARAKAN
BASSEIN
RANGOON
Dalhousie
Mouths of the Irrawaddy
MANDALAY
PROME
Tali Fu
Momein
Kiang-hung
ZIMME
TAVOY
Port Owen
Mergui
Tenasserim
Hastings Harbor
BANGKOK
GULF OF SIAM
B A Y
O F
E N G A L
Gt. Coco I.
(Table I.)
ANDAMAN ISLANDS
ANDAMANESE
NICOBAR ISLANDS
Nancoury I.
NICOBARESE

north-eastern forest creatures

14/12/2018

Location Unknown

Driving on the empty roads with nothing but stretches of forest on either side, I can't help but imagine the spirits that take care of these expanses. Different spirits, called Huai, govern or oversee different aspects of the forest. They are often considered dangerous, with the power to turn people insane or cause severe harm. I think they are deeply misunderstood – I believe they inflict terrible pain on us because we keep trying to encroach upon their land.

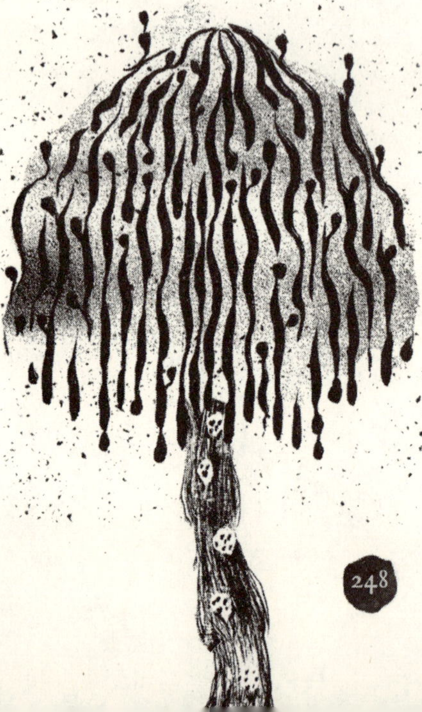

A RAMHUAI is a forest spirit that guards the trees.

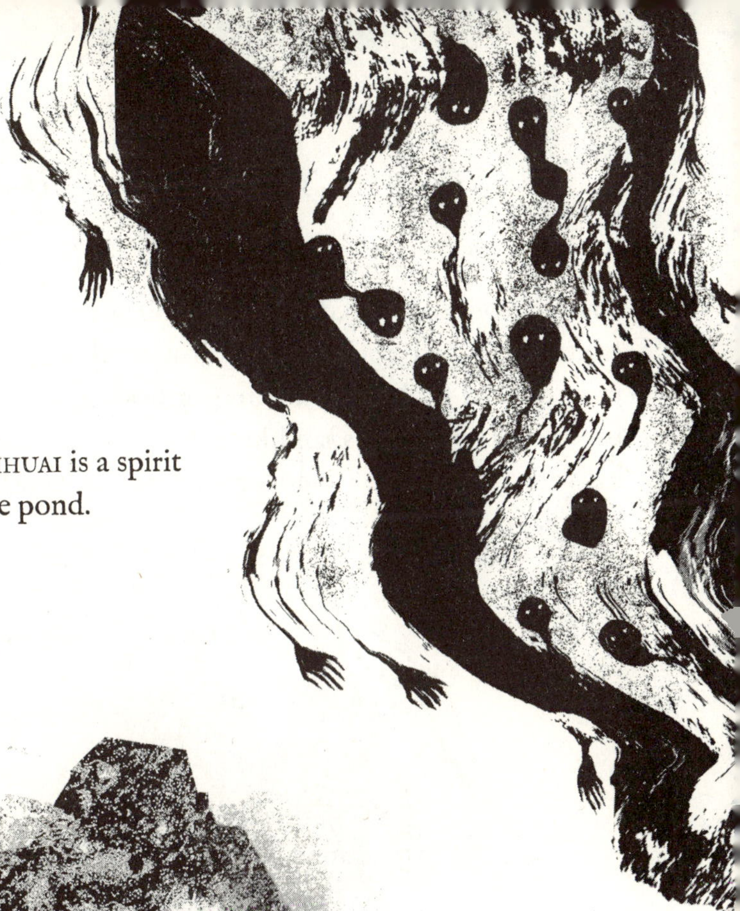

A SIHHUAI is a spirit of the pond.

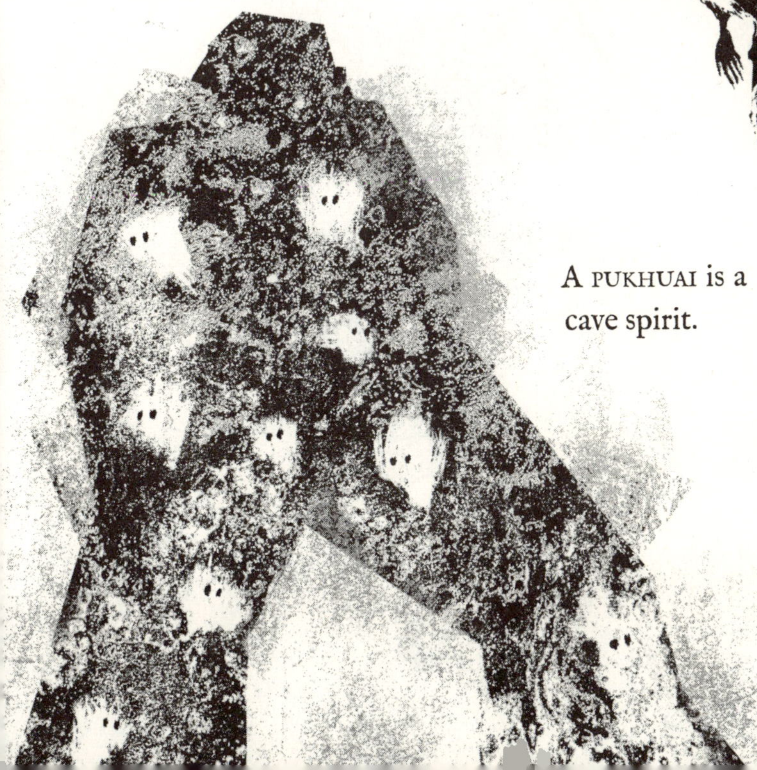

A PUKHUAI is a cave spirit.

NARIPHON

nariphon

15/12/2018

Location Unknown

The Nariphon are trees that give birth to women as fruit. According to Thai Buddhist mythology, they were created by Indra, the king of heaven, to distract the hermits and yogis, and keep them from attacking his wife Vessantaraa. The women fruits were made in her image.

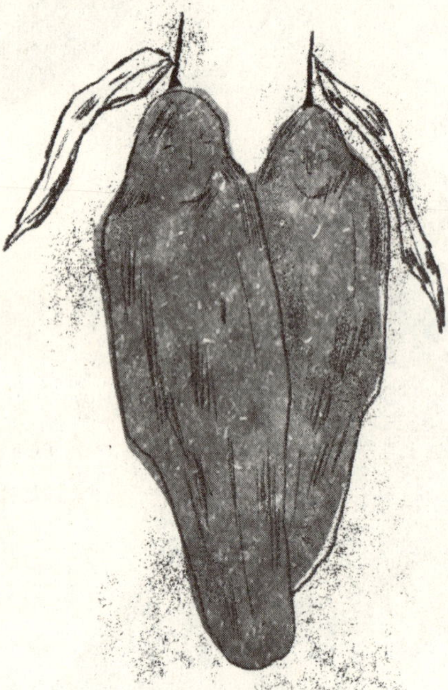

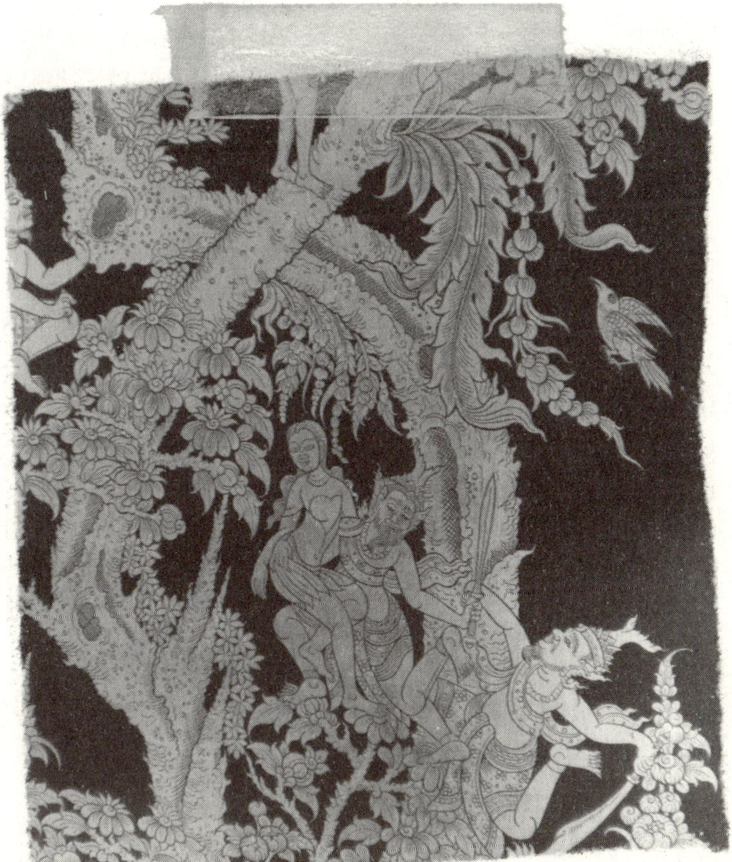

Note: Revisit this topic later...

THE THLEN
the thlen

20/12/2018

Cherrapunji (Sohra), ML

I didn't really think things through before heading to this very wet place. I don't have a raincoat or an umbrella. The floors outside my hotel room are wet and slippery, the pillows and blanket on my bed feel moist, and the walls are damp with fungus.

At least I'm finally here, in the heart of the caves where the Thlen once roamed. The Thlen was a cruel spirit who took on the form of a monstrous man-eating snake and preyed on men, women and children. It killed so many people that one day the villagers who lived around the caves came together and decided to get rid of it, once and for all. They found a brave rebel without a cause – named Suidnoh – to get rid of the beast. Suidnoh travelled through the caves all by himself, feeding the Thlen pork and beef whenever he walked by. Soon, the beast warmed up to the youth. One day, when the Thlen had let its guard down, Suidnoh struck it in the heart with a piping hot metal rod. The boy then cut the giant snake into many pieces and brought it back to the village for everyone to eat. The villagers threw a big feast to celebrate, and by the time they were done, almost all of the Thlen was eaten, except for a chunk of meat that an old woman had kept for her son who was out of town.

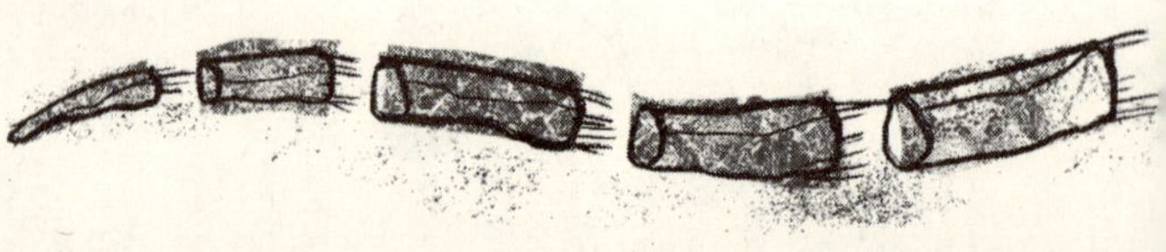

The old woman cut the chunk into smaller pieces but forgot all about them and eventually threw them in the trash. From the discarded pieces of meat, a dozen more Thlen were born, each as powerful as the first.

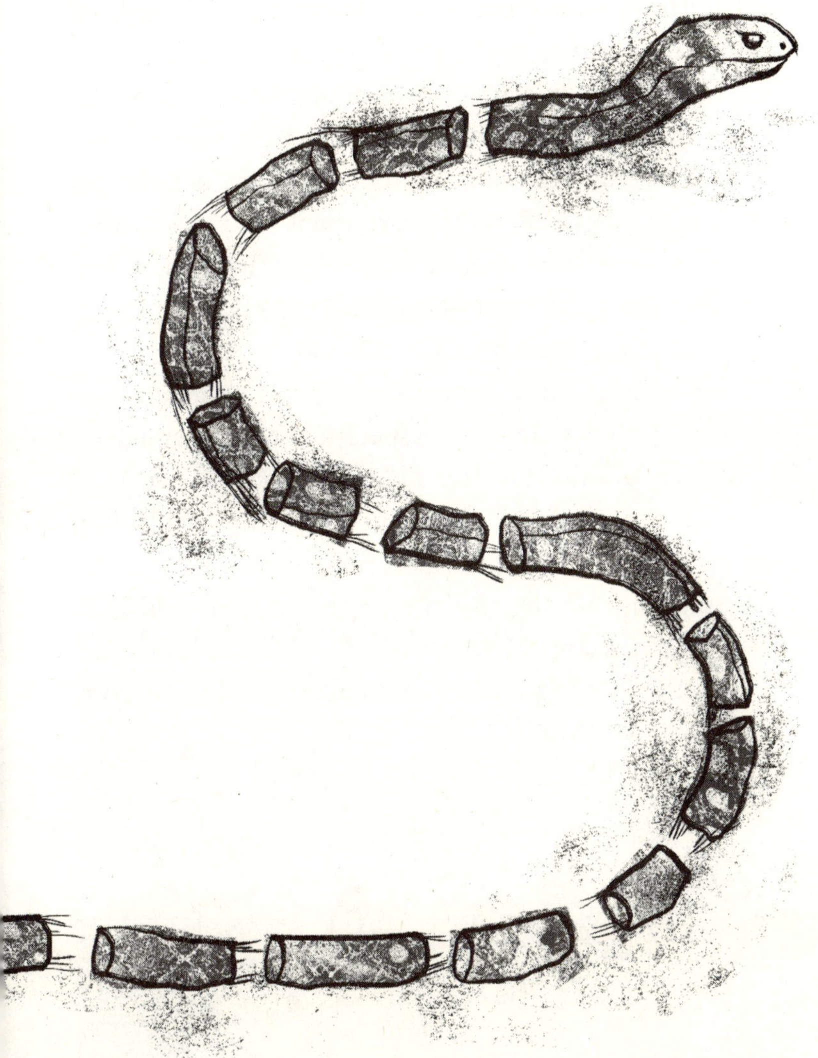

THE NONGSHOHNOH

the nongshohnoh

22/12/2018

ML

Now, considering that there were dozens of Thlen on the loose, or perhaps just one giant Thlen as a result of all the cut-up Thlen joining together, the people of Meghalaya had to find a way to appease the beast.

Enter the Nongshohnoh, meaning 'beaters', who get their name from the club they use to beat their victims. The Nongshohnoh hunt by bludgeoning their victims with a wooden club to prepare them for the sacrifice. The Thlen will not accept the sacrifice if metal has been used to kill the victim – probably PTSD from being stabbed in the heart by a hot iron rod.

Of course, there were rules for the sacrifice. For starters, only a native from a specific tribe in Meghalaya could be sacrificed to the Thlen, probably as penance for their ancestors killing it, and a certain ritual had to be followed. A Nongshohnoh first prepared the ritual by snipping off the victim's fingertips, toes and hair, using silver scissors. He then used a small bamboo knife to slit the victim's nostrils and collect the blood from their nose in a bamboo bowl.

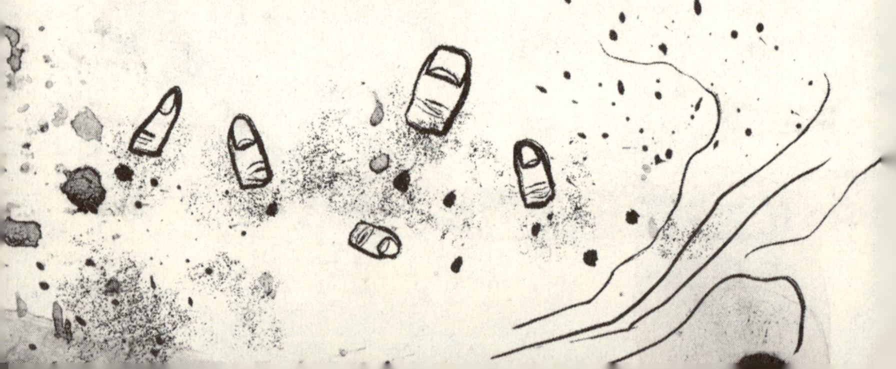

The sacrifice was offered at the darkest time of night. The doors were closed, the curtains were drawn and the Nongshohnoh shed his clothes on the ground, in front of a large brass bowl in which the victim was placed. He then beat a loud drum, summoning the Thlen from its lair. The Thlen devoured the sacrifice within minutes. As a reward, the Nongshohnoh was bestowed with wealth and prosperity.

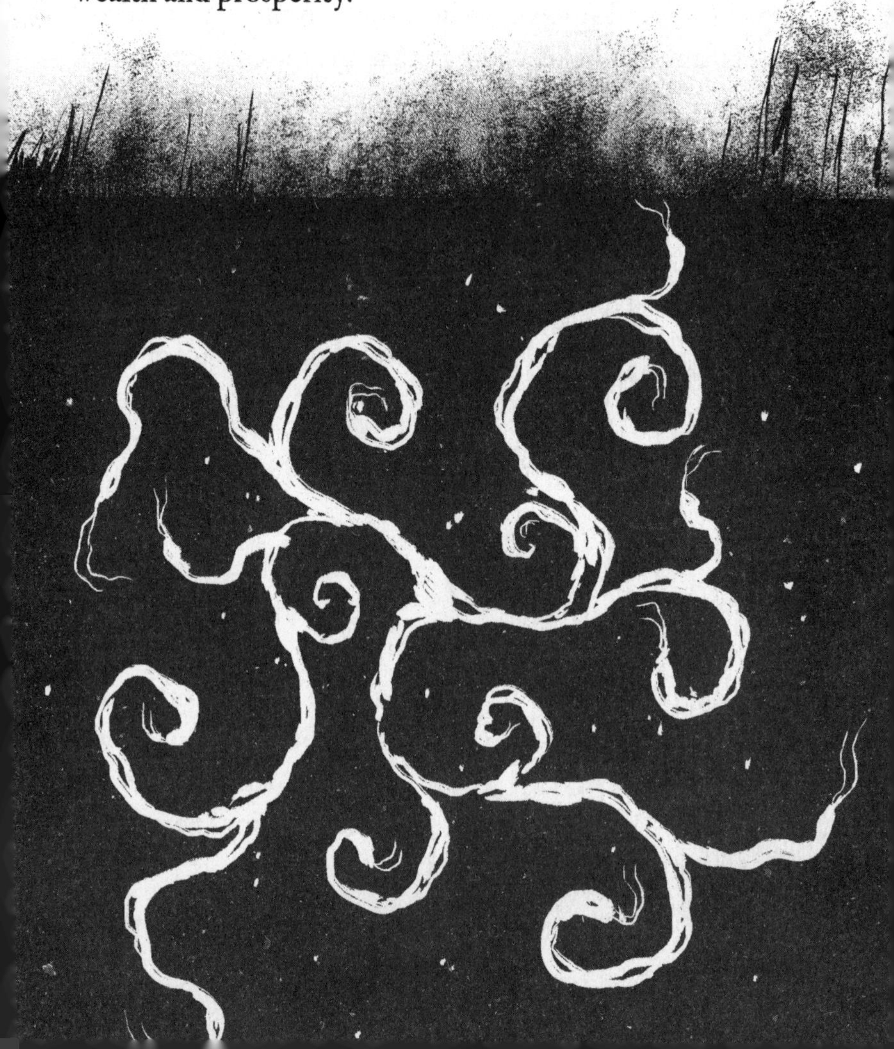

BANJHAKRI AND BANJHAKRINI

banjhakri and banjhakrini

24/12/2018

MZ, en route

The North-East has its fair share of witch doctors, shamans and sorcerers who dabble in the occult. What sets the Banjhakri apart is that they aren't interested in power or material gain – they care about the next generation.

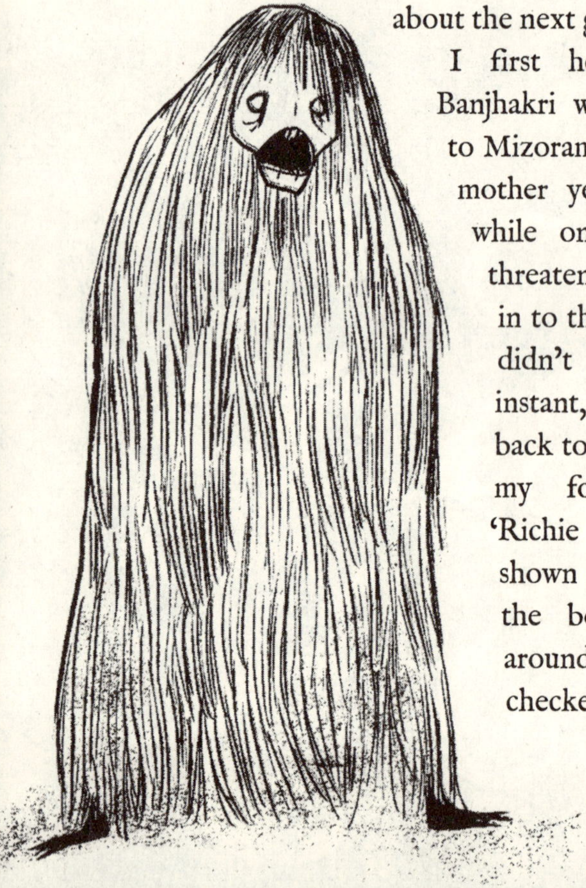

I first heard about the Banjhakri while on my way to Mizoram. An exasperated mother yelled at her son while on the town bus, threatening to hand him in to the Banjhakri if he didn't behave. In that instant, my mind drifted back to the drawing that my former employer 'Richie Rich' had shown me, the one with the boogeymen from around the country. I checked my notes for the copy of the drawings that I had taken, and I was right – the Banjhakri wasn't in there. Here's probably why.

The Banjhakri were sort of in between a shaman and a Boogeyman. Hailing from Sikkim, they were short supernatural beings with ape-like faces and long, matted hair that covered everything but their faces and feet. The Banjhakri would look for children who showed a talent for magic, nab them and bring them back to their cave to train. These children often went on to become the most powerful shamans, and the Banjhakri dropped them back at the very spot of the kidnapping. Not all children survived the training, though. The ones who showed weakness were handed over to the Banjhakri's wife, the Banjhakrini, who killed and ate them.

As for the ones who made it out alive, they acquired skills to cure every disease and perform the most complicated spells. They brought wealth and prosperity to their village. So I guess it all sort of balances out in the end.

I just hope for the sake of the child I met on the bus that he wasn't really offered to the Banjhakri. One look at him, and I could tell he was more likely to be dinner than shaman.

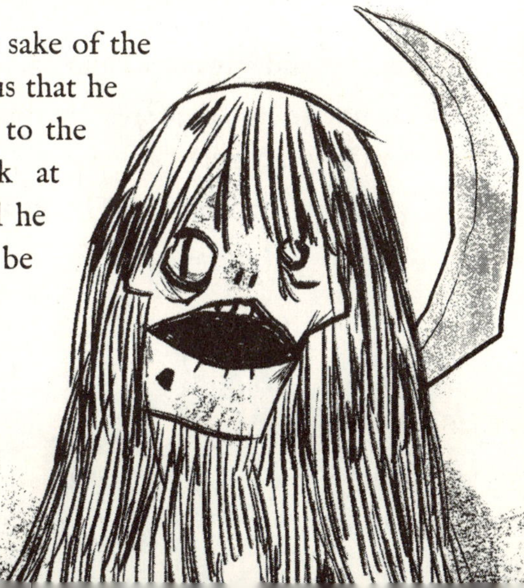

THE KEIMIS

the keimis

27/12/2018

Unknown forest, MZ

Me: Where's the first place you'd look if you were searching for a weretiger?

Werecat Ravi: Are you heading into the forest by yourself again?

Me: No, but let's say that you were looking for one, would you head into the forest?

Werecat Ravi: Of course not – that would be stupid.

Me: Why so?

Werecat Ravi: Have you ever met a tiger? Just a regular tiger? How many people do you know who march into forests hoping to meet a tiger?

Me: Umm...

Werecat Ravi: Exactly! Now picture a weretiger. Stronger, smarter and way more cunning.

Do not go into the forest by yourself! And do not look for the weretiger!

Me: Okay, understood. Thanks again, Ravi.

I get why Werecat Ravi is afraid, and I know why he doesn't want me looking for a Keimi. But a weretiger is half human, so all I need to do when I meet one is try reasoning with it. Besides, I'm already at the Dampa Tiger Reserve, and I've spent a lot of money hiring a cab to get here.

Werecat Ravi was right about one thing, though. Going into the forest alone was a pretty dumb idea, especially if I'm looking for a weretiger. Mizo folklore is in general well rounded, and the beasts that appear in Mizo tales are neither black nor white. They're a lot like humans, meaning that they can be good or bad. But there are two exceptions to the rule, one of which is the Keimis. According to Mizo folklore, a Keimi can only be evil, and is depicted as a human with the power to transform into a tiger. Keimis live in human villages, have jobs and congregate with humans – but only so

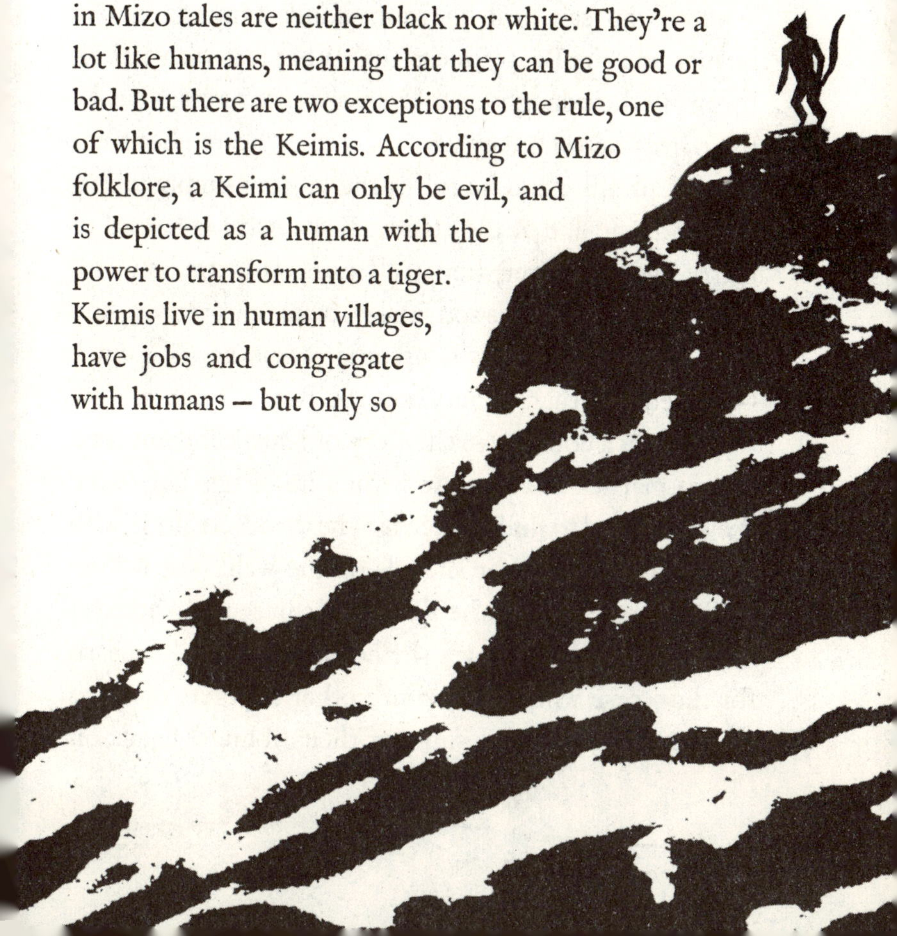

that they can eat them. In essence, they're the proverbial tiger in sheep's clothing.

Yet, being mauled to death by a weretiger is the least of my worries. A worse fate would be to be in the clutches of a Keimi; Keimis have the power to cast magical spells, and are even known to mingle and mate with humans. Like in the story of Kungawrhi, where a Keimi steals Kungawrhi's father's footprint and holds it over the fire, causing him a great deal of pain. Kungawrhi's father announces that he will give his daughter's hand in marriage to anyone who can heal his foot. (Kinda reminds you of Beauty and the Beast, doesn't it? What is it with fathers throwing their daughters to the wolves, or tigers, to make their lives better?) Anyway, the Keimi hears about the father's promise and he fulfils the task by simply taking his footprint out of the flames. Kungawrhi is forced to marry the weretiger, but it all ends well for her. Her father learns about his son-in-law being a weretiger, and they storm the Keimi's house and rescue her – a much better ending than Beauty and the Beast, if you ask me.

Then, as a counter, in the story of Khualtungamtawna, a hero marries a Keimi. And when he brings her home, she's surprised to find the heads of her brothers along with the heads of the other animals on the wall. Not willing to show her true self, the Keimi cries in secret whenever her hunter husband leaves the house. Things take a turn for the worse when the Keimi's other brothers come to visit. Disgusted by the sight of their siblings' heads on the wall, they pounce on Khualtungamtawna, who shoots them down with his gun. I think the story ends with Khualtungamtawna dying at the hands of his Keimi wife, or dying during a hunt because of his wife's interference.

All things said and done, I'm kind of relieved that I never encountered a Keimi in the forest. I am a bit antsy about the footprints I left in there, though.

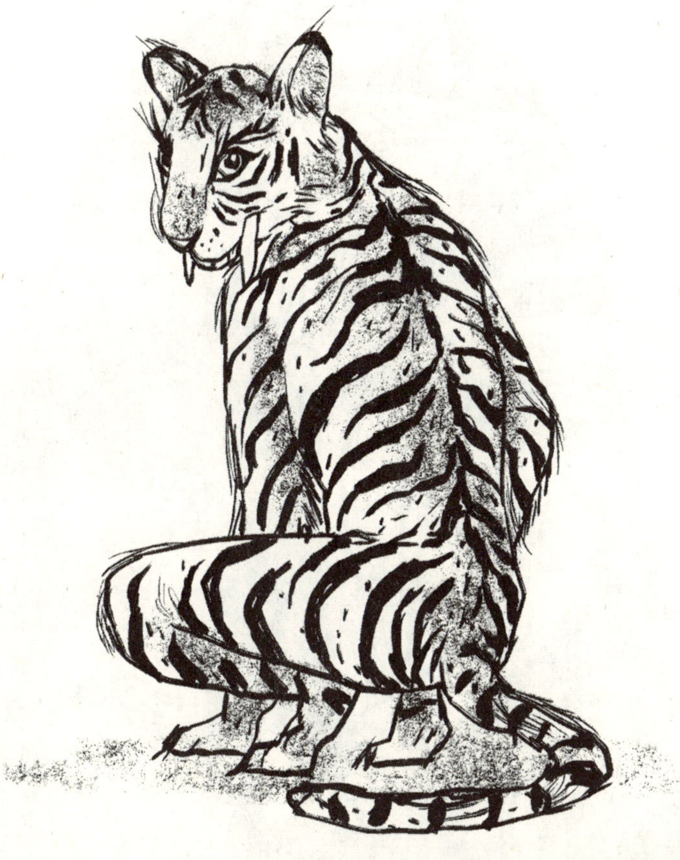

THE PHUNGPUINU

the phungpuinu

28/12/2018

MŽ

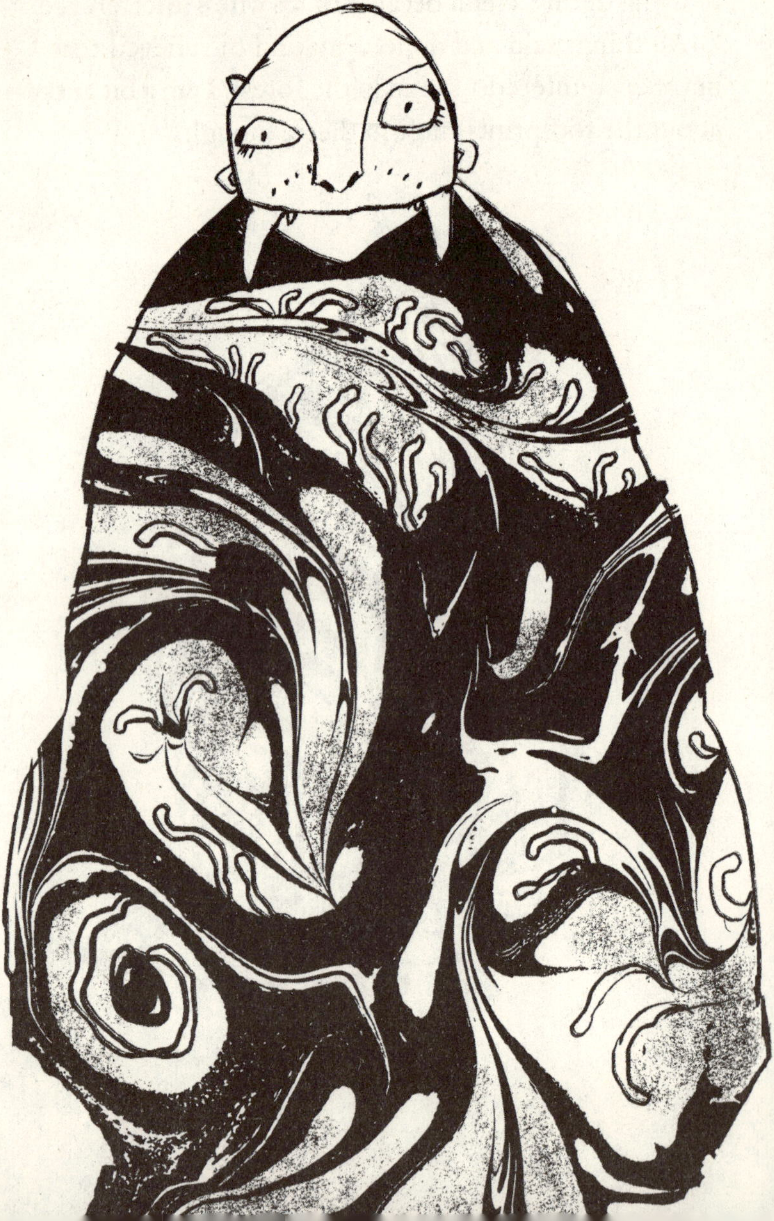

Yet another mythical creature hated in Mizo folklore, the Phungpuinu is a large ogre who, in my opinion, isn't all that bad.

In the story of Chawngchilhi, all the poor ogre wants is to play on Chawngchilhi's swing after he leaves his house. But Chawngchilhi is furious to learn that an ogre has been using his swing, and so he sets a trap for her and pounces on her the moment she steps onto the swing. Chawngchilhi then strikes a bargain with her, and receives a horn that spews out rice on one side and meat on the other. And there's another story of Chawngchilhi roasting the Phungpuinu's children. If you ask me, it would be completely justifiable for the Phungpuinu to come after the human race.

THOMAS IN THE BARDO

thomas in the bardo

Now that I've officially searched for a hundred beasts, I think it's about time I planned my return home. I could fly back to Chennai and still have enough money left to start my next trip. Or I could take the train and have enough to fund my research for a year.

The way back home somehow always feels longer.

Sometimes I feel like I'm stuck in a bardo. Like I'm in a waiting room where I live out the part of my existence that's between death and rebirth. During my journeys home, the berths in my train turn to coffins, and the train itself turns to a burial vault, and yet there is so much life around me. I feel as if I inhabit a place that isn't meant for either the living or the dead.

The tighter I hold on to my ticket, the more detached I am from life, the universe, and everything else...

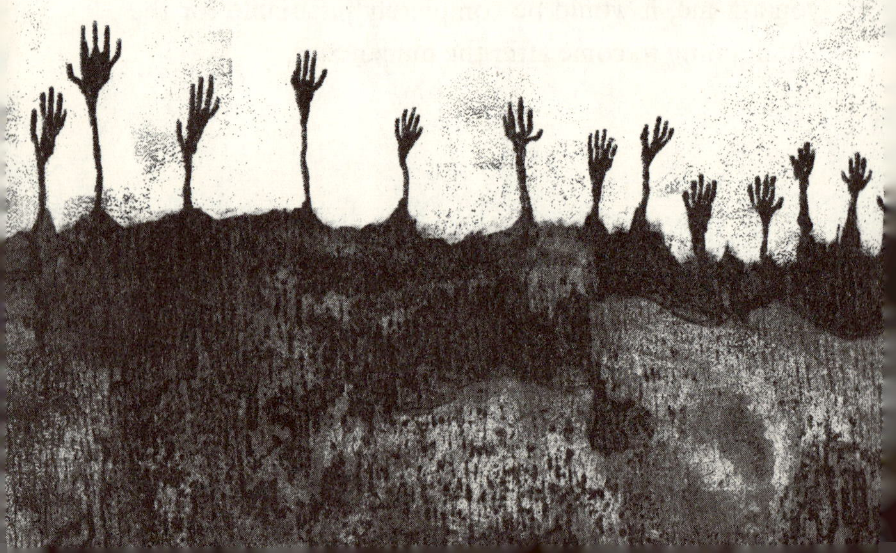

...but before I use that ticket,
I will make one last stop.

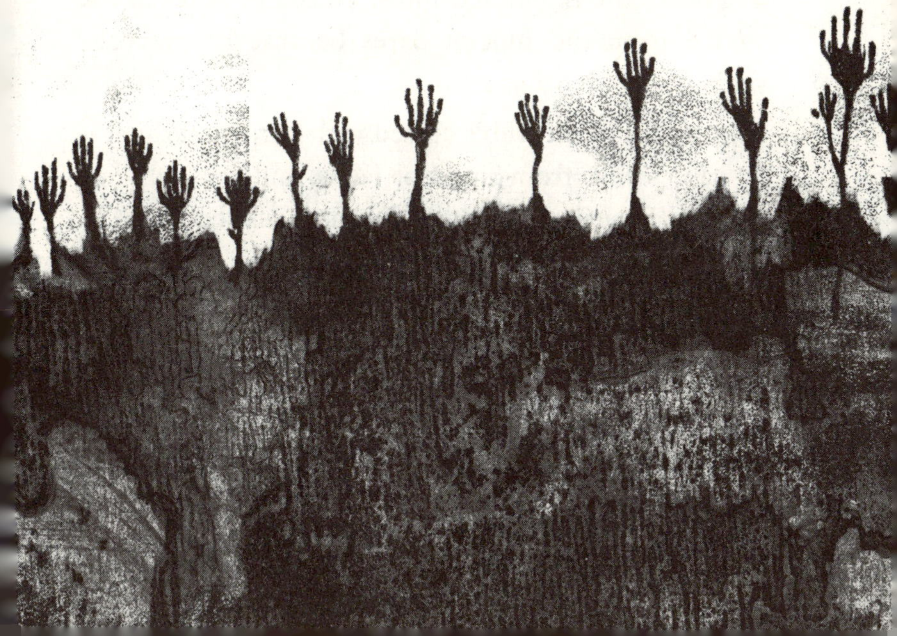

HUNGRY GHOSTS

hungry ghosts

31/12/2018

Tawang, AR

All this talk about bardos and purgatory has got me thinking about Hungry Ghosts. I am sure that they are all around me. Hundreds of them, each slightly different from the other, all cursed to live out a terrible life sentence.

Would you believe me if I told you that I can see them when I close my eyes? Some of them are a foot tall and others as tall as the mountains, but for the most part they're about as tall as me. I can see:

NIMMY, the hungry ghost with a big stomach and a neck as thin as a needle. She's here because she refused to share her food in a previous life.

VATSALA, the big-nosed ghost cursed to feed on the smoke from the funeral pyres because of everyone she'd tortured in a past life.

RAJIV, the ghost who's cursed with perpetual thirst – he can't drink from rivers or lakes, and can only lick drops off the legs of those who have just bathed. His crime? Adulterating food.

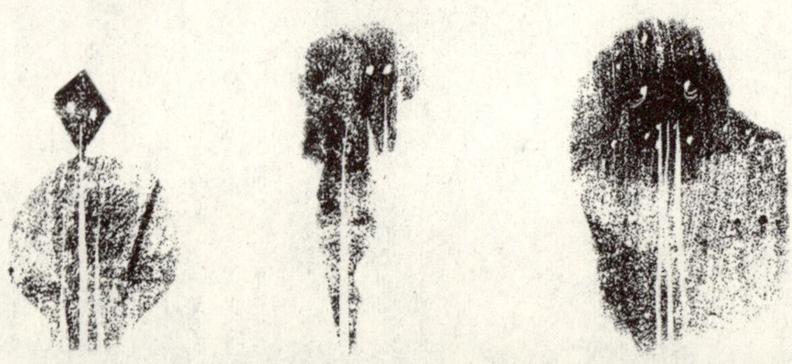

Bijal, the tortured soul forced to eat human babies, all because she faked being a healer in a past life.

Chetana, the soul who embezzled money, must be confined to cemeteries and keep the corpses company.

Ramona, whose murderous crimes have led to a deformed, cauldron-shaped body, a fire in the pit of her stomach consuming her from within.

Sure, I made up their names, but not their appearances. It must be such a curse to live out the rest of their existence engaged in a task so repetitive, to end each day knowing that they would have to start over again. I read somewhere that they live for 500 years, and that each one of their days feels like a month. My calculation may be off, but that's 1,500 years of misery that come to an end only for the cycle to start all over again.

Forget about all my fears and nightmares. Nothing scares me more than being reborn as a Hungry Ghost.

Unless...unless I were fated to spend eternity looking for mythical beasts. That is a fantasy even I would have trouble believing.

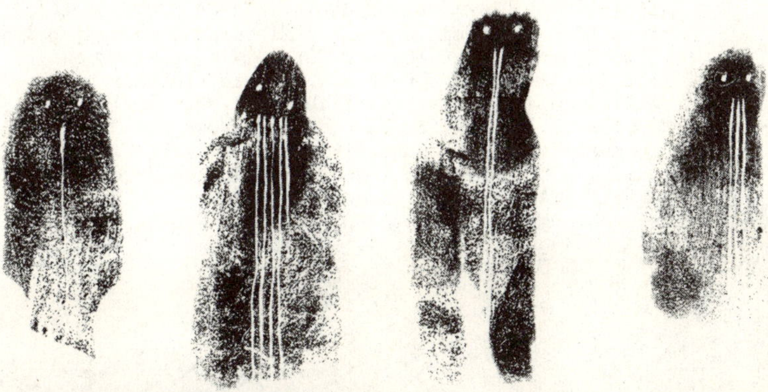

Image Copyright Information: All images from Wikimedia Commons under the following licenses: **p.15:** Yali: Attribution: Richard Mortel from Riyadh, Saudi Arabia; CCA-SA 2.0 Generic License; https://commons.wikimedia.org/wiki/File:Carved_pillar_in_the_16th_century_Thousnad-Pillared_Hall,_Meenakshi_Temple,_Madurai_(2)_(37259217170).jpg; **p.16:** Sarambam: Attribution: Ccmarathe at English Wikipedia; CCA-SA 4.0 International License https://en.wikipedia.org/wiki/File:Peth_sharabha.JPG; **p.17:** top left: Attribution: Leon Meerson; https://en.wikipedia.org/wiki/File:Munneswaram_Sharabha.jpg; CCA-SA 2.0 Generic License; **p.19 & 130:** CCA-SA 3.0; **p. 31:** The Commons; Hunter, William Wilson - Sir, K.C.S, British Library; **p.59:** PD (Public Domain); **p.68:** PD; **p.69:** Internet Archive (archive.org); Uploaded by chris.jones@archive.org; **p.86:** Ambadevi Rock painting: Attribution: Vtingole; CCA-SA 4.0 International; https://commons.wikimedia.org/wiki/File:Ambadevi_Rock_Painting_-_Animal_zoo.jpg; modified; **p.96:** Vasuki: PD; Takshaka: Attribution: LRBurdak; CCA-SA 3.0 Unported/ GNU Free Documentation License; https://commons.wikimedia.org/wiki/File:Taxaka_Statue.jpg; Mucilinda: Gary Todd; PD; **p. 97:** Shesha and Manasa: PD; **p.112:** gift of the Ernest Erickson Foundation, Inc., Brooklyn Art Museum, Asian Collection: No known copyright restrictions; **p.119:** Author name in foreign language; CCA-SA 3.0 Unported; https://commons.wikimedia.org/wiki/File:Homa_Persepolis_Iran.JPG; **p.121:** PD; **p. 125:** Attribution: Dineshkannambadi at the English-language Wikipedia; CCA-SA 3.0 Unported/ GNU Free Documentation License; https://commons.wikimedia.org/wiki/File:Kirthimukha_at_Kasivisvesvara_Temple_at_Lakkundi.JPG; **p.128:** Mooshakraja: British Museum, PD; Uchchaihshravas: PD; Airavata: Indian Art Special Purpose Fund; https://collections.lacma.org/node/240827; **p.129:** Dawon: Detroit Institute of Arts, PD; Garuda: from LACMA, PD; Nandi: ttps://www.britishmuseum.org/collection/object/A_2007-3005-27; PD; **p.136:** Daderot, Linden-Museum, Germany; PD; **p.137:** top: Ashmolean Museum, PD; bottom: Sarah Welch, PD; **p.158:** Rietberg Museum, PD; **p.159:** Gita Press Gorakhpur, PD; **p.160:** Both PD; **p.161:** Harn Museum of Art, PD; **p.183:** Clockwise from left: 1: Brooklyn Museum, PD; 2: British Museum, PD; 3: The Ravi Udaya Vijaya Press Ghatkoper, Raja Ravi Varma; PD; 4: Attribution: User: Adarshkothia; CCA-SA 3.0 Unported; https://en.wikipedia.org/wiki/File:Eran_Boar.jpg; **p.185:** Victoria and Albert Museum, PD; **p.194:** Attribution: Balaji Srinivasan; CCA-SA 2.0 Generic License; https://en.wikipedia.org/wiki/File:Kabandhal.jpg; **p.211:** PD; **p.247:** Map, 1891: Internet Archive Book Images; CCA-SA 2.0 Generic License; https://commons.wikimedia.org/wiki/File:British_India_map_of_Northeast_India_and_Myanmar,_Bengal_Assam_Meghalaya_Arunachal_Pradesh_Nagaland_Manipur_Mizoram_Tripura_regions_1891.jpg; **p.251:** LigerCommon, PD, modified.

C.G. Salamander is a writer and graphic novelist who divides his time between Chennai and the Netherlands. He's one half of the *Maithili and the Minotaur* series, editor of a scientific journal, and is currently working on a fantasy novel.

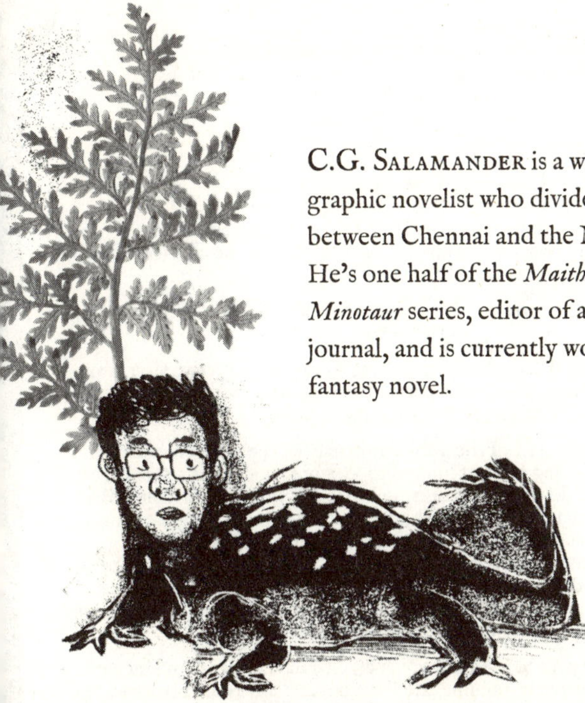

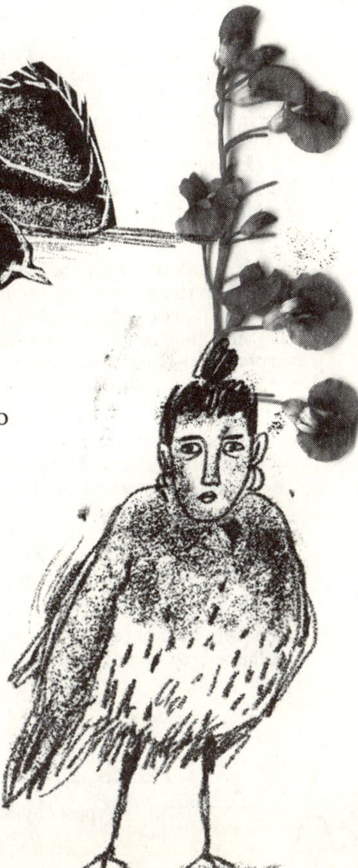

Sheena Deviah is an illustrator who draws inspiration from the natural world. She has illustrated the picture books *Incredible Insects*, *Kuchh Gadbad Hai* and *When I Grow Up, I'll Have a House*. She lives in Bengaluru with a toothless cat, Ramona. You can see more of her work on her website https://www.sheenadeviah.com/

First published in 2023 by Hachette India
(Registered name: Hachette Book Publishing India Pvt. Ltd)
An Hachette UK company
www.hachetteindia.com

1

ISBN 978-93-93701-96-1

Hachette Book Publishing India Pvt. Ltd
4th & 5th Floors, Corporate Centre
Plot No. 94, Sector 44, Gurugram - 122003, India

Typeset by Manmohan Kumar, Delhi

MIX
Paper from responsible sources
FSC™ C043100

Printed and bound in India
by Manipal Technologies Limited

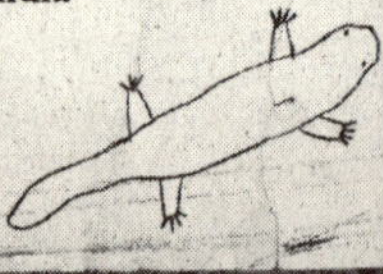